Party
Politics
in the
Age of
Caesar

Inscribed Bronze Bust of Cato Uticensis
Photograph, Museum, Rabat, Morocco. See p. viii.

Party
Politics
in the
Age of
Caesar

LILY ROSS TAYLOR

University of California Press

Berkeley, Los Angeles and London

UNIVERSITY OF CALIFORNIA PRESS
BERKELEY AND LOS ANGELES, CALIFORNIA
UNIVERSITY OF CALIFORNIA PRESS, LTD.
LONDON, ENGLAND

ISBN: 0-520-01257-7

8 9 0

ORIGINALLY PUBLISHED AS VOLUME TWENTY-TWO
OF THE SATHER CLASSICAL LECTURES

PRINTED IN THE UNITED STATES OF AMERICA

TO
K. T. R.

PREFACE

Roman *political parties have been placed in a new light by Matthias Gelzer in a series of epoch-making studies. Party developments of the late republic have been illuminated by the investigations of Anton von Premerstein and Ronald Syme. In publishing a book on the parties of Caesar's time I gratefully acknowledge my obligation to these three scholars. I also venture to express the hope that I have been able, as a result of my analysis of the voting system, to present a new point of view. The chapters were arranged for presentation as lectures, and in consequence I have assumed in the first two chapters the conclusions on the voting which I have set forth in the third. Those conclusions, expanded in certain details in the fourth chapter, are of importance also for the succeeding chapters.*

My colleague in the Latin Department at Bryn Mawr College, Professor T. R. S. Broughton, has placed at my disposal his detailed knowledge of Roman politics. He has also made available to me the unpublished manuscript of his Magistrates of the Roman Republic. *He has read the entire text of the book (though not all of it in its final form) and has made illuminating criticisms and suggestions. Other colleagues in the Departments of Latin and Greek at Bryn Mawr, Professors Berthe Marti, Agnes Kirsopp Michels, and Mabel Lang, have read and criticized certain chapters. Professors Caroline Robbins and Felix Gilbert, of the Department of History, have helped me by their discussions of questions concerned with the development of political parties from the Renaissance to the present day. At the University of California members of the Department of Classics and of other departments who attended my lectures have by their comments and questions led me to alter the text at many points. Professor William Hardy Alexander, Chairman of the Department of Classics (until his retirement in 1948), has been generally helpful and has, through published studies and oral suggestions, contributed much to the final chapter. Professor Max Radin has given me valuable aid on various details, and particularly on the material of the fifth chapter. Professor Walter Allen, of the University of North Carolina, who read a copy of my manuscript after it was in the hands of the printer, saved me from several errors and directed my attention to important foreign bibliography.*

I wish to express my gratitude for the help I have received from the Library Staff of Bryn Mawr College and also of the University of California. I appreciated the opportunity of working in the University's remarkable classical collection.

For permission to use translations from the Loeb Classical Library I express my thanks to the Library and to the Harvard University Press, publisher of the Series. Specific acknowledgements are made in my notes.

To the Editor of the University of California Press, Mr. Harold A. Small, and to Mr. Robert Shafer, Assistant Editor, I am grateful for their careful editorial work, their helpful suggestions, and their interest in seeing the work through the Press. My friend, Miss Alice Martin Hawkins, has made valuable suggestions on method of presentation, and she and Professor Berthe Marti have read the proof and eliminated a number of errors. Another friend, Mrs. George Carland, has given me efficient aid in the preparation of the manuscript and of the index.

To all the colleagues and friends who made my tenure of the Sather Professorship in Classical Literature a memorable experience in my life I express my deep appreciation. It was a great privilege to be associated for a time with the University of California and to see how, in a period when its capacities were taxed to the utmost, it maintained high standards and a vigorous intellectual life.

October 13, 1948   L. R. T.

Results of this book have been in general supported by my later books, The Voting Districts of the Roman Republic *(Rome, 1960)* and Roman Voting Assemblies *(Ann Arbor, 1966). In the latter I discuss a new inscription confirming views presented in Chapter III of this book. Another important discovery is the first authenticated portrait of Cato Uticensis, a bronze bust inscribed CATO, found at Volubilis, now at Rabat, Morocco (R. Thouvenot, Monuments Piot 43 [1949] 71–75). For the photograph showing this man of youthful gravity, the Frontispiece of this reprint, I am grateful to M. Abdeslam Marrakchi of the Musée des Antiquités Pré-Islamiques, Rabat.*

1968   L. R. T.

CONTENTS

CHAPTER I

PERSONALITIES AND PROGRAMS

MY SUBJECT IS the bitter partisan strife of the last years of the Roman Republic, and particularly of the final twenty years of free Roman institutions, 70 to 50 B.C. The period has remarkable parallels with the problems and experiences of our own time. One world had in a sense been realized, for most of the lands known to the Romans were either in vassalage or in unequal alliance with the Roman state. But there was no effective world government, for in the center of that state there was revolution and anarchy. Rival parties were striving by the use of arms for domination, and victory in the strife was to lead to the supremacy of a single party and the identification of that party under a totalitarian system with the whole state.

The party struggles of this period are known to us from more detailed firsthand evidence than we possess for any other period of antiquity. We are not dependent on the historians of later generations, Velleius, Appian, and Dio, or on the biographers Suetonius and Plutarch, although they tell us much that is important. We can obtain our material from men who actually took part in the struggle, from the victorious leader Caesar, who has left us priceless comments in his account of the Civil War, and from his henchman Sallust.[1] In two letters to Caesar, the earlier written shortly before the outbreak of the civil war of 49 and the later several years afterward, Sallust, as a member of Caesar's party, gave Caesar remarkable advice on the reconstitution of the state. It is a great gain for our view of the period that the genuineness of these documents, long questioned, now seems to be established,[2] and they will be a valuable guide in our discussion. From Sallust's later years, when he had withdrawn from political life, we have two monographs on the Jugurthine and Catilinarian wars and fragments of his *Histories*. In these works Sallust looked back on events that he knew from personal experience or from word-of-mouth reports and wrote with at least a measure of that detachment from partisanship which, in his opinion, he had achieved.

[1] For notes to chap. i see pp. 185–194.

But more important than either Caesar or Sallust are the voluminous works of Cicero, his rhetorical and philosophical essays, his
fifty-odd orations before senate, people, and courts, and his correspondence, including his uncensored letters to his brother and his
most intimate friend. It is in Cicero's writings and particularly in his
letters[3] that the political leaders emerge as living persons whose activities we can follow from month to month and often from day to
day. The collection of Cicero's correspondence even includes letters
from Caesar, Pompey, Cato, Brutus, Cassius, and other men prominent in politics.

Our sources of information, extensive though they are, are singularly one-sided. Almost everything we have comes from men of the
senatorial class, and most of what they say concerns their own
group. In the literature of the republic there are no counterparts to
the writers of the empire, Petronius, Martial, and Juvenal, who tell
us what the common man was thinking. The failure of our sources
here is the more serious because the widening chasm between the
upper and the lower classes was a major reason for the decay of the
political institutions of the republic and for the role played by arms
and violence in settling party strife.

Roman republican government, which men of aristocratic sympathies like Polybius and his follower Cicero describe as an ideal
combination—with checks and balances—of monarchy as represented by the consuls, of aristocracy as embodied in the senate, and
of democracy as it was exercised by the popular assemblies, had, in
contrast to the democratic government of Athens, always been
predominantly aristocratic, for the aristocrats not only controlled
the senate of ex-magistrates but also exercised sufficient power over
the assembly of the people to retain an almost complete monopoly
on the consulship for members of their own group. But there once
had been a strong bond of common interest between aristocrats and
people, and in spite of constant strife between the orders in the
state, the sword was said not to have been carried into the Roman
assembly until the tribunate of Tiberius Gracchus in 133.[4]

Rome was a society in which there was, at least for the freeborn,
some measure of personal liberty, but no equality. The citizens were
divided and subdivided into classes based on possession of landed

property, and the classification determined the military service and weighted the votes of the citizens in an assembly that was essentially military. There was a sharp line between the men who served as foot soldiers in Rome's constant wars and those who were rich enough to serve on horseback, that is, in the late republic, the officer class. It was, except in time of revolution, almost unheard of for a man to pass from common soldier to officer. In the late republic the dividing line between officers and foot soldiers was the possession of property valued at 400,000 sesterces (about $25,000).

The senate of ex-magistrates who served for life was composed of men of the officer or cavalry class.[5] The senate was also divided into a number of different groups based not on property but on office: in ascending order, men of quaestorian, tribunitial, aedilician, praetorian, and consular rank. No senator could speak of his own accord; he was asked his opinion on a question put by the presiding consul, who began with the men of consular rank and often did not have time to reach the humbler members of the body. In obtaining election to office, family and heredity had a strong influence; every senator's son expected to reach at least the rank that his ancestors had attained; some of them climbed higher, but the way up was hard. The consulship particularly was closely guarded.

The families which had held the consulship formed the hereditary nobility.[6] The office was once confined to patricians, but after the year 366 it was open also to plebeians. In the next century and a half a good deal of new blood came into the senate and eventually into the nobility, chiefly from the towns annexed to Rome's domain.[7] But eventually the new plebeian nobility proved as tenacious of its rights as the old patriciate had been. The patrician and plebeian nobility became a closed group, letting in from time to time a man whose ancestors had stopped at the praetorship or a lower office, but very rarely permitting the entrance of the new man, that is, the man who without senatorial ancestors rose from the knights. In the last hundred and fifty years of the republic only ten new men reached the consulship, and Cicero was the only one to achieve that distinction between 93 and 48 B.C.[8]

There was in the officer or cavalry class a large group of families whose members had not held public office and did not belong to the senate. This group, which came largely from the municipalities of Italy, was known as the equestrian order, or knights. Sons of these families sometimes became candidates for office, and they could, without too great difficulty, get into the lower sections of the senate; but the great majority, particularly after restrictions were placed on the business activities of senators, were content to remain knights and engage in Italy and the provinces in manifold enterprises as bankers, traders, and public contractors (publicans). They were the capitalist class, and, after Gaius Gracchus gave them the right of jury duty in the criminal courts, they also became a powerful pressure group in politics.

The people who provided the foot soldiers were also divided into a number of classes based on property rating. They voted by classes in the assembly that elected consuls and praetors. The men possessing 50,000 sesterces had a preferential position in the voting.[9] There were four lower classes of small farmers in this assembly. Below these, and practically disfranchised, were the industrial groups of the city and the constantly increasing class of freedmen.

In this predominantly agricultural society, evolved when Rome had a limited territory, no part of it far from the city, senators and knights on the one side and people on the other had once known each other well. They were neighbors at home and they served together in the army as officers and men; they had common interests, interests of national welfare, in the elective assembly. But the old relationship broke down as a result of the extension of Roman citizenship in Italy and of Roman power over Sicily, Sardinia, Spain, Africa, Greece, Macedonia, and Asia Minor. The men of the upper classes and the people no longer knew each other so well.

The prizes of empire enriched and corrupted the senators and the knights, who together exploited the provinces, and at the same time resulted in the impoverishment of the common people of Rome and Italy.[10] Senators, as governors of provinces or as members of the governors' staffs, and knights, as bankers, and also as publicans, brought back to Rome the fabulous wealth of the provinces, the gold and silver of Spain and Macedonia, the riches gained from the bounteous agricultural products of Sicily, Sardinia, and Africa. They also brought back an abundant supply of slaves from every quarter of the empire.

The small farmers meanwhile, as the census records show, declined in numbers. Many of them perished in the long-drawn-out wars overseas, and many who returned home were unable to retain their farms, partly because their property had suffered during their long absences, and partly too because, on the depleted Italian soil, they could not compete with the cheap grain brought in from the provinces. Most of the land in the vicinity of Rome was swallowed up into great estates worked by cheap slave labor. Farmers still had the strongest influence in the assemblies at Rome, but after the extension of citizenship to all Italy south of the Po they were scattered throughout much of the peninsula. If they wished to vote, they had to come to Rome from distant places, and usually special interest rather than national welfare was the determining factor in bringing them.

A disturbing element in the state was also the great growth in the population of Rome. The dispossessed farmers drifted there in considerable numbers and failed to find adequate means of livelihood in competition with slave labor. Many slaves got their freedom and passed with limited rights into the body of citizens. The population seems to have consisted primarily of the well-to-do and the poor, with a very small middle class. The city rabble was not bound to the upper classes by the ties which had once united small farmers and aristocrats. Freeborn and freedmen alike, they were ready to hire themselves out to anyone who could use their services. The Roman constitution had undergone no essential change, but the foundations on which it had been established were no longer there. And so the party struggles developed more and more into armed clashes and broke out repeatedly into civil war.

This was not the first period of intense party strife at Rome. Contests between patricians and plebeians had occupied more than two centuries in early Roman history and had left their lasting mark on the Roman constitution in the characteristic office of the tribunate of the plebs, a magistracy belonging to a state within the Roman state. The ten tribunes elected every year were the protectors of the people under attack, and they acquired the right of vetoing acts of magistrates, decrees of the senate, and bills proposed to the assemblies. They also won the important prerogative of proposing legislation themselves in a nonmilitary tribal assembly, and eventually the laws they initiated were made binding on the whole state. In time, the tribunes acquired membership in the senate and many of them were chosen from the plebeian nobility. With occasional revivals of its ancient independence, the office tended in the third and early second century B.C. to be subservient to the will of the nobles.

As the empire grew, the senate, controlled by the patrician and plebeian nobility, had an ever stronger hold on the state. It had command of the treasury, assigned provinces and armies to magistrates and promagistrates, and was recognized by foreign peoples as the governing power of Rome. Thus, the senate was dominant when in the latter half of the second century party strife once more became intense and passed this time into violence and revolution. It is my purpose in this chapter to consider the character of the parties which then developed and the relative importance of personalities and programs.

In its form and organization the political party is dependent on the society in which it evolves. The modern reader, hearing of an ancient party, is apt to attribute to it the characteristics of the parties he knows in his own society. The European will think of parties as close-knit groups based on specific programs, and, if the party is Social Democratic or Communist, provided with a party line to which disciplined adherence is expected. The American will think of parties in terms not so much of programs as of organization; for, to quote from Bryce's famous account of the American party system, "the fewer have become [the] principles [of the parties] and the fainter their interest in those principles, the more perfect has become their organization."[1] The American reader will also think, when he hears of a party, of the ticket—again, according to Bryce, the essential feature of the American concept of party. Both the European and the American will be wrong if they think of the Roman parties in terms of the political parties they know in their own state.

As Bryce points out, the foreign observer is better than the native in estimating the peculiar characteristics of the party system in any nation, and Ostrogorskiï and Bryce have provided the most significant observations on the American party system and its peculiar development by which under the primaries it has entered into the state constitutions. Now Rome in the mid-second century had a remarkably able and acute political observer in the Greek, Polybius, who spent many years in the city as a hostage and became an intimate member of the noble Scipionic circle. Polybius knew that there had been a time of fierce strife between patricians and plebeians, but in his illuminating account of the Roman constitution he failed to report any comparable struggle in his day.[12]

Yet in his day there was a substitute for a party system, a substitute that persisted and overlapped the other types of party grouping that developed. It was provided by the fierce strife of the nobles for political advancement. The two consulships open every year did not supply adequate opportunity to satisfy the ambitions of all the men who were determined to equal or surpass the glories of their ancestors. In the contest for office each noble depended on his family and his relations by blood, marriage, and adoption. The basis in popular support was the noble's clients and adherents in Rome and in the citizen communities of Italy and his old soldiers. Each noble had masses of such adherents, many of them inherited from his ancestors. But he needed further support, and that he got from his personal friends among the nobility and their clients and adherents.[13]

The old Roman substitute for party is *amicitia,* friendship.[14] *Amicitia* in politics was a responsible relationship. A man expected from his friends not only support at the polls but aid in the perils of public life, the unending prosecutions brought from political motives by his personal enemies, his *inimici,* his rivals in the contest for office and for the manifold rewards of public life. Friendship for the man in politics was a sacred agreement. Cicero, in writing to Crassus to clinch their reconciliation, urged Crassus to consider his letter a treaty (*foedus*).[15]

In the intense strife for office and advantages, bands of "friends" often made deals to secure their own ends and to shut their rivals out. Long before violence entered into Roman political life, such deals led to vigorous political machinations.[16]

In the struggle for office the system of alliances between friends persisted during the republic. The handbook of electioneering prepared by Quintus Cicero when Marcus was a candidate for the consulship indicates how completely personal the whole system was. The burden of Quintus' advice is that Marcus should win friends, first of all among the nobles, but also among the knights and the municipal men of influence. It is through such friends that the vote is brought in. The main point is for Marcus to make senators, knights, and the multitude think that he would defend their interests. And there is specific advice not to take a stand on public affairs either in the senate or among the people.[17] The letter gives no indication of a ticket, no sign of combination with other candidates. Such combinations, designed to shut out a competitor, were, as we shall see later, considered rather disreputable, and Cicero protested in the senate when two of his competitors combined against him.

Modern analogies are notoriously unsafe, but if we have any in America for the Roman election campaign they are to be found not in our contests every four years between Republicans and Democrats but in the preparatory maneuvering and the final decision at the national nominating convention within one of our great parties. The groups that form about candidates for the nomination emphasize personalities and make few pretenses of providing programs, and the final result depends largely on the strength of the friends whose support each of the candidates can muster. A Roman politician would have been completely lost in the complicated organization of an American presidential election, but he could have learned the ropes fairly easily in the type of organization leading up to a nominating convention.

Thus, as in our campaigns for nomination, friendship was the chief basis of support for candidates for office, and *amicitia* was the good old word for party relationship. But with the growth of empire and the chance to secure the spoils of empire, in the late second century there developed long-term groupings in which, as we shall see, programs played a part. The groupings are described by *factio* and *pars,* or more often *partes,* the words from which the terms faction and party are derived. The words do not correspond to faction and party. Faction in English is commonly used to describe a splinter of a party or to indicate a group with personal interests in contrast to the party based on national interests. No such distinction can be drawn between *factio* and *partes*.[18]

Let us consider *factio* first. In Plautus the word means simply a band of friends. But gradually the word acquired an evil connotation. It came to be used for a clique, generally of men of high position, who had common designs for their own advantage in the state.[19] Unanimity of purpose, according to a speech which Sallust puts in the mouth of a tribune, is *amicitia* among good men and *factio* among bad men.[20] In time the word became the designation of the clique of nobles who from the period of the Gracchi controlled the senate. Gaius Gracchus used it in that sense when he spoke of the *factio* of his personal enemies,[21] and Sallust in his earlier letter to Caesar, now convincingly dated 51 B.C.,[22] employed it repeatedly for Caesar's enemies in the nobility. For a definition of *factio* we must turn to Cicero's *De Re Publica,* published also in 51. There Cicero is in the main discussing Greek political theory. "When a certain number of men," Cicero declares, "by virtue of riches or family or some advantage obtain possession of the state," *est factio sed vocantur illi optimates,* "it is a *factio,* but they go under the name of *optimates.*"[23] Or, as St. Augustine paraphrases Cicero, the *factio* represents the unjust *optimates.*[24] In other words, the *factio* is the oligarchy of the eighth book of Plato's *Republic* and the fifth book of Aristotle's *Politics,* a depraved and corrupted aristocracy, in control of the state.[25] It is also used for a group of aristocrats with oligarchical designs that have not as yet been accomplished. This development of the word reminds one of Alexander Pope's definition of party as "the madness of many for the gain of a few,"[26] or of Ostrogorskiĭ's description of the oligarchic tendencies within American parties, or still more of Michel's theory[27] that the essential purpose of the political party is oligarchical.[28]

Factio is a favorite word of Sallust in his historical writing. Although he applies it to other groups like the Catilinarian conspirators (who, to be sure, had oligarchical designs), he employs it most often for the clique of nobles who controlled the senate from the time of the Gracchi. As so often elsewhere in his work, he is here consciously echoing Plato,[29] having in mind depraved aristocrats transformed into oligarchs.[30] Caesar also uses the term for his enemies in the senate, and he indicates the connotation of oligarchy by combining the word with *dominatio* and the genitive *paucorum*. He marched into Italy, he says, *ut se et populum Romanum factione paucorum oppressum in libertatem vindicaret*—to liberate himself and the Roman people, who had been overwhelmed by an oligarchy.[31] Hirtius, who completed Caesar's Gallic commentaries, also employs *factio* coupled with *paucorum* for Caesar's enemies.[32] *Factio* is thus a term of opprobrium, used by Caesar and two of his henchmen, Sallust and Hirtius, to describe the self-styled good men, and the word implies that the group is an oligarchy.

Sallust, and after him perhaps Livy, hold that the Romans of a better day did not go in for *factiones*. They used to be organized, Sallust says, against external foes;[33] the creation of a *factio* within the state is thus a sign of the state's decline. Livy, writing not long after Sallust, is chary about using the word for Roman national affairs. He does employ it in that sense a few times in his first decade, but in his twenty-five books on the years 218 to 167 he admits the existence of a *factio* at Rome only once.[34] Yet in these same books he repeatedly speaks of *factiones* in foreign city-states. He seems to be avoiding the attribution of anything so unseemly to Rome.[35]

Cicero in the *Republic* applies the word *factio* mainly to the Greek oligarchs, giving the thirty tyrants of Athens as an example; he concedes that there was a *factio* at Rome in the second decemviral college three hundred years before his time, but he is apparently not inclined to agree with Sallust that the nobles of his day represent a *factio*. In general he avoids the word *factio* in discussions of Roman politics. In his public orations there is not a single occurrence of the word. In his letters he uses it only once to apply to political groups, and then he is speaking of the deal made by Pompey, Crassus, and Caesar.[36]

Partes is the word that Cicero regularly uses for parties.[37] It is incidentally the word most often employed for parties in the law courts; and in politics, as in the courts, it is generally applied to opposing sides in a two-party division. The meaning comes out clearly in a passage in which Cicero says that the tribunate of Gaius Gracchus divided the state *in duas partes*. It comes out also in similar passages in Sallust and in Caesar.[38] Sometimes in Cicero's mind the

division is between good and bad men,[39] but frequently it depends
on a personal basis. He speaks of the *partes* of Marius, Sulla, Sertorius, and, over and over again, of Caesar.[40] The word thus desig-
nates the split in the state between the followers of revolutionary
leaders. That usage seems to have been adopted by Livy, for although he uses *partes* rarely for Roman political groupings in the
extant books, which end with the year 167 B.C., the word, if we can
trust his epitomator, occurred as a description of the personal parties
of the period of revolution.[41]

While *partes* in Cicero frequently denotes a grouping about a
prominent personality, it is rarely so used in Sallust, who loves
abstractions.[42] For him the state is divided *in duas partes* between
people and senate. He describes the division in rather repetitious
passages in the *Catiline*, the *Jugurtha*, and the *Histories*.[43] *Partes* for
him is a general term for the division, and he alludes specifically to
partes populi and once to *partes populares*.[44] When speaking of the
party of the senate or of the nobility which controlled the senate,
he prefers the invidious term *factio*.[45]

Sallust's *partes* of senate and people correspond roughly to
Cicero's division of the Romans into two classes, *optimates* and
populares, but Cicero never refers to these divisions as *partes*. He
applies the words not to the masses but to men of politics, in general
men of the senatorial class. There have always been two types of
citizens at Rome, Cicero says. "Those who have wished their deeds
and words to be pleasing to the multitude have been held to be
populares, and those who have conducted themselves in such a
manner that their counsels have met the approval of all the best men
have been held to be *optimates*."[46] And from Cicero's letters we hear
constantly of the *optimates*, more often described simply as the *boni*,
the good men, the sound conservatives bent on upholding the
status quo, the rights of private property, and most particularly the
prestige of the senate hallowed by tradition. Sometimes, especially
when he sees some of these *optimates* going over to Caesar, Cicero
suggests that they are not really very good.[47] On the *populares* Cicero
varies in his attitude before and after his exile. Before that event, he
distinguishes between good *populares*, interested in the welfare of
the state (and on one occasion claims to be *popularis* himself in that

sense), and bad *populares,* who are demagogues." After he had been driven from Rome by a law presented by a popular tribune, *populares* are almost always bad. The two words are the closest parallel for the Greek aristocrats and democrats, but the correspondence is closer between *optimates* and aristocrats (or *aristoi*) than between *populares* and democrats. Cicero apparently realized that democracy, as he knew it for instance from the traditions of Athens, did not exist at Rome. Sallust consciously avoids both words; he is unwilling to concede that the self-styled *optimates,* his *factio,* have any good in them."

It is the use of *optimates* and *populares* by Cicero, and the indication in his speeches that they were words that were constantly being bandied about at Rome, that has led modern historians to describe the party contests of the late republic as a struggle between an optimate or a senatorial party and a popular or democratic party. The historian who has done most to perpetuate the parties is Theodor Mommsen, who in his great *History of Rome* (first published in 1854–1856) presented party politics of the late republic in terms of the strife of his own day between liberalism and the reaction that won the battle in 1848. Mommsen identified the Roman *optimates* with the hated Prussian Junkers and aligned himself with Caesar against them. But he fully recognized the lack of principle or program among the *populares.* He well understood the amorphous character of the Roman "parties."" The parties that he knew in Prussia and in other German states were almost equally amorphous. But Mommsen's terminology has passed into the language of other historians, and in the meantime, through the mid-nineteenth century development of party organization and party tickets in the United States and of party lines in Europe, the meaning of party has undergone a radical change. Thus the terms "optimate" and "popular" party are misleading to the modern reader.

Lately there has been protest against the atttribution of such parties to Rome. The protest has gone too far," for, although there was no large-scale party organization, no party caucus or ticket, and no fixed party line, there was a division between upholders of the authority of the senate and proponents of the people's rights. It was not an alignment of senate against people, but an opposition between groups of men of noble or senatorial rank.

The men designated in ancient sources as *optimates* and *populares* are regularly either members of noble and senatorial families or men who had themselves gained admission to the senate through election to office. Romans of lower rank are never described by such terms, though as clients and adherents of senatorials they had an important share in party conflicts.[52]

The strife between *optimates* and *populares* developed in the senate and, as we shall see in a later chapter, in the campaign for laws in the tribal assembly. A set of nobles who called themselves the "good" men gained control of the senate and prevented other nobles and senatorials from obtaining the endorsement of the senate for their measures. The defeated men turned with the aid of tribunes to the tribal assembly and, without the senatorial authority prescribed by the best custom for laws submitted to the people, procured from the people the enactment of laws that accomplished their designs. Such men were described by their opponents as *populares,* demagogues. The strife between *optimates* and *populares* was in theory based on programs, but it was actually no more than a difference in method, as Sallust, once active as a *popularis,* recognizes. He declares that those "who assailed the government used specious pretexts, some maintaining that they were defending the rights of the commons, others that they were upholding the prestige of the senate; but under pretense of the public welfare each in reality was working for his own advancement," *pro sua quisque potentia certabant.*[53] There was, however, a difference, for the *optimates* were working for the maintenance of an oligarchy while the great figures who adopted popular methods were usually attempting to establish personal supremacy.

The best indication of the lack of organized parties at Rome is that there were no generally accepted names for special parties. Names are needed for such political groupings, and the conservatives, in calling themselves the "good" men and their enemies the *populares,* the word being used in the sense of demagogues, found names they could use. But the men who followed a popular course did not consent to the use of these names. They resented the suggestion that the would-be "optimates" had any good in them; instead, they applied to them the invidious term *factio,* oligarchy.

There is nothing to show what they called themselves, but it is significant that neither Caesar nor Sallust uses *populares* to describe Caesar's party.[54]

Let us turn now to the composition of the two groups. From the Gracchi to Caesar the senate was controlled by powerful nobles who were determined to uphold or regain the constitution of their ancestors and to keep for themselves and their associates the great gains of empire. They were the self-styled "optimates" whom their enemies called a *factio*. Closely united by bonds of friendship and by intermarriages of their families, they kept up a fairly continuous bloc, and, if one thinks of them mainly as a group concerned with senatorial politics and legislation, and has no illusions about their excellence as implied in the word *optimates,* it is justifiable to call them an "optimate" party.[55]

The opposition, as Sallust recognizes, was less effectively organized, for there was no continuous popular party. Tribunes who, at least for their year of office, claimed to be *populares* formed the nucleus of a people's party.[56] Then there were men belonging, as many of the tribunes did, to optimate families who, having failed to gain their ends from the senate, used tribunes to obtain from the popular assembly their special designs for armies and military commands and other prerogatives and at the same time provided rewards for the people. Since the popular game depended on the tribunes, it could be played by more than one man at the same time. Thus Pompey and Crassus, after restoring the tribunate jointly, each had rival tribunes in his service who proposed laws aimed to accomplish rival purposes. They were in a sense leaders of two rival "popular" parties, personal parties, and neither of them would have conceded that he was *popularis*. Cicero separates Pompey from the *populares* when he says that it was as well that Pompey had restored the tribunate, since some *popularis* might have brought the office back in a manner that would have been destructive to the state.[57]

A popular policy was often a temporary expedient for a noble, and its temporary character is indicated by the expressions *populariter agere, populariter loqui*.[58] The pursuit of such a policy was often a phase in the rise of an eminent man who, according to traditions familiar to us today, became a sound conservative in later years. That was true of the orator Crassus and in a sense of Pompey, and once Cicero indicates that he has similar hopes for the most consistently *popularis* of all the great leaders, Caesar.[59] There were also opportunists, like the two Curios, father and son, who switched with astonishing suddenness from one course to the other.

Always there were large groups of middle-of-the-road men who tried not to align themselves either with the *optimates* in control of the senate or with the *populares*. When the alignment did take place, it was apt to be established on a personal basis rather than in support of a program.

The conflict between senate and people had importance, as I have indicated, rather in the votes on laws than in elections. Occasionally, as when Pompey in his candidacy for the consulship went to the polls with a promise to restore the tribunate, the conflict affected the elections. But in general the elections continued to be carried out on the old personal basis. Cicero in his candidacy for the consulship hoped that he could get the endorsement both of the *optimates* and of Pompey's *populares*. A few years later, Caelius notes it as extraordinary that, in a contest for the augurate, party (*partes*) rather than personal obligation was the determining factor.[60] *Partes* here represented the party of Caesar which Caelius identifies with the people.

Let us trace the contest between the authority of the senate upheld by the controlling bloc of nobles and the rights of the people maintained by tribunes and the men who sponsored them. When Polybius, about the middle of the second century B.C., wrote the major part of his history, there was as yet no real party conflict. The tribunes were in general subservient to the senate and usually presented their bills first to the senate for approval, although, after the *lex Hortensia* of 287, such action was not required by the laws. The office is described by Polybius as a check on the power of the senate, but it does not loom large in his account of the constitution. There were signs soon afterward of a revival of the office, but it did not come fully into its own again until the tribunate of Tiberius Gracchus in 133.

Tiberius, son of a distinguished plebeian father and of a mother from the great patrician house of the Scipios, was supported for the tribunate by a group of relatives and friends in the high nobility who had been blocked in the senate.[61] After his election, Tiberius, knowing that the senate would not approve his measure, submitted directly to the people, without senatorial approval, a land bill designed to relieve the economic misery of Rome and Italy. The senatorial *optimates* found a tribune to veto the bill, and Tiberius, by action that was assailed as a violation of popular sovereignty, had this tribune deposed from office, and then obtained the passage of the land bill. Bitter strife developed, and Tiberius, in seeking re-election to the tribunate, was slain. His brother Gaius sought the tribunate a decade later and presented a far more comprehensive and radical program of legislation. It included fresh distribution of land in colonies, improvements in the condition of military service, and a state subsidy on the price of grain for the miserable urban poor. It comprised, too, various other measures relating to the knights and the allied peoples of Italy who were seeking citizenship—a subject to be discussed later. The *optimates* found in their number a man, Marcus Livius Drusus, maternal grandfather of the younger Cato, who secured the tribunate and, with the authority of the senate, offered the people more than Gaius could give them and deprived him of much of his support. The senatorial leaders joined this tribune in playing *popularis*.

It was after the end of Gaius' second tribunate that the senate, protesting that it was threatened with violence by Gaius and his followers, used a new device to provide a substitute for the dictatorship by which disturbances had been quelled in earlier times. The senate passed what is commonly known as the "extreme decree," in effect a declaration of martial law, which authorized the magistrates to use arms to defend the state.[62] In a clash between forces levied by the consuls and Gaius' bands, Gaius and three thousand of his followers were slain. In subsequent years tribunes never ceased condemning such use of arms against the people. On other occasions in the next forty years the extreme decree was passed, and on one of these occasions a tribune was slain. The tribune's person was sacrosanct and any violence committed against him was viewed by the popular orators as a violation of the people's sovereignty embodied in the tribune.

In the course of this period three other important factors developed in the political struggle, and all of them became associated with the contest between the authority of the senate and the power of the people upheld by the tribunes. These factors were the establishment of the knights as a political class, the emergence of the great general strengthened by his bands of loyal soldiers, and the agitation of the Italians for citizenship. It was legislation of Gaius Gracchus that gave the knights, the capitalist class, influence in politics. Gaius assigned to the knights the sole right of jury duty in the extortion courts which regulated the conduct of the senatorial governors of the provinces. Safeguarded by a provision of the law which made them exempt from charges of bribery, knights were no less corrupt than the senatorial jurors had been, and they used their new power now to make a deal with the supporters of the senate's authority and now to make common cause with the tribunes as the defenders of the people's rights. By the latter method they brought to power the new man Gaius Marius, who, in spite of bitter opposition from the nobles, succeeded in capturing the consulship and in obtaining from the people the command in the war against Jugurtha.

It was Marius who introduced the personal army as a decisive factor in Roman politics. Before his day the Roman soldier had in general been recruited from the small landholders of Roman territory, but the normal levies failed after the supply of these landholders had been depleted by Rome's long and costly wars. To find the troops he needed for the war against Jugurtha, Marius turned for recruits to the landless poor, the proletariat of Rome and the Italian municipalities. He raised an army of soldiers ready to serve under him in the hope of personal gain, that is, the acquisition of a land bonus. During the war with the Cimbri and Teutones, when Marius was elected unconstitutionally to repeated consulships, the number of his soldiers grew steadily. When in 100 B.C. he was consul for the sixth time, Marius had a large band of trained soldiers and veterans who owed allegiance to him and looked to him for rewards.

Marius established the role of the general in politics, exemplified by the subsequent careers of Sulla and Pompey, a role that led through Caesar to monarchy. Marius and the other generals after him had to stay in politics when their victories were won, and procure for their soldiers, who were in a sense their clients, the bonuses they had promised. When the senate was not compliant, they took to appealing to the people through tribunes who proposed laws rewarding the soldiers. To win victory at the polls the generals began to send their soldiers to Rome to vote or, if necessary, to use violence. When Marius was consul for the sixth time, in 100, the year of Julius Caesar's birth, the agitation of Marius' tribune and his soldiers led to outright revolution which Marius himself as consul had to suppress under the "extreme decree."

The other great divisive force at this time was the agitation of the Italians for the citizenship that Gaius Gracchus had tried in vain to give them. In the year 91 the tribune Marcus Livius Drusus, son of Gaius' opponent, with strong support in the nobility, tried to reconcile the opposing forces in the state by giving citizenship to the Italians, and by other measures, including the removal of the knights as a force in politics. He failed and met a violent death after the senate had declared his legislation invalid. The bloody Social War followed, brought by the disillusioned Italians against the state. The Italians lost the war, but were granted the citizenship for which they had long struggled in vain.

The battles were not over, for the *optimates* who opposed their rights succeeded in having them registered in a manner that made their votes ineffective. A tribune, with knights in his train, rose to fight that registration, allied himself with Marius, and arrayed himself against the new leader of the nobility, Sulla, and the bulk of the old citizens. The issue was complicated by personal rivalry of Marius and Sulla, both of whom wished to conduct the war against Mithridates of Pontus, and both of whom were strengthened by their soldiers. We need not follow the full details of the contest: the "extreme decree" passed against the tribune in alliance with Marius, and the violence that cost the tribune's life, the subsequent victory of Marius, and the attendant murders of many of the most distinguished nobles.

The temporary victory of Marius led not to popular government but to tyranny exercised with great cruelty by Cinna, who, after Marius' death, became the leader of the Marian forces. When Sulla, victorious over Mithridates, came back at the head of most of the surviving nobles, many of the people welcomed him as a liberator. There was a renewal of fierce civil war which ended in Sulla's victory and his bloody proscriptions. In this war the majority of the senators were on Sulla's side, the majority of the knights were with the Marians, and the people were divided. Tacitus sees the struggle as a contest not so much between senate and people as between senate and knights.[63] It was particularly on the knights that Sulla, as defender of the senate, vented his cruelty; sixteen hundred of them were slain in his terrible proscriptions.

Sulla, functioning under a revival of the dictatorship, reorganized the Roman government not as a tyranny but as an aristocracy. He planned his constitution to establish the senatorial supremacy for which the nobles had been striving. To that end he eliminated the knights from politics and abolished legislation without senatorial approval. He got rid of the knights by his proscriptions, by his elections of knights to the senate, and by restoration to the senate—now enlarged—of jury duty in criminal courts. He checked demagogic legislation by weakening the tribunate, first by debarring tribunes from seeking other magistracies, and thus keeping able and ambitious men from holding the office, and second by removing from the tribune the right of initiating legislation.[64] Henceforth only consuls and praetors could initiate laws, and they regularly secured the approval of the senate before presenting the laws of the people.

Yet by restoring popular elections and the functioning of the criminal courts, the citadel of free speech at Rome, Sulla actually brought back, with the rule of the nobility, popular rights that had been lost under the Marians. When Sulla voluntarily retired, the nobles themselves speedily began again their fierce contest for office and for the spoils of empire. Very soon one of the leading *optimates,* Marcus Aemilius Lepidus, adopted a "popular" course and began to agitate for the restoration of the tribunate, and presently led an armed rebellion against the state. He was overcome principally because the young Gnaeus Pompeius, a new general raised up by Sulla and soon to develop into a threat to Sulla's nobles, used his soldiers to suppress the revolution.

After that the senate had three sets of enemies. There were still many Marians fighting in Spain under Sertorius against the government, and they were now strengthened by the remnants of Lepidus' forces. Then there was Pompey, who, confident because of his clients and trained soldiers, got the privilege of sharing with Sulla's most experienced general the task of defeating Sertorius. And then there was a strong group in Rome, aided eventually by the young patrician of Marian connections, Gaius Julius Caesar, who were bent on restoring the full powers of the tribunate. In the year 75 one of the consuls, from the middle of the *factio,* as Sallust states,[65] was coerced into presenting a law removing from the tribunes the prohibition against seeking higher offices.

Two years later an ambitious man, Licinius Macer, author of a history of Rome which magnified the struggle between the patricians and plebeians, held the tribunate, and Sallust gives us a version of a speech in which he harangued the people on the subject of the tyranny of the oligarchs who "have seized the treasury, the armies, the kingdoms, and the provinces and have made themselves a citadel from your spoils. You, meantime, the multitude, like sheep, submit yourselves to their individual service and enjoyment. You have been stripped of every privilege which your forefathers left you except your ballots, and by them, you who once chose your defenders now choose your masters." To redress the wrongs of the people the full powers of the tribunate must, the tribune urges, be restored, and he predicts that Pompey on his return from Spain will come to the rescue. "For I am fully convinced that Pompey . . . prefers to be the first man of the state with your consent rather than to share with them in tyranny over you and that he will take the initiative in restoring the tribunate."[66]

These words about Pompey may be an *ex post facto* statement, put into the tribune's mouth by Sallust. In any case, when Pompey returned he actually did combine with the popular agitators and promise to restore the tribunate. Fortified by the popular support this promise gave him, by the strength of his army, and by a deal with Crassus, Pompey coerced the senate into suspending for him the laws regulating candidacy for the consulship. And as consuls Pompey and Crassus restored the ancient rights of the tribunate.

The whole struggle was to begin over again. The details will be considered in the last three chapters. Here it may be briefly stated that the senate, controlled by the faction of *optimates,* who were determined to save what they could of their Sullan prerogatives, became firm against Pompey, and Pompey used tribunes to obtain from the people the extraordinary commands that the senate would not underwrite. And then, when he returned from his great victories in the East and found all his measures obstructed in the senate, he made a deal with Caesar and Crassus, who had also clashed with the senate, and with them in the so-called first triumvirate, which was, as Cicero recognized, a rival *factio,* secured his ends from the people. Eventually, after Crassus' death, Pompey broke with Caesar and united with his own old enemies in the senate, first to combat Caesar's tribunes in Rome, and then Caesar himself and his mighty army. And the final outcome was civil war and the end of republican institutions.

The men described by modern historians as leaders of the "popular" party at Rome, the Gracchi, Marius, Cinna, Pompey for most of his career, and Caesar, were all opposed by cliques of nobles who were able to control the decisions of the senate against them. All of them would have been glad to obtain the prior endorsement of the senate for their measures, but that proved impossible. They therefore secured their ends by appealing to the popular assembly, sometimes with the threat of armed violence, to override the will of the senate. Although they or the tribunes in their service asserted the rights of the people, they were all, except perhaps the Gracchi, seeking personal power rather than establishment of the rights of the sovereign people.

It is to be noted that with the exception of the new man Marius, who rose from the knights, all the leaders of this series of "popular" parties were not men of the people, but members of the hereditary nobility. But none of them except the Gracchi belonged to a dominant group in the nobility. Cinna[67] and Caesar were descendants of ancient patricians, but their families had long been relatively obscure. Pompey obtained nobility only through his father, one of the great generals of the Social War. After the Gracchi, most of the "popular" leaders were generals with a strong army bound to them in personal allegiance—an army that was more than equal to the hereditary clients of other nobles.

These men were struggling not for the paltry prizes of the yearly magistracies, but for the opportunities and spoils of a mighty empire. They could have used their soldiers to gain their ends by force, but they preferred to employ constitutional means. Since their enemies controlled the senate, they or their tribunes took their measures directly to the assemblies without the authority of the senate. Moreover, because these generals made use of tribunes whose laws were voted on mainly by the urban populace, they became involved in certain programs that were known as "popular." The programs included distribution of state-subsidized or free grain to the urban mob, and agrarian laws which nearly always provided for land for some of the urban poor. These men also favored the extension of citizenship, though thereby they sometimes offended the old citizens. They were inclined, too, to open the offices to more new men, and with the extension of citizenship after the Social War there was a large group of Italians clamoring for such privileges. These are the chief elements of what is commonly described as the program of the "popular party." The program was presented to the people in fiery orations which emphasized the tyranny of the nobles and the slavery of the people.

Opposing this series of popular parties was a fairly continuous bloc of *optimates* in control of the senate, led in the post-Sullan period first by Catulus and later by Cato. This bloc had its own program, the maintenance of the constitution, or rather the restoration of the pre-Gracchan or the Sullan constitution, under which the senate was the chief governing body of the state. The program was conservative; it was likely to be concerned with the protection of the treasury and of private property, threatened by the radical *populares*. At least by Cato it was presented with constant insistence on the responsibilities of the Roman state to subject and allied peoples. It was in the senate that the bloc functioned most effectively, but before the people too the *optimates* were able, through their own tribunes—Cato was one of them,—to secure eloquent advocacy of their policies, and, through frequent use of the veto and of the obstructions provided by the state religion, to delay, or sometimes to defeat, the popular bills of their opponents. The optimate orators also spoke steadily of tyranny, *dominatio,* or more often *regnum,* which in Roman tradition was a tyrannous form of government. Every important popular leader from Tiberius Gracchus to Caesar was accused of attempting to set up a *regnum.*

Liberation of the state from tyranny was thus a major theme in the speeches on both sides. In the emphasis on tyranny neither side went far wrong, for the question at stake was not senatorial versus popular government but the maintenance of the tyranny of an oligarchy versus the establishment of the tyranny of the individual.

All this talk about programs might seem to suggest a large-scale party organization, but nothing of the sort developed. The parties continued to be personal groupings, based in popular support on the noble's clients and strengthened by alliance of friendship with other nobles. That was true also of the generals and the popular leaders, for they added to their clients their personal armies and masses of the urban populace. It is mainly of this group that Cicero uses the word *partes* for a personal party. When three men, Pompey, Crassus, and Caesar, who had soldiers and city populace in their following, united to control the state, Cicero in intimate letters called them *populares,* or sometimes dynasts, and once also referred to them as a *factio,* but they called themselves by the time-honored name *amici.* Even Cato implied the use of that term when he said that it was not discord between Pompey and Caesar but their concord that wrecked the state,[68] and Horace echoes Cato when he speaks of the *graves amicitiae* of leading men.[69]

Our concern in these chapters is primarily not with programs but with personalities—with members of great noble houses attended by masses of adherents. The traditions of these houses and the organization of clients and soldiers will be considered in the next chapter. In the following chapter, I shall present the evidence for a view I have already set forth and try to show that it was in the votes on laws and not in the elections that the program served as a political device for building a personal party in the urban plebs. After that I shall discuss the use the nobles made of the state religion in party politics and the importance of the criminal courts, particularly as they contributed to the rise of the new man Cicero. In the last three chapters I shall attempt to outline the political groupings of the years 70 to 50 and the subsequent emergence of a single party. I shall treat the subject mainly from the standpoint of the optimate opposition, led by the man who strove in life and in his death to maintain the great traditions of the Roman nobility, Marcus Porcius Cato.

The men who play the major roles in party politics are, with one exception, members of noble houses. The people appear as adherents or clients of these leaders. The stage in the political scene is Rome. The action takes place in the midst of intrigue and corruption, and often in violence and bloodshed. And behind the scene and the action lie the provinces, the kingdoms, and the principalities that make up the one world subservient to Rome.

CHAPTER II

NOBLES, CLIENTS, AND PERSONAL ARMIES

THE DOMINANT figures in Roman party politics and party organization were usually members of the hereditary noble or consular houses. By their traditions these houses kept alive the hallowed customs of old Rome, the *mos maiorum*.[1] The noble families considered it their right to provide the men who as magistrates and senators represented the people, the *res publica*. Particularly they held it to be their prerogative to supply the consuls; they passed the office "from hand to hand" and considered that the consulship was polluted if a new man was elected to it.[2] It is with the nobles that we are concerned in this chapter, their inheritance of politics as a profession, their training and experience, their marriages and friendships, their contacts with their clients, and, if they were generals, with their soldiers.

The Roman nobles have often been compared to the so-called British ruling class. There is some similarity in the way the profession of politics was passed down from father to son and in the recurrence of familiar names in high office. But the Roman nobility, unlike the British ruling class, did not constantly renew itself by the admission of new men and by marriages outside its own circle. A far better parallel for the exclusive inbred nobility of Rome is provided by the patriarchate of the Republic of Venice, the oligarchy which for more than five hundred years maintained its primacy, but maintained it by statute such as the Romans never enacted.

To understand the noble houses of Rome one should turn to the sixth book of the *Aeneid*, to the lines where Anchises foretells the glories of Aeneas' descendants and fires his son with love of fame to come (*incenditque animum famae venientis amore*); or one should read the vivid pages on which Livy sets forth the deeds in war and in peace of the great republican heroes. There was a splendid tradition of sternness, discipline, courage, and patriotism, and every noble strove to keep it alive both by recalling constantly

---

[1] For notes to chap. ii see pp. 194–199.

the distinctions of his ancestors and by striving himself to reach an equal eminence. The atrium of the city house was adorned with the wax images of the noble's ancestors, accompanied by emblems and inscriptions recording the consulships and the censorships, the priesthoods, and the triumphs they had held. In the magnificent pageantry of the public funerals of members of these great houses, these images were taken with the dead to the Rostra and were placed on descendants who were thought to resemble their ancestors. And in the funeral orations the achievements of these ancestors were lauded along with the deeds of the man who had died. Polybius, who had seen such funerals, is deeply impressed with the stimulus this "constant renewal of the good report of brave men" provides for the younger generation.[3]

Cicero, the new man, speaks with scorn of the "commendation of smoky wax images" through which an enemy reached high position, and makes fun of the defeated candidate who asks, "What shall I say to the images of my ancestors?";[4] but there is no doubt that he felt deeply all his life his exclusion from the traditions that belonged to the great noble houses. Even when he reached the consulship he was never really accepted, never in the inner circle of nobility. Sallust, another new man, who gave up a political career before he reached the highest office, felt it too, and comments more than once that the nobles considered themselves defiled if an outsider broke into their group.[5]

In the nobility, as everywhere in Roman society, there were classes within classes. The highest class was represented by the princes of the state, the men who could marshal on the Rostra for a family funeral the greatest array of masks with the emblems of the highest distinction. Among these the great patrician houses had a preëminent place, for they traced their ancestry back to the kingship and even sometimes to the expedition of Aeneas. Still prominent in the late republic were the Claudii, the Aemilii, and certain branches of the Cornelii and the Valerii. But the majority of the fourteen patrician houses still surviving from the fifty-odd patrician families whose names we know from the early republic[6] were no longer in the front ranks of the nobility. Cicero notes that the nobility of Servius Sulpicius Rufus, a patrician who expressed his wrath at being defeated for the consulship by a man of less distinguished name, had to be "dug out of ancient records."[7] The same thing was true in less degree of the family of Julius Caesar. Although a collateral branch of his house had reached the consulship in the middle of the second century, none of Caesar's ancestors had held the office for three hundred years, and few of them were really eminent. Vergil went back to the legendary past to provide a glorious tradition for the Julian House. The fortunes of Caesar's family had been improved by the marriage of his aunt with the new man Marius.

Of the patricians it may be noted that a surprising number, like Caesar, embraced popular programs in order to rise in the state. Marcus Aemilius Lepidus, Catiline, and Clodius are other examples. These men had a decided disadvantage if they wished to be *populares,* for they were ineligible for the tribunate unless, like Clodius and certain of his predecessors, they had themselves adopted into a plebeian house. There were other disadvantages for patricians. Only one of them could be elected to the consulship in each year, and sometimes a man, who would otherwise have won, had to withdraw when another patrician had already been chosen.

On a level with the greatest patrician houses and far above the lesser families of the patriciate were certain illustrious houses of the plebeians, the Mucii Scaevolae, the Licinii, the Lutatii Catuli, the Domitii Ahenobarbi, ancestors of Nero, the Livii Drusi, ancestors of Augustus' wife, Livia, the related Porcii Catones, and the most eminent of all, the prolific and wealthy house of the Caecilii Metelli, related through marriage and adoption to many families of the patrician and plebeian nobility.[8] On the Appian Way today a splendid tomb of a lady of this house, wife of Crassus' son, is still a monument of the princely position attained by the family. From these houses and not from the patriciate came the leaders of the optimate opposition to Pompey and Caesar—Catulus, Metellus Pius, Lucullus, Cato, and Domitius. In contrast to houses like these, Pompey, also a plebeian, was a newcomer, with his father his only forerunner in the consulship.

Along with the wealth that made it possible for him to engage in a lifework which at least in theory provided no means of gain, the

noble inherited from his family the profession of politics and he
was expected to pursue it. Late in his life Cicero, proud of the nobility which he had brought to his family, addressed to his son an
essay, *De Officiis*, "On Duty," or perhaps more accurately, since the
essay is filled with practical advice, "On propriety of conduct." In
it Cicero outlines the obligation of the citizen. Although much that
he says is of more general application, he is concerned particularly
with the obligations of the young man whose birthright is participation in the state. His discussion is based, as he frankly says, on an
essay of the Stoic Panaetius, who almost a century earlier wrote on
the same subject for the noble circle of the younger Scipio; but
Cicero writes in terms of the obligations and responsibilities that
his own renown had conferred on the young Marcus. Men who have
the natural endowments needed to conduct public affairs should,
he says, without hesitation seek office and take part in their conduct.[9] They should not be deterred by the toil and trouble of a
political career or the fear of meeting defeat at the polls. They are
justified in not going in for politics if they are too weak to undergo
the strains of public life. Perhaps also, though here Cicero is doubtful, men devoted to learning may be excused from politics, but there
is no excuse for those who, in order to secure tranquillity and ease,
avoid the trouble of a political career.

It was, it may be noted, partly because the Epicureans recommended avoidance of politics that the Roman state was officially
hostile to the sect. The Roman nobility could not countenance the
view of the contemporary Epicurean poet Lucretius when he stood
on the heights and looked down with pity and saw men

> Certare ingenio, contendere nobilitate
> noctes atque dies niti praestanti labore
> ad summas emergere opes rerumque potiri.

> Rivals in genius, or emulous in rank,
> Pressing through days and nights with hugest toil
> For summits of power and mastery of the world.[10]

At least officially the nobles would have rejected the poet's description of public life, with its defeats, as hell on earth.

> We have before our eyes
> Here in this life also a Sisyphus
> In him who seeketh of the populace
> The rods, the axes fell, and ever more
> Retires a beaten and a gloomy man.
> For to seek after power—an empty name,
> Nor given at all—and ever in the search
> To endure a world of toil, O this it is
> To shove with shoulder up the hill a stone
> Which yet comes rolling back from off the top,
> And headlong makes for levels of the plain.[11]

Lucretius might scorn the goals of politicians, but he was undoubtedly right about the incessant toil of public life. It was grueling even for the noblest, who were said to have been elected to the consulship in their cradles. The boy's entire education was planned for public life. The chief emphasis was on physical fitness, training of voice and diction, familiarity with public affairs, and the development of ready ease in speaking. To accomplish this last aim the boy had to store his mind, and that meant familiarity with Greek and Latin literature and with history and philosophy.

As the boy grew older, he had daily exercises in speaking under Greek rhetors, who were useful for technique but could of course teach their Roman masters nothing about statecraft. To learn that art, the boy was taken to the Forum to hear the public speeches and the orations in the law courts, and he sat at the feet of great Romans who had achieved renown in public affairs. At least by the time he was twenty the youth began to appear in court, perhaps as a character witness for a family friend. If he was good at speaking he would even assume the exacting role of prosecutor of a family enemy. Over and over again such public accusations were conducted by men in their youth, by the orator Crassus at nineteen, by Lucullus, Caesar, Calvus, and Asinius Pollio when they were not much older.[12]

Along with the young man's practice in speaking went his first military service, which began when he was about seventeen. The requirement of ten years' military service, which Polybius states as a prerequisite for a political career,[13] seems no longer to have been in force in the late republic, but some military experience was apparently demanded. After initial training at home, the young man often went out to serve in one of the provinces, perhaps as a *contubernalis* (tentmate) of a governor, who was very likely a family friend; later he often served as military tribune, a rank that corresponded to a lower commissioned officer in our army.

With his military training he frequently continued his practice in speaking, seeking out the great teachers of the Greek cities if he was in the East, or, if he was not sent to a center of traditional culture, taking a teacher along with him, as the young Augustus did.[14] Before the day came for his first candidacy—and he often held a minor office or an elective military tribunate before he sought for the quaestorship—the young noble had to make himself known to the electorate, perhaps to journey about Italy and become acquainted with the men of the municipalities, particularly with the richest men, who were most likely to come to Rome to vote.

At his house in Rome, which, Cicero emphasizes, should be a seemly mansion, with plenty of space in it,[15] he had to be ready in the morning to greet the family clients and retainers and friends who came for the daily *salutatio,* and in the Forum he had to appear with a retinue and to be always at the call of any friend who might need him in the courts. If he had good family traditions, he would have no difficulty in securing immediate election at the age of thirty to the office that admitted him to the senate,[16] the quaestorship, and then he would be engaged for a year as an aide to the chief magistrates, either in Italy or, more likely, in the provinces. At that time he might well have further experience in war.

The next obligatory office in the *cursus* was the praetorship, which could not be held until nine years after the quaestorship. In the intervening period the noble would probably seek election to one of the optional offices, the curule aedileship or, if he was a plebeian, the plebeian aedileship or the tribunate of the plebs. All these offices were a great help to the aspirant for the consulship. The aediles had to put on public theatrical and circus games and, if they had enough wealth, or, like Caesar, could borrow enough money, they could attract attention by making the games magnificent.[17] Sometimes the nobles made the aedileship the occasion of gladiatorial games in honor of a member of the family who had died. There was a tendency to postpone such celebrations until candidacy for the consulship was in view, so that the memory of the show would be fresh in the minds of voters. Thus Caesar in his aedileship gave a splendid gladiatorial show for his father, who had died nearly two decades earlier.[18] The tribune, especially after Pompey restored the full powers of the office, had great opportunities to gain popular favor by intervention for citizens under attack, vetoes of unpopular measures, addresses to the citizens, and bills proposed in the council of the plebs. Even though tribunes were not necessarily interested in the people, they claimed to be *populares* when in office.

This intervening period between quaestorship and praetorship was often spent in part in the provinces, usually as legate of a governor in command, and, though many such posts were mainly administrative, there was often opportunity of gaining further military experience under a tested commander like Lucullus or Pompey or Caesar.[19]

The praetorship also was usually secured by the nobles as soon as the law allowed, for, since there were eight of these officers, the competition was not too severe. After a year of service in this office as judge in the urban, peregrine, or criminal courts, the praetor normally went out, the following year, to a province. Although in general the provinces likely to be involved in war were saved for consular governors, the governor of praetorian rank sometimes, like Caesar in Further Spain, had opportunity for military exploits and might occasionally win a triumph. He always had a chance to enrich himself—a chance that was in part legitimate, for the state allowances were far in excess of necessary expenditures. He also had great opportunity for plunder. He returned with his mind completely on the consulship.

The consulship could be held three years after the praetorship, and every noble hoped to hold it in what he called "his year," the year he reached the age of forty-three. Here, since there were only two places and a number of candidates, the competition was intense. It was, moreover, fraught with personal danger, for rivals or their adherents were continually bringing suit in the courts in order to eliminate, through exile or removal from the senate, an opponent who seemed likely to win.[20] The favorite charge was extortion in the provinces, but embezzlement of public funds and treason against the state were also possible charges. With the elections (to be considered in the next chapter) the dangers of an accusation were not over, for, though the man was immune while in office, he could still be prosecuted in the interval between election and entrance into office. In such cases the usual charge was illegal canvassing, including bribery.[21]

After the consulship there was regularly another provincial governorship, again with opportunities for enrichment and new dangers of accusations. Often, too, there were chances to conduct a war, and if these came his way the noble's ambition was whetted again. He wished the senate to vote first a thanksgiving to the gods for any victories he had won, and then the great distinction of a triumph, which would enable him to array himself in the costume of Jupiter the Best and Greatest, drive with a splendid procession in a chariot along the Sacred Way, and lay his spoils at the feet of Jupiter on the Capitol. Cicero, a peaceful man, after his lieutenants won some victories, longed for that honor, and for years during the Civil War went about accompanied with the laurels he hoped to bestow on Capitoline Jupiter.

The man of consular rank might occasionally, after an interval of ten years, seek a second consulship, and repeated consulships were a great honor.[22] He might also seek the censorship, to which every five years two of the most eminent *consulares* were elected.[23] The censor's task of reviewing the list of senators and overseeing the enrollment of citizens enabled him to eliminate his enemies from the senate and to make alterations to the advantage of his associates in the registration of citizens. But the office was even more valued for the honor which the censor, resplendent in the purple toga that belonged to this office alone, conferred on the family. The other great distinction of Rome, coveted by all the high nobility and limited almost exclusively to them, was membership in the great colleges of priests. This distinction might be achieved at any time after the noble took the toga of manhood, and men of the most distinguished houses were apt to be chosen when they were very young.[24]

Even if he fell short of the distinction of a triumph or a second consulship or a censorship or a priesthood, the ordinary *consularis,* with an influential place in the body that was, for purposes of empire at least, the ruling body of the state, was in a position of great prestige. It was in no sense a position of leisure, for now he had to think of the maintenance of his *dignitas,* his rank, and he also had to concern himself with his family and particularly his sons, who must achieve a career like his own. And that meant that he had to keep powerful friends and make new ones, that he had in fact to be a candidate all over again, this time for the younger generation.

To carry on the traditions of the house the noble counted on having a son to succeed him, but he rarely had a large family; he did not wish the responsibility of a number of sons who had to be brought to the consulship and of several daughters for whom he had to find noble or consular husbands. The family of Metellus Macedonicus, which consisted of four sons, all of whom reached the consulship, and two daughters, who married into families of the high nobility, was exceptional. So also was the family of Appius Claudius Pulcher, consul in 79, who died and left in relative poverty three sons and three daughters. Through the interest of relatives and friends these children prospered. One of the sons reached the consulship, and two others, one of whom was Cicero's enemy Clodius, were on the way to the office when they died. The three daughters, one of whom gained immortality as the Lesbia of Catullus, all married husbands who reached the consulship. Another comparatively large family was that of the younger Cato, who had two sons and probably three daughters.[25] In contrast to these families, most of the other nobles about whom we have information either had no issue or small families of one, two, or three children. Thus Pompey had two sons and a daughter; Crassus, two sons; Caesar, one daughter; Catulus, probably two daughters; Lucius Domitius Ahenobarbus, one son; Metellus Scipio, one daughter; and Metellus Pius, no children.

It was through intermarriage and adoption from one family to another that the closest bonds between the noble houses were established. As Horace tells us, one of the questions asked about a candidate was whether people had heard of his mother.[26] The nobles considered carefully the political importance of the family connections, when arranging the marriages of their sons and daughters.[27] In consequence the princely houses were an inbred group, bound to one another by relationships going back for generations. The great family of the Caecilii Metelli intermarried with the patrician Aemilii, Claudii Pulchri, Cornelii Scipiones Nasicae, and Cornelii Sullae, and with the plebeian Mucii, Servilii, Licinii Luculli, and Licinii Crassi. The relations of two houses joined by marriage frequently continued when, as often happened, there had been a divorce. Cicero maintained friendship with two former sons-in-law from whom his daughter Tullia was divorced. The attitude toward divorce is illustrated by the fact that Cato agreed to give up his wife Marcia to his friend Hortensius, and then, after Hortensius' death, married her again himself. According to Caesar, she came back to Cato much richer than she was before.[28]

To unite families, adoptions were as important as intermarriages.[29] A noble without an heir frequently adopted a son, and he regularly chose from a distinguished family the child, or often the full-grown man, whom he wished to carry on his name. Thus the conqueror of Macedonia, Lucius Aemilius Paullus, allowed two of his four sons to be adopted by the Cornelii Scipiones and the Fabii Maximi, two other great patrician houses; and then, tragically, his family became extinct through the death of the two remaining sons. Sometimes a noble who had no heir adopted in his will the son of a relative or friend. Caesar supplies an illustration, for he adopted his great-nephew, the young Gaius Octavius. By such adoptions the two houses were brought closely together, and the man adopted was thought to belong to both families. Thus the younger Scipio Africanus, son of Aemilius Paullus, the leading figure in Cicero's essay on the state, speaks of *both* his fathers, and is proud of the family tradition of both his houses.[30]

A remarkable example of such a double tradition in the days of Cicero was Publius Cornelius Scipio Nasica. He belonged to a line of the Scipios that was collateral to the Africani, and he could trace his house back for at least eleven generations in which all his paternal ancestors except two, who had probably died too young, had reached the consulship; some of them had been censors and had triumphed. His inheritance had been enriched by intermarriages of his ancestors with the line of the elder Africanus, the Caecilii Metelli, the Licinii Crassi, the Mucii Scaevolae, and the Laelii, all great consular families. He himself married Lepida, daughter of Mamercus Aemilius Lepidus Livianus, a relative of Cato (whom she jilted for Nasica), by birth an heiress to the traditions of the noble plebeian Livii, the family of Augustus' wife, and by adoption to the glories of the patrician Aemilii. To this splendid heritage from patrician and plebeian nobility Scipio Nasica added glories by accepting testamentary adoption from Quintus Metellus Pius, *pontifex maximus,* consul, and *triumphator.* By this adoption he gained another direct line of six consular ancestors. His atrium, with the wax masks of two long lines of consular ancestors and with many more added from the female side, must have been a showplace of Rome. His daughter, married first to a son of Crassus and later to Pompey, was the great catch of Rome.[31] In Lucan's epic on the Civil War Pompey addresses her as *femina tantorum titulis insignis avorum.*[32]

The noble's family, with his connections by marriage and adoption, was strengthened into a party grouping by his bonds of friendship with other noble houses.[33] We have already seen that *amicitia* was the time-honored substitute for party. Friendships were often passed down from one generation to another. The strength of inherited friendship is illustrated by the array of counsel and character witnesses that rallied to the defense when the son of the first man of the senate of Marius' time, Marcus Aemilius Scaurus, was accused in 54. Party rivalry, then strong between the "triumvirs" and the *optimates,* was laid aside, and among the nine men of consular rank who appeared were Pompey and Crassus and some of their strongest opponents. In the group also were the two fierce rivals, Milo and Clodius, whose adherents were busy murdering each other at the time.[34]

Nobles in politics not only inherited friends; they constantly made new friends. They also inherited personal enemies (*inimici*) and, as a result of their political activities, acquired new enemies; from time to time, too, they made their peace with former enemies. The news of fresh alliances of friendship, of enmities, and of recon-

ciliations looms large in the political gossip of the Ciceronian collection of *Letters.*

Obligations of friendship often led to conflict with other friends,
but it was accepted procedure that a man should pay his personal
obligations, whatever the conflict. Thus, after Milo had risked his
life to bring Cicero back from exile, Cicero had to pay his debts,
though at the time he was in the orbit of Pompey, who had clashed
with Milo. Cicero gave vigorous support to Milo's candidacy for
the consulship, which was opposed by Pompey, and in court defended Milo against the charge of violence. Cicero later acknowledged Pompey's understanding attitude on this occasion.[35] When
the Civil War came and Cicero was debating his own course, the
fact that Pompey had also helped to bring Cicero back from exile
was the deciding factor in leading him to join Pompey. As Cicero
puts it, *ingrati animi crimen horreo.*[36]

"Friends," as we saw in the first chapter, often joined together in
closely knit cliques. The short-term unions of candidates, *coitiones,*
designed to shut out competitors, will be considered in the next
chapter. Long-term combinations, "bad friendships," were known
by the invidious term *factio.* We have seen that the word came to
mean oligarchy or to suggest oligarchical designs, and that it was
applied to Caesar's enemies in the senate and on one occasion to
Caesar's deal with Pompey and Crassus.

There were also various associations of men of the senatorial class
which had political importance. Among these were the colleges of
priests, in our period made up of nobles, and the brotherhoods like
the *Luperci* and the *sodales Titii.*[37] We hear also of *sodalitates* that
functioned in the law courts, apparently for both prosecution and
defense. Quintus Cicero, in writing to Marcus, speaks of such
groups, which were committed to support Marcus' candidacy because he had taken their cases in the courts.[38] But at Rome such
sodalitates seem to have been less important than the Athenian
clubs which played a major role in politics and in the courts.[39]

Occasionally there was a revolutionary organization of prominent men bound together, as the members of the Athenian clubs
often were, by a joint oath. That may have been true of the senators
who were accused of having conspired with Marcus Livius Drusus

in 91 to obtain citizenship for the Italians,[40] a subject to be considered later in the discussion of clientage. The best-attested example of a *coniuratio* is the conspiracy of Catiline which included, with knights and disaffected city and country people, a number of senators, among them two men of eminent patrician ancestry. The steadfastness of the members in refusing to reveal the details of the conspiracy was taken as proof that the Catilinarians were living up to an oath they had taken.[41] The group of sixty-odd senators who united to murder Caesar was, we are explicitly told, not bound together by oath.

Political associations were also cultivated outside the nobility and the senate. Of first importance were the knights, men with property valued at 400,000 sesterces (about $25,000) or more. The knights included members of the senatorial class who had not yet entered upon a political career. Most senators' sons were enrolled in the eighteen centuries of knights with public horse, comprising men of the officer class in the army who looked forward to a political career. They voted as a separate unit in the major Roman assembly. They had great prestige with the electorate, for they were cultivating it in the hope of future advantage for themselves. Older men sought to enhance their prestige by having as many younger men as possible in their group of friends.[42] Cicero's fame in the law courts brought many young men of prominence into association with him, and he valued their support both in his elections and in maintaining his position in subsequent years.

Then there was the great body of knights, men theoretically eligible for office, who in general preferred to remain knights because they were not restricted, as senators were, in their business activities. Some of the knights, like Cicero's friend Atticus, while not engaging in political life, had enormous influence in a wide circle of friends among the nobles. Cicero considered Atticus' aid of great importance in his own candidacies and in his time of peril. As a group the knights did not, in the late republic, regain the full measure of political influence that they had wielded when they controlled the juries from the time of Gaius Gracchus to the dictatorship of Sulla, but their votes counted heavily in the assembly that elected consuls and praetors. Among the knights a particularly well organized group was composed of the public contractors who worked in societies in the various provinces and had their representatives at Rome. Every provincial governor became involved with these societies, and Cicero, who frequently handled the business of the publicans in the law courts, carried on an extensive correspondence in their interest.

The knights and the public contractors were, in large part, drawn from the aristocracy of Italian municipalities. With this aristocracy, the leaders of their communities, the Roman nobility often established rights of hospitality. Municipal leaders could be helpful in swinging the election districts for the noble and his friends, and the noble himself provided his *hospes* with a place to stay and with suitable entertainment when he came to the city. *Tesserae* recording such rights of hospitality between prominent Roman houses and municipal families have come to light in Italian excavations.[43]

An example of a municipal leader who had such ties with various Roman houses is provided by Sextus Roscius from an Umbrian town, of whom Cicero says: "By birth, descent, and fortune he was easily the chief man not only in his own town but also in the neighborhood, while his influence and relations of hospitality with those of the highest rank enhanced his reputation."[44] Cicero goes on to note his relations of hospitality with the Caecilii Metelli, the Servilii, and the Scipiones in Rome and to point out that, in the struggle between Marius and Sulla, Roscius had favored the Sullan side, that is, the nobility, for "he thought it his duty to fight for the honour of those to whom he owed it that he was reckoned a most honourable man among his fellow citizens."[45] It is an indication of the close relationship of Rome to the municipal aristocracy that both in the Hannibalic and in the Social War, when their fellow townsmen revolted, the chief men of the Italian towns often maintained fealty to Rome.

The Roman nobility found in the municipal leaders the same conservatism that they themselves represented in Roman politics. Thus Cicero's grandfather, a leader of his native town, Arpinum, fought, and with more success than the nobles did at Rome, against the institution of the secret written ballot at Arpinum, an institution that curbed the influence of the aristocrats on the vote. According to Cicero, Marcus Aemilius Scaurus, the first man of the Roman senate in Cicero's grandfather's day, expressed regret that the elder Cicero had preferred to devote himself to his own town rather than to the Roman state.[46]

Sometimes Roman nobles, to strengthen their relations with municipal men, married their children into municipal houses. Such alliances were a good thing because they brought new blood into the nobility, but they were usually considered unworthy.[47] In spite of the use of the term *hospitium,* technically a designation of equality, to dignify the relationship, the Roman noble looked upon even the wealthiest man from a municipality as an inferior. That attitude was shown even toward men who secured high office, like Cicero. Catiline dubbed Cicero an *inquilinus,* an immigrant, and a patrician opponent in the courts called him a *peregrinus rex.*[48]

To maintain their contacts with their friends of their own class, with the knights and the municipal aristocracy, and with the inferior group of clients, to be considered later, the nobles had to have an elaborate organization. The Romans understood the need of organization in politics, but the organization was personal. It was in line with the "rugged individualism" that prevailed in the republic.

There was no police force, no postal or freight service, and, except in the treasury, practically no civil service. The nobles looked after their personal safety by keeping up bands of followers and attendants. They communicated with the cities of Italy and the provinces through personal messengers, using vehicles, horses, or ships which were their private property. They often made their means of communication available to their friends, but in doing so they were conferring a personal favor. Every important man had a staff of slaves and freedmen to aid in political activities. The staff included a secretariat to keep up the voluminous correspondence that was necessary.

Cato must have needed a number of aides to keep up his assiduous exchange of letters not only with the men in the provinces but with allied peoples in whose concerns he showed interest,[49] especially if there were any suggestion that they were being exploited. Cicero also was constantly writing to men in the provinces, recommending people to them, and assuring them that he was looking out for their prestige in Rome. When he was governor of Cilicia he carried on an immense correspondence, not only with Roman senators who, he hoped, would secure him a thanksgiving and a triumph, but with men who had special interests in his province. He exchanged many letters with the young Marcus Junius Brutus, future leader of Caesar's assassins, who kept recommending a certain Saufeius.[50] This man was trying by pressure and force to collect money at an exorbitant rate of interest from a city of Cyprus, and Cicero was appalled to learn that the money had really been lent by Brutus himself.

Cicero, as we know from the letters of introduction included in his correspondence, was involved through his own personal agents in the affairs of other provinces. He writes to one provincial officer about a slave of a certain Lucius Egnatius, a knight who often did business for him. "I commend him to you with no less warmth," Cicero says, "than if the business I commend to you were my very own."[51] To show Cicero's relations with a leading municipal man I quote a letter written to Brutus when he was governor of Cisalpine Gaul. "L. Castronius Paetus, by far the most important member of the municipality of Luca, is an honourable, sterling and most obliging man, a thoroughly good fellow, and graced not only with all the virtues but also, if that has anything to do with the matter, with a handsome fortune. Besides he is on very good terms with me, so much so indeed that there is no member of our order to whom he pays more particular attention. I therefore commend him to you as being both my friend and worthy of your friendship; and whatever you do to oblige him will assuredly give pleasure to yourself and in any case be a favor to me."[52]

Caesar's organization of his contacts at Rome through the loyal Balbus was remarkably efficient during his years of absence in Gaul. There was a steady stream of messengers between Rome and Gaul, and Caesar was informed of everything, *omnia minima maxima.*[53] Balbus, later aided by the equally efficient Oppius, did wonders in upholding Caesar's influence and seeing to it that the men whom Caesar supported lived up to their obligations.

In maintaining this great private organization, the noble aimed to keep up his own influence at Rome when he was away and in the provinces when he was at Rome; he was seeking, too, through patronage to add steadily to the group of men who had received favors which they might be expected to repay. When Cicero writes to a friend about some senator, public contractor, or provincial, he frequently adds, "Please tell him I wrote to you about this."

Particularly important for every noble was the organization of his contacts with the members of his own voting group or ward, his *tribules,* whom he counted on being able to carry for his own elections or those of his friends. This group will be discussed in the next chapter.

I turn now to the admittedly inferior group, the clients, for whom also the maintenance of organized contacts was essential.[54] These were the men for whom the noble, as *patronus,* a word related in origin to *pater,* was expected to take paternal responsibility. The clients, men said to be in the *fides* of their patron, provided the Roman politician with a basis in popular support. The institution of clientage went far back in Roman history. In a passage that seems to depend on a monograph of Caesar's time,[55] the Greek historian Dionysius of Halicarnassus attributes the institution to Romulus, who "placed the plebeians as a trust in the hands of the patricians by allowing every plebeian to choose for his patron any patrician whom he himself wished." The relationship of *fides,*[56] trust, loyalty, theoretically entered into voluntarily, was at the root of the institution. Dionysius describes the duties of both sides, the obligation of the patron to explain the law to his client, to look out for him and his family, to bring suit for him and defend him, and the client's responsibility to serve his patron in every way. The relation of mutual loyalty between patron and client (*fides* again) is further demonstrated in Dionysius' account. "For both patrons and clients alike," he says, "it was impious and unlawful to accuse each other in law suits, or to bear witness or to give their votes against each other or to be found in the number of each other's enemies; and whoever was convicted of doing any of these things was guilty of treason ... The connections between the clients and patrons continued for many generations, differing in no wise from the ties of blood relationship, and being handed down to their children's children. And it was a matter of great praise to men of illustrious family to have as many clients as possible and not only to preserve the succession of hereditary patronage but also by their own merit to acquire others."

These clients had once been serfs in the power of their noble patrons, but that condition had ended several centuries before the age of Caesar. The relationship in our period is frequently not an exclusive one. A client could have a number of different patrons. We know more about the whole class under the empire, for Martial and Juvenal tell us a great deal about the inconveniences and difficulties of the morning *salutatio,* for which the poor man had to climb up the hills to the great houses of Rome. The class was equally strong under the republic, and more useful to the patron in the days of free elections.

To understand the importance of clients in the late republic, we have to go to a passage like the following in Cicero's speech for Murena: "Men of slender means have only one way of earning favors from our order or of paying us back and that is by helping us and following us about in our campaigns for office. For it is not possible and cannot be asked of men of our class and of the Roman knights that they should for entire days follow after their friends who are candidates. If they come in numbers to our houses and sometimes accompany us down to the Forum, if they deign to walk with us the length of a public hall, we think we are securing great attention and respect. It is the men of rather slender means, men with free time, who supply the steady attention that is regularly given to good men and to benefactors. Don't take from the lower class of men this fruit of their devotion. Let the men who hope for everything from us have something themselves to give us."

Cicero goes on to indicate that to have influence the men of lower station have to do something more than cast their ballots for their benefactors. "As they often say, they can't talk for us or make speeches or offer bail or invite us to their houses. These are all things they secure from us and they can make return only by their services."[57] In this passage Cicero appears to be protecting the humbler people from restrictions on electioneering, but he clearly shows the value the nobles placed on the assiduous service of the client class. That value is also shown in Quintus Cicero's advice on Marcus' candidacy for the consulship.

Quintus classifies the clients who show attention to candidates for office into three groups,[58] the throngs that come to the morning *salutatio* and that often journey about from one candidate to another, the men who accompany the candidate down to the Forum, and the men who follow him about as he goes around asking for votes. The second class, the *deductores,* are apparently more respectable than the other two, and Quintus advises Marcus to go to the Forum at a regular hour every day, so that they will not be kept waiting.

Both Marcus and Quintus seem to be speaking mainly of the urban populace which provided most of the people that thronged the houses of the great and followed the leading men around, especially when they were candidates, but in smaller numbers also at other times. The urban plebs, especially after it had been increased by men evicted from their lands, by vagrants who came to the city to enjoy the games and to benefit from the grain dole, and by the steady manumission of slaves, had in it a large group of people who possessed no means of livelihood except what could be had from attachment to nobles of the great houses and to popular leaders like Caesar or Clodius—who, by advancing popular measures in the assemblies, were actually building a personal party.

Sallust, in a rather sweeping statement, says that every man of a people that was once sovereign has made private arrangements for slavery.[59] Plenty of them were actually hired out to individuals, and they could be used not only for legitimate campaigns, where they followed the candidate about, but also, as we shall see in the next chapter, for violence. It was easier to gather such men together because many of them, including slaves and freedmen, were, under the free right of association that prevailed at Rome, already organized in guilds or *collegia,* primarily burial colleges for men in the same trade or adherents of a common cult. There were also neighborhood guilds, centering about altars at the crossroads where annual games were celebrated in religious organizations. Such groups, made up of men associated in their trades and cults, or living in close proximity, could easily be brought together for political purposes.

Catiline seems to have used these guilds to terrorize his opponents, and it was apparently during his campaign for the consulship in 64 that the senate passed a decree disbanding all the guilds except such as contributed to the public welfare.[60] Clodius as tribune in 58 revived the guilds and even created new ones; he armed the members with sticks and stones and sometimes with swords, and employed them as a private army in politics. The senate attempted again to dissolve the guilds, but apparently without success.[61]

The client class went far beyond the bounds of the city. It included inhabitants of towns, and in fact of whole regions, over which the nobles assumed patronage because they or their ancestors had conquered them in war, or had aided them in obtaining citizenship and other advantages. Thus the descendants of the commissioners who had established Roman colonies—the city founders, who in Roman tradition functioned in groups and not individually—thought of themselves as the patrons of the towns their ancestors had established. As Rome's empire extended, the nobles numbered among their clients not only Italians but inhabitants of conquered territory overseas—provincials and even peoples of client kingdoms.[62] The Claudii Marcelli, descendants of the conqueror of Syracuse, considered themselves the patrons of all Sicily. Lucius Domitius Ahenobarbus, grandson of one of the conquerors of Narbonese Gaul, thought that that region was in his care and for years looked with jealous eyes on Caesar's tenure of the province. Every man who had been a provincial governor strove to maintain relations with the people, and especially the "best" people, of the province he had administered. When Flaccus, who had governed Asia, was tried for extortion, many Asiatics were there to testify for him.[63]

All the great noble houses had great numbers of clients in their service. Crassus and Pompey each had a band so large that he could raise an army in Sulla's service. Crassus had built up his inherited riches by his policy of continually annexing more clients.[64] It is the fashion of modern historians to single Crassus out as the weakest of the three men in the so-called triumvirate, but it is noteworthy that both Caesar and Pompey thought he counted. The reason he counted is that in his great following of clients he was a rival of the strongest of the nobles who combined against the three men.

Pompey's clients were perhaps more numerous than Crassus', but they were probably less well distributed in the voting districts. From his father, a leading general of the Social War, and a man who once threatened to take the state over by force, Pompey had inherited a large band of loyal veterans who had been richly rewarded by the elder Pompey; he had also inherited masses of clients in Picenum, where his father had vast estates, and in the Social War had managed to conciliate the richest elements in the population. In the elder Pompey's bodyguard, as we know from an inscription, was a group of young Picene officers,[65] and men from that region appear later in his son's entourage. One of them was Caesar's most trusted lieutenant in Gaul, Titus Labienus, whose defection to Pompey at the beginning of the Civil War is to be explained by his Picene origin.[66] The elder Pompey had also won a large following both in the Gallic cities south of the Po and in the teeming and vigorous population north of the Po, where he had, under a consular law, bestowed Latin rights on the towns. He also had numerous clients in Spain, to many of whom he gave citizenship.

The younger Pompey himself increased his inherited clients through his enlistment of soldiers, his bestowal of citizenship, and his conciliation of many individuals and groups. His adherents were so numerous in Spain that his sons were able to make the peninsula a base of resistance not only against Caesar but later against Caesar's heir. Pompey's eastern conquests also added to his clients huge forces of allied peoples—barbarians, and not Romans, as the opposing side took care to point out.

Extension of citizenship was a favorite means of adding to one's clients. Gaius Gracchus had tried to give citizenship to the Latin communities (towns whose magistrates acquired Roman citizenship through election to local offices) and Latin rights to the other Italian people, and at the end of his career, when he was hard pressed by his enemies, he seems to have encouraged Latins and Italians to rally to his defense. His example was followed by the tribune Marcus Livius Drusus, who in 91 B.C. attempted to enfranchise all the Italians. We have an extraordinary document of

Drusus' activity in an oath of fealty that the Italians took in Drusus' name. The text of the oath, quoted by the Greek historian of the Augustan Age, Diodorus Siculus, has generally been rejected because it was considered inconsistent with Roman religious formulae, but the recent discovery of an inscription has provided strong reason for believing it genuine.[67] It reads: "I swear by Jupiter Capitolinus and the Vesta of Rome and by Mars, the ancestral god of Rome, and by the Sun, the founder of the race (*Sol Indiges*), and by earth, the benefactress of living and growing things, and by the demigods, who are the founders of Rome, and the heroes who have contributed to increase her domain that I will hold the friend and enemy of Drusus to be my friend and enemy and that I will not spare possessions or the life of my children or of my parents if it be to Drusus' advantage and to the advantage of those who have taken this oath. If I become a citizen by the law of Drusus I will hold Rome as my country and Drusus as my greatest benefactor, and I will share this oath with as many citizens as I can. And if I swear faithfully, may all good things come to me; if falsely, the reverse." If, as I believe, this oath is genuine, it is clear that Drusus was building a very powerful body of followers among the Italians, who were then more numerous by far than the Roman citizens. There was some basis for the nobles' fear that Drusus was striving for personal supremacy.[68] It was as swearers of a joint oath that, aroused by the murder of Drusus, the Italians rose in revolt in the Social War.[69]

When the Italians acquired citizenship after that war, the next group clamoring for the right was the Transpadane people, the inhabitants of the cities across the Po, the country of Catullus, Vergil, and Livy, the richest and most populous district of Italy. The Latin rights given them by the elder Pompey meant that the men elected to magistracies in the towns—that is, the richest inhabitants, like Catullus' father, for instance—already had such rights, but plenty of noncitizens remained, and there were men at Rome who wished for the credit of enrolling them with full franchise. Pompey was interested in them because of his father's benefactions, and so was Crassus, who tried to give them citizenship when he was censor, but failed because of the opposition of his colleague Catulus.

Caesar, who had shown his concern for the subject as early as the year 68, was able to make progress with the awards during his long Gallic proconsulship. Many of the men had acquired citizenship through enlistment in his army, and others through the colony he established at Novum Comum.[70] Sallust, in the letter to Caesar written in 51, urged Caesar to adopt a general policy of enfranchisement, acknowledging that the nobles would, as they subsequently did, oppose his policy bitterly.[71] Sallust supported the enrollment of new citizens as a means of purifying the state, but he did not deny that the awards would greatly strengthen Caesar's position. The Transpadane region was enfranchised in 49 under a law proposed by one of Caesar's praetors.

We do not know how usual it was for the client to swear allegiance to his patron, but the example of Livius Drusus may indicate that it was customary procedure for new citizens. The humbler followers of Catiline, as well as the senators and knights, took such an oath. They included a large group of the city plebs, hard pressed by misery and debt, and another in the country, where Sulla's veterans, who had not proved to be good farmers, and the men who had been dispossessed made common cause.

The most important group under oath to individuals was the personal army.[72] The Roman soldier, recruited in earlier times for a year's service under a consul who also functioned for a year, though the command might be prolonged, had regularly taken an oath of allegiance to his general. The relationship was a close one, but, since terms of service were often brief and generals constantly changed, the citizen soldiers had been distributed in military allegiance among various generals of the nobility. When Marius instituted the army of the proletariat, which remained under arms for years, the old military oath seems to have been administered for the entire period of service. The soldiers were turned into clients of the general; while they were in the army they looked to him for rewards, and after they were established in colonies with grants of land they continued as veterans to regard him as their patron, to look to him for aid, and to respond to his call in time of need. Certainly Caesar, and perhaps Sulla and Pompey before him, settled the veterans in colonies according to their military units so that it would be possible to call them out for renewed service in their old formations. And they had an advantage over other clients, for they already knew the art of war. They were the most important and decisive accretion to the personal party.

From 70 to 49, Pompey's veterans constituted a major factor in Roman politics. The union of Pompey, Crassus, and Caesar brought them into the service of the three men, where they were added to the strong forces of inherited clients belonging to Pompey and Crassus. Caesar, with an ancestry that had in recent generations been less distinguished, probably inherited no such large group of clients, but he had built his personal following out of the old Marians, both the upper classes, who had been debarred from public office by Sulla, and the populace, who revered the memory of Marius.[73] Caesar had also, by conciliating the urban plebs and sponsoring laws that looked out for their interests, added greatly to his adherents. These three men were opposed by the great mass of the nobility, men like Cato and his wealthy brother-in-law Lucius Domitius Ahenobarbus and the influential Cornelii Lentuli, all provided with inherited clients, of whose strength Sallust warns Caesar.[74] There were fewer trained soldiers in this group, but there were plenty of men available to provide armed bands to oppose the forces of the "triumvirs," and to keep the streets of Rome and the popular assemblies in a state of confusion for a decade.

When Pompey broke with Caesar, he united his clients and his veterans with the forces of the men who had been his enemies for years, the *optimates* of the senate. The combination made a strong party, but not strong enough to prevail against the party that Caesar had built for himself alone. That party included the urban plebs to whom Caesar and his tribunes had for years presented popular laws, but the plebs no longer counted when arms took the place of legislation. What did count was Caesar's army, ten legions, most of them tested by years of victorious fighting and devoted to their leader. And after he won the war, Caesar attempted to turn all Italy into a single unit bound in personal loyalty to him. He failed, but his successor Augustus, by administering an oath of fealty to himself, succeeded. That development, to be more fully discussed in the last chapter, was not clearly understood until a German, and,

I feel confident, an anti-Nazi German, Anton von Premerstein, writing under the domination of a leader and a party which had become identified with the whole state, interpreted Roman politics in terms of the scene in which he was living and showed how the totalitarian party of the empire (which the Romans were not so illogical as to call a party) evolved from the personal parties of the old Roman nobility.

CHAPTER III

DELIVERING THE VOTE

EVEN THE MOST HARDENED modern party organizer would have quailed at the problem of getting out the Roman vote, for it had to be done so often and many of the voters lived so far away. Every year six regular magistracies, made up of colleges of two to ten men, and various minor offices had to be filled at elections that took place mainly on different days and often, because of postponements, in different months. Besides, from time to time important special officers like censors or public priests had to be elected. In addition, since every law was a referendum to the people, voters had to be summoned to the polls whenever a consul or a praetor or a tribune proposed a bill. And the polls were in Rome, while the voters after the Social War were spread through the whole of Italy south of the Po.

Obviously the people of Rome, always on hand, found it easier to exercise suffrage, and, although it has been recognized that the bulk of them were registered in such a way as to make the individual vote count little, the general view has been that the city populace often decided the issue at the polls. That view has been disputed by Professor Frank Burr Marsh, and his rather sweeping statements have in turn been questioned by Professor Hugh Last.[1] For an understanding of the political strife of the late republic it is important to consider what proportion of voters outside the city came to Rome to cast their ballots.

THE ROLE OF THE CITY PLEBS AND THE ITALIANS IN THE VOTING

The Romans had a group voting system. The voting unit was the *tribus* (tribe or ward). There were thirty-five tribes in the Roman state, four urban and thirty-one rural. The majority of the city population, always on hand to vote, was registered in the four urban tribes, and, though many more men could have voted in each of these tribes than in the rural tribes, each urban tribe had no more effect on the election than each rural tribe.[2]

[1] For notes to chap. iii see pp. 199–211.

The original distribution of the tribes went back to a day when the people of Rome consisted of the farmers who had plots, often small ones of two acres or so, in the surrounding country and of the nonlandholding industrial groups who lived in the city. The system deliberately put the chief political power in the hands of the farmers and subordinated the industrial population of the city. The industrial workers were placed in the four urban tribes, and in those tribes too were men under a stigma—for instance, illegitimate children, and eventually the freedmen. Originally each rural tribe represented a district in the neighborhood of Rome.[3] The men who owned the land either lived in the city or could easily come in from a short distance to vote.

The steady extension of Roman territory and Roman citizenship made a radical change in the situation. For a time new tribes were added for new citizens, but after the year 241, when thirty-one rural tribes had been created, no additional tribes were organized. New colonies and municipalities were placed in the old tribes, which gradually ceased to occupy continuous geographical areas. Voters now lived farther and farther from the city. Besides, the region about Rome, which had once supplied the men who came to the assemblies, became more and more depleted of voters as it was swallowed up into large estates, worked by slaves who had no vote.

A great change in the tribal organization resulted from the bestowal of citizenship on all the Italians south of the Po, a statesmanlike measure that followed Rome's victory over her allies who were fighting for citizenship in the Social War. Sulla's party of nobles tried to make the award of citizenship ineffective by putting the Italians into new tribes which were to vote after the old tribes had cast their ballots,[4] but in the end all Italy achieved registration in the old rural tribes. All the freeborn inhabitants of a community acquired citizenship in the tribe to which the community was assigned. Henceforth not ownership of property but free birth became the distinguishing mark of the rural tribe, though it was conceded that the rural tribesman was more apt to have property than the urban tribesman.[5] After the new registration was worked out, many of the tribes were divided; parts of a tribe then coexisted in several sections of Italy. Thus Cicero's tribe, the Cornelia, consisted of at least five sections, in as many areas.[6] There was the old territory near Rome, once the estate of the Cornelian family, by this time inhabited by few freemen. Then there was Cicero's own territory about Arpinum in the Volscian mountains, another section on the edge of the Samnite territory, another down in the toe of Italy, and yet another in Umbria.

Not all the Italians were registered after the Social War. In the censorship of 86–85, held under the domination of Sulla's enemy Cinna, who had supported the favorable registration of the Italians, only about seventy thousand men were added to the citizenship rolls. Men apparently had to come to Rome to register, and no great effort seems to have been made to bring them. As dictator, Sulla made no change in the attribution of the Italians to the old tribes, but by his suspension of the censorship he seems to have made sure that there should be no great addition to the number of citizens registered.

It was no doubt in part dissatisfaction with the static condition of the registration lists that made the *populares* of the seventies clamor for the restoration of the censorship.[7] As consul in 70 Pompey revived the office and brought about the election of two of his henchmen as censors.[8] Throngs came to Rome to register,[9] and the citizen rolls were practically doubled. The geographical distribution of the voters must have been radically altered, doubtless with a great increase in Pompey's strength in the assemblies.[10] Yet even so, according to Frank's calculations, not more than half the eligible Italians seem to have enrolled.[11] Among those registered there was no doubt a preponderance of men possessing the higher property qualifications, whose votes counted heavily in the major elections.

By this time the populous communities north of the Po were clamoring for citizenship, and Crassus, Pompey, and Caesar were all interested in giving it to them. If the Transpadanes had been enrolled in the old tribes, as they eventually were by Caesar, they would have created another great change in the distribution of votes in the assemblies. The *optimates* opposed giving them citizenship, and on this question Catulus clashed with Crassus, his colleague in the censorship in 65.

Before we discuss the make-up of the Roman electorate, we must consider the registration of the men who were residents of Rome. That was the voting place, and the tribes had headquarters and representatives in the city. But most of the city people, registered in the four urban tribes, had little effect on the vote. There were, how-ever, a good many rural tribesmen living in Rome. Their numbers had been increased in the second century by many of the small landholders, who drifted to the city after they had lost their farms. These men apparently kept their old registration, but for each rural tribe the number remained far smaller than the numbers in the urban tribes.[12]

Besides these impoverished rural tribesmen in Rome, the prop-ertied men in Rome—senators, knights, and the lower-income group known as *tribuni aerarii*[13]—were, with the exception of a few who voted in the urban tribes and served as patrons of the urban masses,[14] registered in the rural tribes. These propertied men were, I believe, distributed fairly evenly among the thirty-one rural tribes, for the lists of jurors who served in criminal trials were drawn up on a tribal basis.[15] Those lists, after the jury law of 70 B.C., consisted of three hundred men each from senators, knights, and *tribuni aerarii*.[16] It has been doubted whether the senators could have been thus distributed among the tribes,[17] but it is significant that the gradually increasing list of names of senators coming to light from inscriptions, the chief source of knowledge about tribal connec-tions,[18] gives us men in all thirty-one rural tribes, and that one list of fifty-five names includes senators and knights from twenty-five rural tribes.[19] It is probable that the censors, who were apparently empowered to shift men from one tribe to another in which they held property,[20] made a definite effort to effect equitable distribu-tion of the propertied men in Rome among all the rural tribes.

There was endless scheming to have citizens shifted from the urban tribes where their vote did not count to the rural tribes. Prom-inent citizens could be very helpful in such matters. Quintus Cicero tells his brother to make use in his election of those "who have secured from you or hope to secure a tribe or a century or some other benefit."[21] Such changes were made from time to time as rewards for special services. Thus under the Roman system by which the successful prosecutor was rewarded, a subject to be considered in a later chapter, men who had taken part in an accusation that led to conviction could be rewarded either with citizenship, if they were noncitizens, or with transfer to the tribe of the accused man if it was a better tribe than that of the man who took part in the accusation. Apparently by this method Caesar's trusted agent Balbus, a new citizen from Gades, was transferred from an urban to a rural tribe.[22] Similar changes also came about, especially after Marius' reorganization of the army, when men of the proletariat belonging to the urban tribes enlisted and seem thereby to have passed into a rural tribe.[23] Other changes were brought about through pressure and influence. Some censors made wholesale revisions in tribal registration. They also used registration as a means of punishing citizens, transferring men from a rural to an urban tribe.[24]

A very large element in the urban tribes was composed of the freedmen, and from the late fourth to the second century there seems to have been a persistent effort on the part of the nobles to increase their own prestige by having their property-owning freedmen registered in the rural tribes. Before the censorship of the father of the Gracchi in 169 B.C. many of them were so registered. Gracchus succeeded in placing most of them in an urban tribe.[25] In the days of Caesar all the freedmen were apparently in the urban tribes; that was where the rest of the populace seems in general to have wished them to vote. As a result, foreign minorities, which made up a considerable section of the population of Rome, were not, as they have been in the United States, a group that could be manipulated in elections. Groups of Phrygians and Mysians might shout in the public meeting and Jews might demonstrate around the tribunal in the Forum, as they apparently did when Cicero defended Flaccus and they did not like the defense,[26] and plenty of men of foreign origin could be recruited from the urban mob to serve in the bands that kept the city in anarchy in the fifties.[27] But, except under special conditions in legislative assemblies (to be considered later), their votes did not count. In the late republic the freedmen were useful not so much to the *optimates* as to demagogic leaders. Clodius and, before him, three tribunes of the plebs of the first century, eager to gather in votes that they might control in the city,[28] proposed to distribute the freedmen in the rural tribes, but the proposal was not taken up by any responsible popular leader like the Gracchi or Caesar, doubtless because too many persons believed in Rome for the Romans. The freedman's son with property seems, however, to have obtained registration in a rural tribe, and it is likely that in this way a good many men of servile stock swelled the registration in those tribes in the city.

The striking thing about the city population as we know it is the lack of a middle class. The sons of freedmen and the countrymen who had not lost everything may have provided a small group of men of moderate means, but in general Rome was inhabited by the rich and the poor, with few men in the middle group. Yet, as we shall see, it was the vote of the middle income group which counted particularly in the elections of consuls and praetors. Such men had to come mainly from outside the city, and since in our period the immediate vicinity of Rome, which once supplied the voters, was now almost denuded of freeborn men, most of them had to come from a considerable distance. A representative system might have been the solution, but no one seems to have proposed that, though such a system existed in Macedonia.[29] Augustus later devised a plan for absentee ballots,[30] but by that time votes had ceased to have any real validity. In our period voters had to go to Rome and they made the journey not as representatives of their communities but on their own initiative or because someone arranged to bring them. Whether it was important to have them come depended on the type of election. And that brings us to the complicated subject of the Roman assemblies.[31]

The assembly which chose the lower magistrates and which in our period had become the chief legislative body was the *comitia tributa*. In it each tribe voted as a unit, and the problem was simply to carry a majority of the tribes. Although the votes of individuals in the rural tribes carried more weight than that of the proletariat in the urban tribes, the organization was far more democratic than that of the other Roman assembly, the *comitia centuriata*, the old military organization which met in the Campus Martius to elect consuls and praetors, the officers with military *imperium*. According to Cicero this assembly was organized by Servius Tullius in such a manner that "the votes were in the control not of the multitude but of the men of property."[32] That characteristic of the assembly was retained even after a democratic reform of the third century.[33] In this assembly the tribal vote was taken separately in five classes arranged in centuries according to property qualifications, and the men without property, all lumped in a single enormous unit, were practically disfranchised.[34] The vote that really counted here was the first class,[35] the men who had property amounting to perhaps 50,000 sesterces ($3,000) or more.[36] There were seventy centuries of the first class, two from each of the thirty-five tribes, made up respectively of the men of military age and the older men. They voted and had their votes announced before the rest of the assembly cast their ballots.[37]

Before the whole first class voted, there was a special preliminary ballot by one century of that class chosen by lot after the citizens had gathered in their voting units. This century was known as the *praerogativa*, and it accounts for our word prerogative.[38] The result of this century's vote had an effect on the outcome that was once attributed in our elections to the advance vote of the State of Maine. There was among the Roman voters a superstitious feeling that the men chosen by this century, and particularly the man put in the first place, were lucky, or rather were blessed by Heaven,[39] and that feeling was influential in winning votes for him at the last minute. Cicero says that the man put in the first place by the *praerogativa* always did get the consulship.[40] The importance of the *praerogativa* is shown by two incidents in our period. When Cato was the choice of the *praerogativa* for the praetorship, Pompey, who did not wish Cato to be elected, suddenly heard thunder and dissolved the assembly.[41] In a time of scandalous bribery in 54, two candidates for the consulship announced in advance that they would pay ten million sesterces for the vote of the *praerogativa*.[42]

The persuasive effect of the *praerogativa's* vote and the heavy weighting and separate announcement of the vote of the entire first class gave a great advantage in this assembly to the middle income group among the Italians. There seems in the balloting to have been something of the bandwagon psychology that we see in our nominating conventions. The consul chosen first was, in several elections on which we have information, elected by all the centuries, though the final decision for the second consul might depend on a plurality of very few centuries.[43]

There was recognition of the undemocratic character that the centuriate assembly retained even after the third-century reform, and there were proposals for a further reorganization. The institution of the written ballot instead of the oral vote was a step in that direction. Gaius Gracchus is said to have suggested as a new reform that the five classes be placed together indiscriminately, and apparently that the *praerogativa* be chosen from all the centuries. This proposal was renewed in the sixties and again by Sallust in 51, but nothing came of it.[44] Cicero in an oration of 63 gives the view of "honorable men influential in their communities" who objected to having "all distinctions of dignity and influence removed."[45] It is noteworthy that it is the objections of municipal men that Cicero stresses.

Because of the importance of the first class and of the century selected from that class to vote first, the contestant for the consulship or the praetorship had to have strength throughout all the tribes in the first class,[46] and the majority of the men in this class lived outside of Rome. In these elections the city populace was never the decisive factor. There was a large attendance of men from the towns of Italy; as Cicero puts it, *cuncta Italia* elected him to the consulship.[47] The candidate's problem was to bring the right men, the propertied men who were the backbone of the Italian municipalities.

Hence the contestants for praetorship and consulship kept up their contacts with every section of Italy and particularly with the richest men of the Italian towns. Especially important were the populous regions not too far away, which were connected with Rome by a network of excellent roads—the region from the Alban Hills down to Campania, a section representing about a dozen tribes, easily accessible by the Via Appia and the Via Casalina; also Umbria, united by the Via Flaminia and the Tiber to the city. There were nine tribes here, and the tribesmen seem to have come in large numbers to vote for the consulship of Murena, who had treated the region generously when he held levies there.[48] But even more distant sections also counted, for instance the cities south of the Po, one of the most populous regions. Cicero, when a candidate, contemplated a journey there because the district, he tells us, seemed to be very powerful in the elections.[49] This region was part of Caesar's province of Cisalpine Gaul, the only Roman province which had in its population a large body of citizens. These citizens were distributed in no fewer than fourteen of the rural tribes.[50]

Caesar does not, in his brief notes on his winters in Cisalpine Gaul, tell us anything about his cultivation of the voting body there, but his friend Hirtius, who completed the commentaries after Caesar's death, made some revealing observations.[51] He says that Caesar started out on a visit to these cities in the year 50 in order to urge them to vote for Mark Antony for the augurate, and then, learning that Antony had already been elected, he continued on his way, to thank them and ask them to vote for his own second consulship. He was welcomed with extravagant enthusiasm by the townsmen. This comment of Hirtius indicates that Caesar may have been similarly occupied during other winters of his nine-year Gallic proconsulship; it also throws light on his success in getting his candidates into office. He was not, in his Gallic province, removed from electioneering; he could not go to the *comitia* himself, but he could send down instructed delegations of voters, and of soldiers, most of whom were enrolled from Cisalpine Gaul.

It was important for the candidate to know his Italy well. Cicero's brother, advising him on his campaign for the consulship, writes: "Have in your mind and in your memory the tribal divisions of all Italy so that you won't let there be a single municipality, colony, prefecture, or place in Italy in which you have not strength that will be adequate; seek out and search for men in every region, learn to know them, strengthen them, encourage them, see to it that they canvass for you in their vicinity, that they are, as it were, candidates for you."[52]

It is noteworthy that in this essay the municipalities receive far more attention than the urban plebs.[53] Cicero's strength in the equestrian order, which was made up largely of men from Italian towns, and his influence in the municipalities in general are emphasized. It would be advantageous for Cicero's candidacy, Quintus says, to have from the municipalities a throng of men who had come on his account.[54]

The consular and praetorian elections, for which considerable numbers of men in the first class must have come to Rome from all Italy south of the Po, were normally scheduled in the latter part of July immediately following the games for Apollo, an attraction that doubtless aided in getting out the voters. The curule aediles, the quaestors, and the military tribunes were elected by the tribal assembly, usually just after the praetors had been chosen; and the officers of the plebs, the plebeian aediles and the tribunes, were ordinarily chosen in the same period.[55] The crowd that had assembled for the consular and the praetorian elections was likely to be in the city still for these minor elections, but in the more democratic assembly, where the richer men counted less, the outcome was much less predictable. Cicero points this out in his defense of Plancius, who was prosecuted after his successful contest for the curule aedileship.[56] Cicero's own election to the aedileship had proved this, for he won the office in spite of the machinations of Verres, who had been able with his bribes to control the consular and the praetorian elections.

It seems likely that the rural tribesmen in the urban plebs, most of whom probably did not belong to the first class, had more effect on elections in the tribal assembly. This view is borne out by the evidence of the votes on legislation. It was to the tribes that the officer most active in legislation, the tribune of the plebs, proposed his bills.[57] The other two magistrates who initiated legislation, the consul and the praetor, could call either the tribes or the centuries, but during the last two hundred years of the republic they usually proposed their bills to the tribes. Aside from the regular censorial laws, only one bill, that for Cicero's restoration from exile, to be considered later, is known to have been proposed to the centuries in the years 70–50.[58]

Legislation was limited to periods when the throngs of Italians were not on hand for the elections. Under laws passed in the middle of the second century,[59] no bill could be proposed in the twenty-four days[60] before the elections were to be held. After elections were over, no bill could be voted on for another twenty-four days, the required interval between the proposal and the ballot on the law.[61] By that time most of the Italians who came for the elections would have gone home. At other seasons there was not enough time between the announcement of a bill and the vote on it (again twenty-four days) to summon a large crowd from Italy. If men were to be brought in, the officer presenting the bill had a special advantage, for he knew in advance, as others might not know, when he was going to make the proposal and could send for just the voters he needed. Tiberius Gracchus did that for his land bill, and Saturninus, tribune of 100, was careful to have Marius' soldiers on hand when he proposed a bill for their land bonus.[62]

The presiding officer for tribunitial laws, regularly the tribune who proposed the measure, had special means of influencing the vote in the tribal assembly. It was obligatory to have all tribes represented, but sometimes there was no one in attendance from certain rural tribes, and at such times the presiding officer could ask men from another tribe to vote in their place.[63] Naturally he picked men who would vote the way he desired. According to Cicero, even freedmen and slaves were used in this manner.

The *optimates* sometimes obtained the support of the Italians for their bills by arranging through senatorial decrees to suspend the laws which prohibited legislation just before the electoral assemblies. By that method some conservative laws were carried by the vote of the Italians.[64]

The fundamental distinction between the tribal and the centuriate assembly is shown in the legislation for Cicero's exile and restoration. It was to the tribal assembly that Clodius as tribune proposed that the man who had put Roman citizens to death without trial should be interdicted from fire and water.[65] There is no doubt that the urban mob, with which Cicero had been unpopular since the Catilinarian episode, was on the side of Clodius, who was incidentally strengthened by armed thugs and by Caesar's soldiers at the gates. Cicero charges, moreover, that the bill was passed by armed slaves.[66] The senators, though they sympathized with Cicero, urged him to depart in order to avoid bloodshed, and, after toying with the idea of raising a force of his own, he yielded and went away to voluntary exile before the bill was passed.

Cicero's friends among the nobles began at once to agitate for his recall. Various bills for Cicero's return were prepared, and friendly tribunes tried to assure their passage in the tribal assembly. The efforts were unsuccessful, chiefly, Cicero holds, because Clodius was filling the sewers with dead bodies and soaking the Forum with blood that had to be mopped up with sponges.[67] The nobles tried to decide the issue by counterviolence under Milo, but in the end they decided to submit the bill to the centuries instead of the tribes. Cicero comments in his *Laws* on the decision to call the centuries: "When the people are divided according to wealth, rank, and age, their decisions are wiser than when they meet without classification in the assembly of the tribes." Then Cicero goes on to say of the law on his exile that, although a prominent consular held that it was invalid, his brother and other prominent men "thought it better that all Italy should declare its opinion of a man against whom slaves and brigands claimed to have enacted a law."[68]

It is striking that in this passage the tribal group that exiled Cicero is described as slaves and brigands, and the centuries which recalled him are equated with *cuncta Italia*. Every effort was made to get out the vote when the centuries were summoned to take action on Cicero's case. The consul who presented the bill was authorized by the senate to send letters to the Italian towns to urge all who desired the safety of the state to come to Rome to vote for it. Pompey joined in the effort, making speeches on the subject in Italian towns and sponsoring a decree in Cicero's favor in his new colony of Capua.[69] The Italians—particularly, of course, the richest of them, who valued Cicero's tireless defense of private property— came in throngs. Not only shops, but municipalities, Cicero says (doubtless in exaggeration), were closed for the occasion.[70] All Italy, in the same centuries which had once elected him consul, now voted for his restoration. Cicero never ceases to glory in the honor that united Italy paid him.[71]

The bills for Cicero's exile and for his restoration reveal the essential difference in the role played in the late republic by the urban plebs and the Italians in elections and in legislation, in assemblies of the centuries and of the tribes.[72] In this period of decay, when the country about Rome was denuded of its voters, when the city was swollen to a turbulent metropolis which had practically no middle class, and when all Italians south of the Po had the franchise, the Italians of the first class, the men who provided the *praerogativa,* were brought by nobles and senators to Rome to vote for consuls and praetors in the centuriate assembly. It was these Italians, most of them bound to the leading houses of Rome, and not the city plebs, who decided the issue and kept the chief offices in the hands of the ruling class. Unless there was a postponement of the *comitia,* the Italians were still on hand when most of the lower officers were chosen; but in the more democratic assembly they could not prevent the election of men whom the nobles did not like. The Italians were not in Rome when most of the laws were voted on by the tribes. It was in the legislative assembly that the urban plebs was really powerful. The plebs could be manipulated by popular leaders, and it was to counter the influence of such men that the senate decided to summon the centuries—*cuncta Italia*—to vote on Cicero's recall.

The Campaign for Election and Legislation

The candidate for office was interested in carrying as many tribes as possible. If he was seeking an office elected in the centuriate assembly—consulship or praetorship,—he was concerned primarily with the vote of the first class, which usually decided the contest. If he was trying to win a lower office elected by the tribal assembly he would seek support from all classes in the tribes. In his campaign the candidate might make a preliminary journey to various sections in Italy. But his major activity was in Rome, for all the tribes had headquarters there.[73] In Rome, too, were the politicians who had great influence with their fellow tribesmen, their *tribules.*

Every man of prominence in Roman political life maintained close relations with his *tribules.*[74] He looked out for them in the law courts and concerned himself with their business in Italy and the provinces. When his fellow tribesmen came to Rome for games and elections, he got them seats at the games and gave them dinners and gifts of money.[75] In return, he expected his *tribules* to vote for him at elections and, on his request, to vote for his friends.

Of course, the tribes did not always vote as a unit. The rival activities of Caesar and Lucius Domitius Ahenobarbus, two men of lavish generosity and of divergent aims in politics, must have split the vote of their common tribe, the Fabia.[76] The lack of geographical continuity in the tribes also contributed to disunity in the tribal vote. Municipal men were frequently influenced by personal knowledge of a candidate who was a native son of a community bordering on their region; *vicinitas* was sometimes as effective for winning votes as common membership in a tribe.[77]

Yet the nobles were remarkably successful in carrying their tribes not only for themselves but for their friends. Particularly in the major elections of consuls and praetors, the close relations that the nobles maintained with the richer men in the Italian towns, who had a weighted vote in the centuriate assembly, had a strong influence on the election results. By their hold on these richer men of the first class the nobles were able to bar new men and pass the consulship about from hand to hand among themselves. They operated what Professor Marsh has with some justice called a "machine."[78] The political workers, who kept up this "machine," were largely personal adherents of the nobles, often freedmen. Such men must have been in constant contact not only with local communities but with the tribal officers, the *curatores,* the *tribuni aerarii,* men with a census just below the knights, and the *divisores,* who distributed the gifts to the tribesmen in Rome. We know little of the details of organization, but the results indicate that the system was efficient.

The old noble families had close relations not only with their own tribes but with many other tribes in which they had clients and old soldiers and family contacts with whole communities.[79] The nobles sometimes made gifts and gave dinners not only to their own tribes but to the tribes in general. Such actions were prohibited by the laws on malpractice. The proper way to carry a tribe not one's own was through friends who gave the dinners and the gifts of money.[80] "Name any tribe," Cicero says, defending his friend Plancius, "and I will tell you through whom he carried it."[81] It was legitimate to win a tribe through a friend. Such methods were hallowed by custom. "We must not forbid our children," Cicero says, "from showing attention and affection to their fellow tribesmen, from being able to deliver the vote of their tribes (*conficere tribus*) for their intimates, and from expecting a similar service in their own candidacies from their intimates."[82] The combinations with friends led to charges of malpractice, a subject to which we shall return later.

The campaign for election took account of the personal character of Roman political associations. In general, as has already been pointed out, there was no program. Cicero's brother warns Marcus against expressing himself on public affairs during the campaign.[83] If the election was conducted legally, there was also no ticket. Two men sometimes combined to shut out competitors and win for themselves the two places in the consulship, but in the late republic such combinations were classed among malpractices. There were no regular election speeches,[84] though there might be orations against competitors in the senate or, if a magistrate provided access to the Rostra, before the people. A candidate might accuse a competitor in the courts and prosecute him, but Cicero recommends against such procedure, since it would divert the candidate from the campaign.[85] Such speeches as were made dealt mainly with the family and the virtues of the candidate and the iniquities of his competitors.

It was on the individual canvass for the vote carried out by the candidate and his friends that the campaign depended. The first essential was that the candidate should have a large and influential group of friends. The campaign, Quintus says, depends on the zeal of one's friends and the good will of the people, and in the discussion the zeal of friends has the chief emphasis; it is the determining factor in gaining the good will of the people. Friends should, Quintus holds, be won from many walks of life. Various groups that cut across the tribal organization should be cultivated; among them magistrates, nobles, and senators, and senators' sons too, who voted in the special equestrian centuries, were very important for their wide influence.[86] Then there were the knights and particularly the public contractors, the group in which Cicero's support was strongest. These men, it may be noted, came largely from the municipalities and would have influence with their home communities. Besides, there were certain powerful freedmen, and various clubs and the guilds whose leaders the politician must cultivate.

Quintus also holds that account should be taken of lowlier men of influence in their tribes; Marcus is advised to find out which men are loved and which are hated by their fellow tribesmen and choose his associates accordingly.

The divisions between *optimates* and *populares* that marked the legislative activity of this period did not prevent Quintus from hoping that his brother could get the support both of the *optimates* and of the group of *populares* associated with Pompey. The nobles and the *consulares,* Quintus says, must be convinced that "we have always agreed with the *optimates* in public affairs, that we have been by no means *populares,* that, if we seem at any time to have spoken in a popular manner, we have done it to unite Gnaeus Pompeius to us, so that the man who has the greatest power will either be our friend in candidacy or at any rate not our enemy."[87] Thus Cicero's support of Pompey's command against Mithridates is presented simply as a means of gaining the support of another friend, and a powerful friend, for Pompey controlled many votes. Similarly the urban plebs must be made to realize "that Gnaeus Pompeius has the greatest good will toward you and that it is very much to his interest for you to win your campaign."[88] As things worked out, Marcus seems to have had the personal commendation both of the *optimates* and of Pompey's popular group, who united to prevent the victory of another popular figure, Catiline. Such were the circumstances under which Cicero, the only new man to reach the consulship in thirty years, was elected.

Cicero's case, as Quintus emphasizes, was not typical, for he was a new man and did not inherit the network of relationships that made it easier for the noble to attain high office. The mobilization of friends would have been much simpler for a Caecilius Metellus.

Friends often sent their endorsements of candidates in written form. This must have been usual in communicating with distant communities. It was also customary for a Roman official who was far away to send back written endorsements of candidates. Caesar sent them back in large quantities during his years in Gaul, always exacting from the men he endorsed a promise to look out for his interests.[89] Cicero requested Caesar's commendation for a number of candidates and guaranteed that a man he endorsed for the consulship would be satisfactory to Caesar.[90] The method followed by Caesar after he became dictator and assumed the right of choosing half the lower magistrates is probably based on earlier custom when commendation was not equivalent to a command. At that time he wrote to each tribe as follows: "I commend to you such and such men that by your vote they may attain the dignity they deserve."[91]

The commendation of nobles was probably painted on signs along the roads leading to Rome and all over the city and the municipal towns. On tombs along the roadside there are inscribed warnings to candidates not to use the monument for sign posting.[92] And all over the town of Pompeii are painted notices of candidates still canvassing for local offices[93] when elections in Rome had either been discontinued or were little more than a sham. The form of recommendation accords with the personal character of the endorsement as we know it in republican politics. Many of them are painted on the walls of houses or shops and give the recommendation of the owner. He asks for votes (*rogare, orare*) and recommends his candidate in rather vague terms as a good man or one worthy of the republic, terms so conventional that they could be abbreviated. A little variation is supplied by the statements "this man will preserve the treasury," or "make so and so aedile and he will make you one." In the days of Cicero's campaign, when the fame of the orator throughout Italy was the chief basis of his strength, we can imagine similar recommendations in the municipal towns and along the roads over which the voters journeyed to the city. The inscriptions of Pompeii also include endorsement from groups such as teamsters, muleteers, hucksters of every type, dyers, barbers, and also from certain districts of the town. It is possible that such groups, both in Rome and in the Italian towns, placarded their cities with notices of favorite candidates for the elections in Rome. There are, it may be added, a few Pompeian notices that present a ticket, but that represents a development that was not typical of republican politics.

Let us now consider the details of the campaign. The advantages of a well-known name and the long-term preparation for candidacy have been considered in the previous chapter, and we may confine ourselves here to the actual events of the campaign. Cicero began his

solicitation of voters about a year before his election to the consulship, starting at the tribunitial elections of the previous year when
many Italians were in Rome.[94] The candidate went down to Forum
and Campus and journeyed about to tribal headquarters, seizing
the hands of voters and begging for their support. He was expected
to humiliate himself and plead.[95] At the same time he mobilized his
friends to plead for him. The candidate was constantly occupied.
He was saluted at his house each morning by a large crowd, was
accompanied down to the Forum by another and more distinguished group, and was followed about by a throng as he asked for
votes.

The campaign became really intense after the formal announcement of candidacy twenty-four days before the scheduled date of
election. From that time on, the candidate was conspicuous in a
toga artificially whitened with chalk, a custom from which our
word candidate is derived. By that time many Italians had arrived
in Rome to witness the games for Apollo. The Forum with its
groups of candidates and their retinue must have presented a busy
scene.[96]

We turn now to election abuses. The most common was bribery,
that is, the distribution of money throughout all the tribes. The
tribal *divisores* once did a legitimate business in distributing money
from leading tribesmen to their *tribules,* but as time went on they
came more and more to be employed in handing out money given
by candidates for all the tribes. Verres used them, Cicero charges, to
defeat him for the aedileship. "I found out," Cicero says, "that
baskets full of Sicilian money were handed over by a certain senator
to a Roman knight ... and that the *divisores* of all the tribes were
called to him by night."[97] Bribery increased rapidly in the succeeding years, when the sixty-four men expelled from the senate by the
censors in 69 were trying to be reinstated through election to office.
The consul of 67 attempted by his law on malpractice to check the
evil by making not only the candidates but the *divisores* responsible,
and the latter appeared in the Forum in a great body and drove the
consul away from the assembly. But the consul came back with his
own armed force and got his law through.[98]

Neither the consul's legislation nor later laws, including one that

Cicero proposed as consul, curbed bribery and other malpractices. The matter was constantly discussed in the senate, and candidates made counteraccusations of the severest sort. In the year 61, when Pompey was pouring out money to elect his man to the consulship, Cato charged in the senate that the money was being distributed from the house of the Pompeian consul in office.[99] But even Cato, it is asserted, yielded and chipped in to bribe when, the next year, Pompey was backing Caesar and Lucceius for the consulship,[100] and the result was that Lucceius, who had supplied the funds for his joint campaign with Caesar, was defeated and the *optimates'* man, Bibulus, was elected with Caesar.

In succeeding years, even when Caesar, Pompey, and Crassus were united against them, the *optimates* continued, by effective use of bribery as well as influence within the tribes, to bring some of their candidates to victory. As consul in 55 Crassus attempted to check the power of the *optimates* by a law against *sodalicium,* organization of associations to distribute money within the tribes and deliver the vote for certain candidates. The law was ineffective.[101] It was in the following year that two candidates offered in advance the great bribe to the *praerogativa* that has already been mentioned. At that time corruption reached such proportions that the rate of interest was doubled. There was an effective check on bribery in Pompey's third consulship in 52, but after that free elections had only three more years to run.

In laws on malpractice, account was also taken of the deal, the *coitio,* most commonly carried out between two men to get an office like the consulship or aedileship for which there were only two places.[102] Such deals were regularly accompanied by bribery; prosecutors sometimes pointed out that the men carried the tribes with the same number of votes.[103] Such deals were made repeatedly: by Pompey and Crassus for the consulship of 70, by Verres' candidates for 69, by Catiline and Gaius Antonius for 63—when the deal formed the subject of a speech delivered by Cicero in the senate,— by Caesar and Lucceius for 59, and by two candidates in 54.

Along with bribery and *coitiones* went intimidation of the voters through violence, threatened or real. It became more and more the custom for candidates to have hired followers, *sectatores,* to aid them in canvassing.[104] Here the urban mob, particularly as it was organized by Clodius, was useful, although it played a more important role in the campaigns for laws. Gladiators, purchased and armed by candidates, provided men experienced in fighting. Such bands of hirelings paraded the streets in the fifties and eliminated candidates by chasing them out of Forum and Campus, sometimes with bloodshed.

In the terrible year 54, when violence was a constant accompaniment of bribery, things became so bad that Sulla's son, campaigning for his half-brother Marcus Aemilius Scaurus,[105] announced that he was going about with three hundred armed men and that he would use them if need arose. The climax came in the year of revolution, 52, when the ruffians Milo and Clodius were trying to get consulship and praetorship. Both of them, and other candidates as well, were accompanied by private armies, and Clodius and many of his associates were murdered and the senate house was burned. Even the consul conducting the election at times appeared with an armed guard (occasionally provided by decree of the senate). Thus Cicero, anticipating violence while Catiline was seeking the consulship for 62, came to the Campus Martius accompanied by a strong bodyguard, and he himself wore a breastplate that he carefully let the assembled throng see.

Sometimes the generals used their personal armies for intimidation of voters. Pompey was loath actually to employ his soldiers for coercion (he preferred large-scale bribery), but he had them on hand when he demanded the consulship in 70 and he had either his soldiers or his veterans on call during the years of anarchy. For the election of Pompey and Crassus in 55, which had been postponed until the fighting season was over, Caesar sent many of his soldiers down from Gaul, ostensibly to vote.[106] And when it came to election time Pompey no longer contented himself with a show of force but actually used his men to chase the opposing candidates and their adherents from the field. That was the first time in our period when intimidation of voters resulted in bloodshed not merely in the campaign but on the election field. This was complete anarchy, in the face of which the voters brought to the polls from the city and from Italy were powerless.

The political boss, who had to be cultivated because he had strength throughout all the tribes, is not unknown. In the seventies, the heyday of the Sullan constitution, a certain Cethegus, probably through organized bribery, got such control of the assemblies that nobles who wanted offices and special commissions had to make up to him in order to get votes. Lucullus, when he sought the command against Mithridates, got it by winning the favor of Cethegus' mistress and having her intercede for him.[107] But Cethegus was a unique instance. He was out of the picture by the year 70, and no one man in the last twenty years of the republic had such power over all the tribes and their votes. Pompey and Caesar seem to have tried something of the sort, pouring into Rome the great wealth of their foreign conquests, but, as we have seen, there was generally strength enough in the opposition to prevent them from getting all their candidates into office.

There were various other abuses that accompanied the actual election. As in our own day, there were marked ballots, ballot-box stuffing, and false counts. The men of the upper classes who served as poll watchers and tellers of the votes (*custodes* and *diribitores*) sometimes employed the actual moment of balloting to solicit votes for their favorite.[108] These men were chosen by the presiding magistrate to exercise general supervision and by the individual candidates to look out for their interests. After 70 B.C. they were selected from the nine hundred senators, knights, and tribal representatives on the official jury lists.[109] They served and apparently voted in a tribe that was not their own. Before the institution of the written ballot in 139 these men, known then as *rogatores,* took the votes of citizens orally and were often able to influence the voters. Even after that time they seem to have considered it their privilege to inspect the ballot before it was handed in. Regulations passed to lessen their influence[110] seem to have had some effect, and in our period the greatest value of the *custodes* was the prestige they could give to a candidate.

The presiding magistrate, regularly a consul except in the election of plebeian officers, also had considerable power in the election, and in earlier times he often abused his power to bring about the choice of a candidate he favored.[111] Though his power had diminished, the presiding officer still retained influence in our period. The optimate consul Piso in 67 made it known that he would not, whatever the vote, announce the victory of a new man supported by Pompey.[112] The presiding consul could also postpone the elections for religious reasons or dissolve the assembly because of an omen or violence. Sometimes he postponed them because he wished the troublesome voters to go home, or to have new voters arrive on the scene who, like Caesar's soldiers, could affect the issue. The other consul in office, and also the tribunes, could effect postponements for religious reasons. Such use of the state religion in party politics will be discussed in the next chapter.

The major elections for consuls and praetors were almost entirely controlled by the nobles, and the struggle was mainly between rival groups in the nobility. In the election of lower officers, which took place in the comparatively democratic tribal assembly, the nobles were strong enough to bring about the election of their men in colleges of magistrates that usually had a number of places, but they were often unsuccessful in keeping out of office, and particularly out of the tribunate, men whom they did not like.

Even after Pompey, Crassus, and Caesar made their deal in 60, and attained their supremacy as *populares,* the elections were not a struggle between *optimates* and *populares.* The "triumvirs" were themselves nobles, and they conducted their campaigns by the old methods of personal commendation, aided by bribery and violence. The *optimates* used similar methods, and the campaigns continued to be carried through with little or no emphasis on programs.

It was in the campaign for laws that the program loomed large in Roman politics; the program submitted was usually a camouflaged design, a machination of an individual or a group—in our period, of Pompey, Crassus, or Caesar, or of all three together. The most active legislative officer, the tribune of the plebs, who was usually in the service of a prominent leader, constantly stressed the program. Under the Sullan constitution, when the tribune could not initiate laws, there was a brief respite from the feverish tribunitial legislative activity that had characterized the half century after the Gracchi. But after Pompey restored the powers of the office in 70, tribunes began once more to propose bills and, to quote Tacitius, "in the most corrupt period of the republic there were the most laws."[113]

The tribune, whose authority was limited to the city and a radius of a mile about the city limits, was peculiarly the officer of the urban plebs. He proposed laws at any season of the year when the religious calendar permitted laws to be submitted to the people. They were voted on in the tribal assembly when few Italians were on hand and when the tribune in charge could fill up empty tribes with his own henchmen. The laws often included special inducements for the urban plebs, who provided the majority of the voters. Thus when bills were formulated to give lands to veterans, they usually included provision of bonuses for members of the urban plebs.

The campaign for legislation, unlike that for election, depended largely on speechmaking. Tribunes and their supporters held public meetings from the Rostra and set forth to the people their view of the long, complicated bills that had been posted up for the people to read.[114] The speeches were demagogic and were answered by opponents in rival speeches at other public meetings. The popular tribune and his associates would declare that their measure would liberate the people from slavery to an oligarchy, and the opposing *optimates* would assert that the popular group was setting up a monarchy. The people who attended the public meetings are scornfully described by Cicero as the "meeting-going leeches of the treasury, the poor starveling people,"[115] that is, recipients of the grain dole. They included many foreign groups. Scipio Aemilianus declared that he had brought to Rome in chains the men who were shouting for the laws of Tiberius Gracchus,[116] and Cicero speaks of bands of Phrygians and Mysians demonstrating in public meetings.[117]

The character of the public meeting is indicated by the rabble-rousing speeches that Roman historians put into the mouths of tribunes. The oration of Licinius Macer has already been quoted to show the way a popular tribune played on the emotions of the crowd and emphasized the tyranny of the nobles and the misery and slavery of the commons. A speech of Cicero to the people, in opposition to an agrarian law, is interesting because it shows the type of argument that could be used against such mob oratory.[118] The argument was apparently successful, for the bill did not pass. The bill was designed to provide land both for veterans and for the miserable city populace, and the tribune who offered it, presumably a tool of Crassus, had presented himself as a vigorous *popularis*. In speaking against the bill, Cicero tried to show that he, the consul who rose from the knights, was truly *popularis,* that is, interested in the people's welfare, while the tribune masquerading in that guise had a scheme to set up a tyranny.

He himself, Cicero asserts, is not one of those who look askance at agrarian laws and think it a crime to praise the Gracchi, and, when he heard that a new agrarian law had been proposed, he was not, like some consuls, inclined to reject it because a tribune had proposed it. But after studying it sympathetically he learned that "through the agency of a tribune of the plebs, whom our ancestors wished to be the guardian and champion of liberty, kings are being set up in the state."[119] The whole bill, he goes on, is an attack at the same time on the position and prestige of Pompey, the man, it may be noted, who at that time was the particular darling of the people. As for the people who expected to benefit from the law, Cicero warns them that it is the tribune's design to settle them in barren and pestilential districts where they will find no pleasure and no means of livelihood. Cicero urges them not to be tempted, but to retain possession of "influence, liberty, suffrage, dignity, the city, the Forum, the public games, the holidays, and all the rest of your advantages."[120]

Opposition to the popular legislation of the tribunes was conducted not only by speeches like this but by the veto and the use of religious obstructions. Among the ten tribunes there was always at least one, and sometimes several, who would be willing to exercise the veto.[121] But to avert violence the optimate tribune was sometimes persuaded to desist from his veto; for example, the tribune who vetoed the bill for Pompey's command against the pirates in 67 finally gave up his veto.[122] The *optimates* had opposed Gaius Gracchus by having their tribune, Marcus Livius Drusus, propose a rival and more attractive popular law, but in our period the *optimates* seem to have refrained from such a policy. They were perhaps too unreconciled to the restoration of the tribune's legislative powers to be willing to seek popularity in that manner. But Cicero's speech on the agrarian bill of 63 shows how the *optimates* attempted to prove that they, the best men of the state, were the true *populares,* really interested in the good of the people. The *optimates* also derived advantage from the lack of a unified popular party. Thus Pompey's and Crassus' tribunes were often in conflict with each other in the sixties. The use that the *optimates* made of religious obstructions and the claims of their opponents that they also represented the will of the gods will be discussed in the next chapter.

With the exception of Caesar, who was accused of acting like a tribune in his consulship,[123] consuls and praetors submitted comparatively few laws in the years from 70 to 50. Several of their laws were presented just before the election, the senate having by decree suspended the law that forbade legislation at this time.[124] A tribune in Pompey's service, Gaius Cornelius, attempted in 67 to curb this power of the senate and make suspension of the laws depend on the people.[125] He was not successful, but he was able to pass a bill requiring that a quorum of two hundred should be necessary for senatorial meetings which dealt with suspension of the laws.

Many of the irregularities familiar from the electoral assemblies were known in the legislative assemblies, but generally intimidation of voters and violence were far more common here than bribery. The public meetings in which rival orators addressed the people on new laws were frequently disorderly, and both sides began going to the meetings accompanied by armed thugs and gladiators. The strife in a public meeting in which Cato exercised the veto will be considered in a later chapter. In our period no sacrosanct tribune was murdered, as in the half century before Sulla several had been, but clashes between armed bands were common on the city streets, in public meetings, and even while voting was in progress. In the fifties the gangs of Clodius, recruited from the guilds of the urban plebs, and the rival thugs of the *optimates'* man Milo, probably drawn from country people, kept the city in a constant uproar. Even more effective than such private armed forces were the experienced soldiers and the veterans of the great commanders. Frequently, their presence was enough to turn the voting into a sham and a mockery.

But even before the ballot became a complete farce, political leaders had been able to manipulate the vote both in the electoral and in the legislative assemblies. At the elections, where the Italians normally had the preponderant influence, nobles and senators determined the outcome under the system of personal commendation. In the legislative assemblies, where the urban plebs supplied the majority of the voters, popular leaders were able to decide the issue by offering programs that won them a great following among the city dwellers. A popular leader could try to win an election by having it postponed until Italians went home and favorable voters like Caesar's soldiers could arrive. Nobles opposed to popular programs could combat radical legislation by vetoes and by obtaining special dispensation to propose their laws while the Italians were in Rome; they could also call the centuries, in which the middle-class Italians predominated, as they did when presenting the bill for Cicero's restoration. As we shall see in the next chapter, the opposing groups found in the state religion a useful tool for the manipulation both of elections and of legislation.

CHAPTER IV

MANIPULATING THE STATE RELIGION

THE ROMAN state religion, inseparably bound up with politics, was in the hands of the governing nobles and could be manipulated by them in the interests of the entire body or for the benefit of one group in rivalry with another. Men who as magistrates celebrated the great games for the gods, performed the chief sacrifices, and took the auspices—which determined the will of the gods—served also as priests to interpret the gods on earth. In the early republic the patricians, who seem really to have believed that they were the representatives of heaven, used the state religion to keep the plebeians in subjection. Later the plebeian nobles, who as magistrates and priests were entitled to a part in the religious control of government, shared with the patricians the same attitude toward the masses.

The comments of Polybius on Roman religion as he saw it in operation in the second century are revealing: "But the most important difference for the better which the Roman commonwealth appears to me to display is in their religious beliefs. For I conceive that what in other nations is looked upon as a reproach, I mean a scrupulous fear of the gods, is the very thing which keeps the Roman state together. To such an extraordinary height is this carried among them, both in private and in public business, that nothing could exceed it. Many people think this is unaccountable; but in my opinion their object is to use it as a check on the common people. If it were possible to form a state wholly of philosophers, such a custom would perhaps be unnecessary. But seeing that every multitude is fickle and full of lawless desires, unreasoning anger, and violent passion, the only resource is to keep them in check by mysterious terrors and scenic effects of this sort. Wherefore, to my mind, the ancients were not acting without purpose or at random, when they brought in among the vulgar these opinions about the gods, and the belief in the punishment in Hades; much rather do I think that men nowadays are acting rashly and foolishly in rejecting them."[1]

---

[1] For notes to chap. iv see pp. 212–216.

Thus the aristocratic Greek familiar with the city-states of the Peloponnesus, where restrictions of the state religion had weakened, praises the Roman system, where he sees religion being used as the "opium of the people." Writers from the ranks of the Roman ruling classes agree with Polybius that religion is valuable for the masses. The renowned *pontifex maximus* Quintus Mucius Scaevola, who was slain by the Marians, declared that three types of gods had been handed down, one from the poets, one from the philosophers, and a third from the leaders of the state. Only the third type was salutary for the people, and it was expedient to deceive them in matters of religion.[2]

Marcus Terentius Varro, who dedicated his *res divinae* to Julius Caesar as *pontifex maximus,* agreed with Scaevola. If he were founding a new state, he would, Varro concluded, organize religion more in accordance with nature, but for a people with a long tradition it was better to maintain the accepted gods and worship them according to the *mos maiorum*.[3] Cicero also presents a similar view in his political and philosophical essays. A member of the college of augurs, he did not himself believe that there was any way of ascertaining the will of the gods, but he favored maintaining the ancient system of divination in the interests of public welfare.[4] And although he was himself a skeptic, he dwelt frequently in his speeches to the people on the ceremonies and ritual of the state cult and sought to show that the will of the gods accorded with the policies of state adopted by senate and magistrates.

The nobles in their magisterial offices took care to carry out the ceremonies with the magnificence that aroused Polybius' admiration. They entertained the gods, and incidentally the people, with elaborate dramatic and circus games, opening them with splendid processions in which magistrates and priests accompanied the images of the gods to special seats from which the gods and the nobles who served them could, in the view of the populace, enjoy the great spectacles provided. They feasted the gods, and often the people too, at banquets and sacrifices. They reported to the people signs and omens by which the gods had manifested their ill will and then allayed any fears that may have been aroused by putting on elaborate expiatory rites. Meanwhile the nobles, in contact with Greek rationalism, were themselves steadily developing skepticism toward the religion of their ancestors, but they were not deterred from exploiting religion for political purposes. The rival manipulation of religion by opposing groups in the nobility, each seeking to show that heaven was on its side, must have weakened the confidence of the people. But even in the days of anarchy faith was strong enough in the masses to make religion an effective political weapon.

RELIGION AND DIVINATION IN POLITICS

The state religion had a particular importance in elective and legislative assemblies. The time when such assemblies could be held was regulated by the will of heaven, and the nobles interpreted that will, sometimes against popular movements and sometimes in rivalry with each other. The calendar, controlled by the college of pontifices, restricted severely the days on which magistrates could call the people together. The restriction went far beyond the one day a week eliminated from our secular calendar. The ancient Roman calendar, which was still in force, marked every day with a special sign. The most common marks, as we know them from thirty-five odd calendars preserved on stone or plaster, were $N(e\text{-}fastus)$, wrong in the sight of god, $F(astus)$, right in the sight of god, and $C(omitialis)$. On the days marked *nefastus* it was not right to attend to secular business, or, in early times, to engage in litigation; on the *fasti dies* such business could be conducted. But only on the days marked *comitiales* was it permitted to call the people together in centuriate and tribal assemblies. The calendars provided only 192 such days in the year[5] and their number was further limited, for any of them which fell on a market day, the last day of the Roman eight-day week, was ruled out,[6] as also was the period devoted to the seven great seasons of public games. By these arrangements the number of comitial days was reduced to about 150 a year.[7]

The comitial days available could be increased by the insertion of the intercalary month needed to bring the Roman lunar year of 355 days into harmony with the sun. In theory, that month was inserted in February every two years; but in the early second century the pontifices obtained the right of putting it in at will, and thereafter they used this power of intercalating to lengthen or shorten, according to their own interests, the magisterial year, the time needed for litigation, and the period required for public contracts in which they were concerned.[8] During Cicero's provincial government, when the calendar was badly in arrears, Cicero, eager not to have his absence from the city prolonged, wrote constantly to Atticus, who had good friends among the pontifices, to see to it that an intercalary month was not inserted (*ne intercaletur*). For other interests than Cicero's no intercalation was ordered that year, and the refusal of the pontifices to put it into effect is given as one of the many reasons why the fiery tribune Gaius Scribonius Curio, eager for more time to propose laws, suddenly began to support Caesar.[9] This failure to intercalate was an abuse that Caesar's reform of the calendar terminated in the year 46, but the political value of the change was slight since free legislation was at an end.

To interfere with the calendar, other devices besides intercalation or failure to intercalate were used by magistrates with the support of pontifices and augurs. Early in 56 Cicero writes to his brother: "Lentulus is an excellent consul ... He has removed all the comitial days, for even the Latin festival is being performed over again and there has been no lack of thanksgivings. In that way resistance is offered to ruinous laws."[10] This means that Lentulus, presumably with the support of the pontifices, had found that something had gone wrong with the ceremony of the Latin games; perhaps someone had stumbled in the procession or had stuttered or misspoken in repeating the prayers or had failed to hold the sacrificial knife properly in offering up the victim.

The possibilities of such mistakes were infinite; they were so common in the days when Plautus' plays were popular that many of the theatrical games at which the plays were performed had to be presented all over again.[11] The pontifices, whose function it was to see to it that state ceremonies were performed at the prescribed time and place and under the prescribed ritual, could report to the senate that the games had not been properly performed and could recommend their repetition. In the year 56, when tribunes were proposing troublesome laws, the Latin festival that was repeated was doubtless scheduled on a stretch of comitial days. Cicero also mentions thanksgivings, celebrations voted for deliverance from danger, usually from a foreign foe. In such periods all the temples were open and the people could go from one temple to another to offer thanks to the gods. No assemblies could be held during the celebrations.

The thanksgivings increased constantly in length, and the one that Cicero referred to in 56 was probably the fifteen-day *supplicatio* voted for Caesar's victory over the Nervii, a celebration of unexampled duration, as Caesar notes in the second book of the Gallic Wars.[12] Caesar's enemies voted it, partly, it would seem, because it hampered legislation in which Caesar might have been interested. Later they gave him even longer thanksgivings for Gallic victories.

Cicero also had a thanksgiving voted for the victories won by his lieutenants in Cilicia, but there was a good deal of discussion about it. The *optimates* wanted it to stop Curio's legislation. Curio, who was personally friendly to Cicero, did not want it, because he needed the comitial days, and Cicero's agent Caelius finally arranged a deal by which it would be voted but not scheduled during the year of Curio's tribunate. Thus Caelius got it through the senate, supported by some of Cicero's enemies and opposed by some of his friends.[13]

If no thanksgivings were available, the consul could also interfere with legislation he did not like by putting on comitial days the movable festivals which he had a right to fix. This scheme was tried against Sulpicius Rufus, radical tribune of 88.[14]

Both Clodius and Caesar were aware of the difficulties provided by the calendar, and Clodius as tribune passed a law which made it legal to hold assemblies on days marked *fasti* as well as on comitial days. This law seems to have become a dead letter, but Caesar may have intended to observe it when in his reform of the calendar in 46 he made all the days he added to the year *dies fasti*. The change, like the reform of the calendar, was not important politically, for free assemblies were over.

But the most common means of stopping elections and legislation was provided by the auspices. The auspices belonged to divination, one of the most characteristic features of ancient religion.[15] The theory on which the auspices were based was not that the gods foretold the future but that they had means of letting the people know whether a certain action was in accord with their will. The auspices were taken to determine the will of Jupiter, chief god of the Roman state. With the *imperium,* the right of command conferred by man, the *auspicia,* conferred by deity, were an essential prerogative of the consul and the praetor. While taking the auspices was the function of the magistrate, their interpretation was in the hands of the augurs, a priestly college as august and ancient as the pontifices. On entering upon office, before setting forth to war, and before calling the people together by centuries or tribes, the consul or praetor had to ask the will of Jupiter, and he had to do it under the most carefully prescribed forms.

The circumstances attending the calling of assemblies concern us particularly.[16] The presiding magistrate pitched a tent at the place where the assembly was to be held, and went there between midnight and dawn to watch for the proper sign, carefully prescribed by augural discipline. He took along an attendant, and if the magistrate wanted to hold the assembly, the attendant, who watched for the signs, duly declared that he had seen the proper sign in the heavens. But if the magistrate did not wish to hold the assembly, perhaps until troublesome voters went home, the attendant would fail to see the necessary sign, and the magistrate would then declare that the auspices were unfavorable and would postpone the assembly.

In conducting the assembly the magistrate might take account not only of the auspices that he had sought on demand from the gods (*auspicia impetrativa*) but also of any that he himself or some other person, and most particularly an augur, declared that he had observed before the assembly was over (*auspicia oblativa*). The particular sign that always dissolved a Roman assembly was a flash of lightning. Thus when Pompey, consul and augur, was conducting the praetorian elections in 55, he declared, after Cato had been chosen for the office by the *centuria praerogativa,* that he had heard thunder. Pompey dissolved the assembly and reconvened it after having forcibly kept out the good men who would have voted for

Cato.[17] Thus Antony, as consul and augur, dissolved the consular *comitia* on one occasion when the voting had progressed to the second class.[18]

Moreover, these chance manifestations of divine will could be used by one magistrate to dissolve an assembly conducted by another. They could from the earliest times be employed by a consul against his colleague, and by provisions of laws passed in the middle of the second century they could also be used by a tribune against the consul holding an assembly,[19] and by a consul against the tribune holding a legislative assembly, but not against the tribune who was holding an assembly to elect plebeian officers.[20] In consequence, during the period of anarchy in the fifties the plebeian aediles and the tribunes of the plebs were regularly elected when the choice of other officers was long delayed.

The auspices of magistrates, according to Cicero, were "intended to bring about the adjournment of many unprofitable meetings of the assembly through plausible excuses for delay; for the immortal gods have often put down unjust assertions of the people's will by means of the auspices."[21] This was the method by which Bibulus, Caesar's colleague in the consulship in 59, tried to forestall the legislation of Caesar and his tribunes. It was sufficient, according to the Roman system, for a consul or a tribune to announce that he was watching the heavens; anyone watching usually saw bad signs, and that announcement regularly called off an assembly. Bibulus therefore shut himself up in his house and declared that he was watching. But Caesar and the tribunes went ahead with the assemblies and passed the laws.

The use of this type of religious obstruction seems to have increased in the late republic and to have been substituted often for the veto power, perhaps because the employment of that power had so often led to violence. Clodius tried to curb these tactics by forbidding *obnuntiatio,* that is, the reporting by a magistrate of such unfavorable omens and by forbidding also the watching of the heavens by a magistrate when an assembly was at hand.[22] And though Cicero objected to Clodius' disregard of Roman religion, Cicero's friends in the senate, when the bill for Cicero's recall was to come up, passed a decree forbidding anyone to watch the heavens.[23] In general, Clodius' prohibition of heaven watching did not last, and *obnuntiatio* was in succeeding years used repeatedly by consuls against tribunes and by tribunes against consuls. It was employed both by staunch *optimates* and by *populares,* seeking to rouse the people against the *optimates.*

In the year 57 the optimate tribune Milo wished to prevent the consul Metellus from holding an election. Before midnight on the day when the election was to be held, Milo with a strong band arrived in the Campus Martius to "obnuntiare." He stayed there until midday and thus prevented the assembly, which had to begin before that hour, from being held. The next day Metellus decided to try deceit. He sent word to Milo that the notice of the *obnuntiatio* could be served on him in the Forum and that he would be there to receive it at the first hour. And so the next night Milo went to the Forum and Metellus played him false. He sneaked off in a devious course to the Campus at dawn, hoping to hold the assembly before Milo arrived to announce a religious obstruction. But Milo found out about it, rushed to the Campus and served his notice, and the assembly was postponed again.[24]

Because of the constant employment of such obstructions,[25] several times in this period the year opened without consuls to take the auspices. Under these conditions an *interrex* had to be chosen to ask the will of the gods and to hold the assembly to elect the chief magistrates. Only a patrician, a member of the group that had once held a monopoly over the higher offices, could serve as *interrex*. He could function only five days, after which, if no consuls had been chosen, a new *interrex* had to be appointed. In the worst year of anarchy, 53, obstructions prevented the election of consuls until July, and the supply of patricians seems to have been practically exhausted.[26]

An augur was regularly present in the assemblies to advise the presiding officer, either by directing attention to an omen he had chanced to see himself or by urging the magistrate to take account of an omen reported by someone present. After the assembly was over, the augurs could also be called on to pass on the validity of the action in the event of a belated report of an omen or a *vitium,* a mistake in the procedure of the auspices. Cicero, who after 53 was a member of the college, describes the augurs as "the highest and most responsible authority in the state ... For if we consider their legal rights, what power is greater than that of adjourning assemblies and meetings convened by the highest officials ... or that of declaring null and void the acts of assemblies presided over by such officials? What is of graver import than the abandonment of any business already begun if a single augur says 'On another day'? What power is more impressive than that of forcing the consuls to resign their offices? What right is more sacred than that of giving or refusing permission to hold an assembly of the people or of the plebeians or that of abrogating laws illegally passed?"[27]

Cicero goes on to specify the incidents in which the augurs, like a supreme court, had passed on the constitutionality of laws. The Titian law, an agrarian law to reward Marius' troops, was abrogated because the augurs decided—undoubtedly to the great advantage of private property—that it had not been properly passed. The Livian law, the great omnibus bill of the tribune Marcus Livius Drusus, was rendered invalid when the consul of that year, himself an augur, declared that it was *non iure rogata*.

The augurs sometimes declared an election invalid. In the year 163, when the father of the Gracchi as consul held the election of his successors, there was some question about the validity of the election, but Gracchus upheld it. Later, from his province, perhaps because he was not satisfied with the policies of his successors, he wrote back to the college of augurs, to which he belonged, that he remembered he had not taken the auspices when he crossed the *pomerium* to go to the Campus Martius for the assembly. The augurs solemnly decided that the election was invalid, and the two consuls, unable to face the charge that they were in office without the will of Jupiter, resigned.[28] On the marble list of Roman magistrates set up under Augustus in the Forum the event is recorded with the words *vitio facti abdicarunt*.

The power of declaring laws and elections invalid seems not to have been used in our period, chiefly because, as we shall see, the college of augurs lacked unity. But even when the augurs did not act, a magistrate who disregarded the traditions of the state religion had to face public opinion if he refused to bow to the will of heaven.

Caesar alone was strong enough for that, but there is some reason to believe that he suffered in public confidence because of his boldness. There is no doubt that Crassus was weakened with the public because on his departure for the disastrous Parthian War he disregarded the auspices. There had been bitter opposition to Crassus' expedition and to the huge levies provided in the tribunitial bill that authorized his command. When Crassus left the city, the auspices that he took were reported to have been unfavorable, and accordingly a tribune in the service of his political opponents followed him to the gates and tried to keep him from leaving. Crassus disregarded the omens and went forth, pursued, according to later writers, by curses and imprecations. Several years afterward, a censor who was also an augur charged the tribune with having falsified the auspices and having thereby brought a terrible calamity on the Roman people.[29]

Besides the auspices, there were various other means of determining the will of the gods. Appeal could be made to the Sibylline Books, sacred oracles in Greek that were preserved in the Capitoline temple. The Roman priests authorized to consult these books were among the chief officials of Roman religion, hardly less distinguished than the pontifices and the augurs. In 56 the statue of Jupiter on the Alban Mount was struck by lightning, and the senate, because of the omen, authorized the priests in charge of the oracles to consult the books. They did so, and were forced by a tribune in the service of Crassus to make the oracle public. It read as follows: "If the king of Egypt come asking for any aid, do not refuse him friendship, but do not support him with a multitude; otherwise you will incur both toils and dangers."[30]

Now this oracle was amazingly pertinent, for Ptolemy the Flute Player, father of Cleopatra, who had been restored to his throne by the "triumvirs" three years before, had been driven out and was back in Rome begging and bribing his patrons there to reinstate him again in his kingdom. There were several prominent men who wished to go out with an army and put Ptolemy back on his throne; among them were Cicero's friend and benefactor Lentulus Spinther, then governor of Cilicia, and Pompey and perhaps Crassus. Certainly Crassus did not want Pompey to go, and he was responsible for the publication of this oracle, forbidding aid to the king with a "multitude," which was taken to mean an army. Crassus had probably had the oracle invented. We know a good deal about the subject from Cicero's letters to Lentulus, whose heart was set on restoring the king to his throne.

Cicero did not doubt that the oracle was a fraud;[31] nevertheless he did not think that Lentulus could, in defiance of it, use force to restore the king. He suggested that Lentulus might try to bring back the king if he was sure that there would be no difficulty, but he warned that if anything went wrong the consequences might be serious.[32] It may be noted here that Lentulus lost the contest, and that Pompey arranged for his adherent Aulus Gabinius, governor of Syria, to restore the king. Pompey's enemies were able to stir up trouble for Gabinius, for the Tiber conveniently overflowed and the flood was interpreted as vengeance taken by the gods for the disregard of their oracle. Pompey had to coerce or bribe the jurors to acquit Gabinius of charges that he had violated the majesty of the Roman people.[33]

The Romans, with their persistent wish to know the will of the gods, also went outside the governing class and called in special priests trained in Etruscan lore, the *haruspices*. These priests explained the omens provided by entrails of victims; it was a *haruspex* who warned Caesar of the unfavorable omen in the victim that he sacrificed shortly before his death. The *haruspices* were also summoned frequently to report their findings on other types of portents.

When the Capitol was struck by lightning in the year 65, the *haruspices* were consulted. They declared that, if the gods were not appeased, conflagration and civil war and the end of the city and the empire were at hand. They recommended that expiatory games of ten days' duration should be celebrated for Jupiter and that a new and bigger statue of Jupiter should be set up on the Capitol, facing the east, that is, the Forum; if this advice were followed, the *haruspices* expressed the hope that secret plots against the safety of the city and the empire would be apparent to senate and people. When two years later in his third Catilinarian oration Cicero made a report to the people on the detection of the conspiracy, he declared that, that morning, as the conspirators and the witnesses against them were on the way to the meeting of the senate in the temple of Concord, the statue was being set in place. "Now that it has been put in place and turned toward you and the senate, both the senate and you have seen the plots against the common safety clearly revealed ... If I should say that it was I who resisted [the conspirators] I should be taking too much upon myself and I should be unbearable." *Ille, ille Iuppiter restitit.* The words were doubtless accompanied by a gesture toward the new statue. "It is his will that the Capitol, it is his will that these temples, the whole city, all of you should be secure. With the immortal gods as my guides I reached this state of mind, this determination, and obtained these significant proofs."[34]

This passage shows how a Roman consul could present himself to the people as the agent through whom the gods were operating for the welfare of the state. Here, Cicero is using the state religion to justify the position that he believed would be taken by the senate as a whole. But in other situations he employed religion to advance his own case against an enemy. In the long personal conflict which he waged with Clodius the two men constantly appeared before the people as rivals in piety.

In the course of an affair with Caesar's wife, Clodius had violated a sacred ceremony of the state when in masquerade he broke in upon the rites of the Good Goddess, held at the house of Caesar as urban praetor. It was, as the pontifices solemnly declared, a *nefas* against the state religion for a man to witness those sacred mysteries, entrusted for the state to the Vestal Virgins and the matrons of the senate. The *nefas* was the more serious because Caesar was *pontifex maximus,* the head of Roman state cult, and his house beside the Forum was not a private dwelling but the public house of this priest. Caesar declared that he knew nothing about the matter; but he divorced his wife.

Clodius was tried on a religious charge, *incestus,* by a special commission, and Cicero, who had been visited at his house by Clodius on the day of the scandal, destroyed his alibi. Through bribery of the jury Clodius was acquitted, but he became Cicero's bitter enemy, and Cicero was vulnerable because he had put Roman citizens to death without a trial. As a result the patrician Clodius began to agitate for transference to the plebeians in order to secure the tribunate and take vengeance on Cicero.

Here religion entered again into the situation, for, before Clodius could be adopted into a plebeian family, he had to forswear the gods of his own family and take those of the new house into which he passed, and that required a curiate law, a law passed in an ancient assembly presided over by the *pontifex maximus*. Caesar in his consulship officiated at that assembly, with Pompey serving as augur. At the time, as during most of that year, Caesar's colleague Bibulus was watching the heavens, and that was supposed to make any action illegal. The question was never formally submitted to the augurs,[35] but Cicero repeatedly called in question the legality of the adoption. Clodius got the tribunate and effected the passage of a law exiling Cicero.

Then Clodius entered into the religious controversy. He tore down Cicero's splendid house on the Palatine, and dedicated on the site a shrine of Libertas, the goddess whom Cicero had supposedly injured when he put the Catilinarians to death.[36] Cicero, on being restored to the state, naturally wished to have his house lot returned to him, but Clodius insisted that it was now the property of Liberty. The senate referred the matter to the pontifices, and Cicero delivered before them a lengthy oration, the *De Domo,* setting forth the claim that Clodius' transference to the plebs was invalid, that the survival of the patriciate, essential for the state religion, was endangered by such transferences, that Clodius' tribunitial laws had violated the auspices, that the laws themselves, including the two providing for Cicero's exile, were invalid, and that the dedication of the shrine of Liberty had not been carried out under the proper form. The pontifices had turned out in large numbers—thirteen of the fifteen members were there—and they uttered a solemn and rather obscure opinion seeming to indicate that, since the site had not been properly dedicated, it could be returned to Cicero. By vote of the senate the house lot was restored. But Clodius had not finished. He kept trying, by violent assaults on the site and on the builders who were reconstructing Cicero's house, to regain Liberty's land.

In the following year the *haruspices,* who were consulted about a mysterious sound heard in the neighborhood of an Italian city, explained that many things were wrong with the Roman state. Among other details they noted that sacred and religious places had been made profane. That was Clodius' chance and he proceeded to address a public meeting. His speech is lost, but we know about it from another of the interminable orations that Cicero prepared to inform posterity on the circumstances of his exile and restoration.[37] "Religious observances and rites, conscript fathers," Cicero declares, "were the matters which Clodius, if you please, laid before the mass meeting; yes, Publius Clodius complained of the neglect, the violation, the desecration of rites and sanctities! It is not surprising that this should seem to you a fit subject for laughter; why his own meeting laughed at the thought that a fellow who, as he himself often brags, was paralyzed by a hundred decrees of the senate, all of them pronounced against him for sacrilege, who had made the sacred banquet of the Good Goddess the scene of his adultery and who had polluted rites which it is a crime for men's eyes to gaze upon ... should protest at a mass meeting against a want of regard for religion. So now we look forward with keen anticipation to his next meeting on the subject of chastity ... He read to the meeting that response recently delivered by the soothsayers with regard to the strange noise that was heard ... the statement ... to the effect that 'sacred and hallowed sites were being turned to secular purposes.' In the course of his argument he asserted that my house had been consecrated by that most scrupulous of priests, Publius Clodius."

Cicero proceeds, taking up the decree clause by clause, to explain that it was not to him but to Clodius that the decree of the *haruspices* applied. Sacred games had been carelessly performed and defiled. Those were the Megalesian games which Clodius had presented as aedile; he had loosed a band of slaves on the stage during a theatrical performance. Sacred places were profaned. That meant not the shrine of Liberty on the site of Cicero's house, but other places, including the temple of Tellus which Clodius had violated. Ancient and secret sacrifices had been polluted. That of course concerned the rites of *Bona Dea*.

The rivalry in piety between Cicero and Clodius was a sideshow

in the party struggles of their time; it demonstrated the use that
could be made of the state cult in partisan politics. But it also showed
that the official religion was suffering from the state of anarchy that
characterized Roman politics in the days of the "triumvirate." The
state religion was no longer the cohesive force that it had been when
Polybius came to Rome a century before.

POLITICS AND THE PUBLIC PRIESTHOODS

The weakening of the state religion is reflected in the priests who
interpreted the will of the gods on earth. Because of changes in the
colleges, the priests no longer presented a solid front to the people.

The official priests were not, as has already been stated, a separate
caste. There were a few relics of such a caste in priests like the *rex
sacrorum* and the *flamen Dialis,* but they were mere figureheads.
The real power in Roman religion belonged not to them but to the
members of the great colleges of priests recruited for life from the
very same nobles who held consulships and censorships, governed
provinces, and celebrated triumphs. The acquisition of these priesthoods imposed no restrictions on the political or military activity
of the holder.[38]

Besides the two most ancient and powerful priesthoods, the pontificate and the augurate, the four colleges included the board of
fifteen men in charge of the Sibylline Books, and the *epulones* who
prepared the great banquets of Jupiter. All these priesthoods were
valued for the prestige they gave to the holders and their descendants, but the pontificate and the augurate were particularly important for the power conferred upon their members. The two
colleges served in effect as standing committees of the senate to
whom matters of religious import could be referred. Of the two
colleges in the late republic, the augurs possessed more political
influence than the pontifices, for their power over the auspices,
exercised either as a college or as individual advisers of magistrates,
was more far-reaching than the authority of the pontifices.[39]

But the head of the college of pontifices, the *pontifex maximus,*
had a more exalted position than any member of the augural college. The *pontifex maximus* was in fact a special kind of magistrate
who differed from other magistrates because he held office not for

a year but for life, not with a colleague but alone. Although he no longer possessed in the late republic the authority he had once had in civil law, he still chose the Vestal Virgins, the *flamines,* and the *rex sacrorum,* and presided over the curiate assembly at which they were inaugurated. He also presided at the same assembly when adoptions like that of Clodius were confirmed and when wills, like Caesar's, that provided for adoptions, were validated. In religious matters the *pontifex maximus* often acted for the whole college, using its members in an advisory capacity. He was the real heir to the religious power of the king; his office was the Regia, the king's dwelling beside the Forum, and he lived close by in a house that was state property.[40] The Roman who held this priesthood was truly a prince of the state; only the *princeps senatus,* the man at the head of the citizen rolls, could rival him, and in several instances the two positions went to the same men.[41]

The colleges of priests were originally self-perpetuating bodies which elected their own members. In the early republic patricians alone were eligible. For more than half a century after the plebeians gained access to the consulship, the patricians succeeded in barring them from the coveted pontificate and augurate. Plebeians could not, the patricians held, interpret the will of the gods. Even after the plebeians, through an increase in the size of the priestly colleges, acquired access to priesthoods, the patricians maintained a strength in the colleges that they could not keep in public office. Approximately half the places in each college—seven out of a total of fifteen—were still in the possession of patricians in the late republic. The plebeian families who obtained priesthoods were tenacious of their privileges, and it was almost impossible for new men to break into the colleges.

The power and exclusiveness of the priestly class were recognized, and there were repeated proposals that the priests should be elected by the people. The objection was made that the will of the people was not valid in religion. Finally, someone thought up a plan under which first the *pontifex maximus* and later the rest of the priests were chosen in a special type of popular election. The solution, as it was applied to the election of the *pontifex maximus* in the third century, was that he should be chosen not by the people as a whole but by a minority of the people, and that the pontifices should then ratify the choice. A special assembly was created for the purpose. It consisted of seventeen, that is, less than half of the thirty-five tribes, the tribes to take part in the voting being chosen by lot, apparently just before the election. But even then there was not free choice, since only men already serving as pontifices were eligible for the office. After that the periodic election of a new *pontifex maximus* was one of the hardest-fought contests of the Roman state.

For more than a century after the *pontifex maximus* had been regularly elected by this tribal vote, the priests continued, like exclusive clubs, to select their own members; they maintained something of the solidarity of a club, refraining from electing to membership anyone who was a personal enemy of a priest already in the college.[42] Tribunes agitated from time to time to institute popular election to the priesthoods, and finally in the year 104 Gnaeus Domitius Ahenobarbus, father of Caesar's enemy, angered because the pontifices had not taken him into their college, carried as tribune of the plebs a law which gave to the special assembly that chose the *pontifex maximus* the right of electing the members of the four great colleges of priests. The priests themselves still maintained some influence in the election, for the candidates had to be nominated by members of the individual colleges.

This right of the people was revoked by Sulla and the choice of priests was restored to the colleges.[43] It is generally believed that Sulla also restored to the college of pontifices the right of choosing the *pontifex maximus,* but there is nothing to prove that he did. It is more likely that he let the people continue to elect the *pontifex maximus.* For some years after most of the aristocratic features of the Sullan regime had ended, the colleges continued to be self-perpetuating bodies, but in the year 63 the tribune Titus Labienus effected the passage of a bill which gave back to the special tribal assembly the choice of priests.

Caesar supported that bill, and the acclaim he got from the popularity of the measure aided him in his own candidacy for the office of *pontifex maximus,* which had lately fallen vacant. Since that office went regularly to a distinguished elder statesman, it was generally expected that it would go to Catulus, a pontifex of long standing, the restorer of the Capitol, and easily the most revered member of the Roman senate. In contrast to him, Caesar was a young man who had not yet held the praetorship or demonstrated his ability except in the intrigues of city politics. But Caesar had popular support both from his sponsorship of Labienus' law and from the demagogic activity he had pursued in recent years. He also had, or borrowed, funds enough to engage in wholesale bribery. It is doubtful whether he would have won if the election had been held in the centuriate assembly, but in the tribes he could make his influence felt. We may have a trace of the publicity accompanying this campaign in the story that Iulus, mythical founder of the Julian line, was *pontifex maximus* at Alba Longa. It was always helpful in Roman politics to prove that an ancestor had held the office that was being sought. Caesar's victory, a bitter blow to Catulus, gave him his first position of primacy in the Roman state.

After Labienus' law was passed, the elections of public priests were major political contests. Members of the high nobility often obtained priesthoods for their sons very early in their careers. Thus Cicero's friend Lentulus got the augurate for his son when the boy had just taken the toga of manhood and presumably was only about fifteen years old.[44] But new men either did not get them at all or, like Cicero, had to wait until late in life for election. Cicero longed for membership in Pompey's college of the augurs and, at a time when he was opposing the "triumvirs," suggested to Atticus that he might be tempted by the augurate to support the men in power.[45] But it was not until six years later, when he had for some time been subservient to the wishes of Pompey and Caesar, that he received his reward. In his last years Cicero, confident in the nobility he had brought to his family, wrote to Brutus to ask support for the election of his twenty-two-year-old son to the pontificate.[46]

In elections to priesthoods the so-called triumvirs were more successful in bringing their candidates to victory than they were in the contests for the consulship. They were better able to control the tribal vote than the less democratic vote of the centuries. One of the fiercest contests was that between Domitius, brother-in-law of Cato, favored by the *optimates,* and Caesar's candidate, Mark Antony, in

50. Although in that year Caesar's candidate for the consulship was defeated, Antony won the augurate, and Caelius writes to Cicero that party interest (*partes,* in this case support of or opposition to Caesar) determined the stand of most people, and that very few did their duty by their friends. Caelius says he is one of those few.[47] He was a personal friend of Antony and canvassed for him, but he was also held to be an optimate, and Domitius did not forgive him for the defection.

We know a good deal about the membership of the two most important colleges, the pontifices and the augurs, in the fifties. We know in fact the names of all the fifteen men in the pontificate in the year 57, for Cicero lists thirteen of them, arranged by order of entrance into the office (the group that passed on the status of his house lot), and the names of the other two members are known. One of them was the *pontifex maximus* Caesar, who was away in Gaul. The group included eight men of consular rank, four of whom (Servilius, Marcus Lucullus, Metellus Creticus, and the elder Curio) had had the distinction of a triumph. It comprised, among younger men, Metellus Scipio, whom I have described as the heir of the most aristocratic traditions of two Roman houses, Marcus Aemilius Lepidus, the future triumvir, and Crassus' son.[48] The augurate, for which we have the names of about half the members in the same period, seems to have been an equally eminent college, including Lucius Lucullus, Pompey, Hortensius, Clodius' brother, and Sulla's son.[49] Few of the names of the other priests are known, but the board of fifteen men had a very distinguished member in the younger Cato.[50]

The divisions in the nobility were reflected in the priesthoods. A recent writer[51] has argued that the opening of the priesthoods through popular election to a wider group contributed materially to cleavage in the colleges, and so to the decay of Roman religion. It is true that, after popular election came in, the old-time custom of not coöpting into a priesthood a man who was a personal enemy of anyone in the group was abandoned. But the men chosen by popular election, after Labienus' law, did not actually come from a wider group in the state. Although on at least two occasions a man who was not a member of a noble family tried to get a priesthood,[52] the office always—so far as the records show—went to a noble. Even before Labienus' law, enmity between Catulus and Caesar among the pontifices and between Lucullus and Pompey among the augurs had destroyed harmony in those groups, and there must have been a good deal of strain in the official meetings of the colleges and in the magnificent banquets provided by the state for the priests. Popular election probably increased that strain by bringing into the colleges more adherents of Pompey, Caesar, and Crassus, men who were completely at variance with most of the older members of the colleges.[53]

Most important for the political events of the fifties was the lack of unity of the augurs. It was the auspices, under their jurisdiction, that Caesar and his tribunes disregarded. They seem not to have violated the state ceremonial that Caesar directed as *pontifex maximus*. One of the tribunes in Caesar's service during his consulship in 59 announced in the senate at the beginning of his term that the decisions of the augurs and the arrogance of that college would not obstruct his actions as tribune.[54] Perhaps he was depending on Pompey, a member of the college, to stop such obstruction. In any case, the best men withdrew from the senate that year, and, with Caesar in control, the legality of his laws was not submitted to the augurs.

The laws were, to be sure, questioned by the demagogue Clodius when he was opposing Pompey in the following year. Clodius called Bibulus to a public meeting and asked him whether he had watched the heavens while Caesar was passing laws. Bibulus replied that he had, and Clodius then called in some augurs and inquired whether laws were properly passed under such conditions. The augurs replied that they were not. In this manner Clodius indicated that Caesar's laws—which, it may be noted, benefited Pompey—were unconstitutional.[55] But that was just a demonstration in a public meeting which could take no action, a demonstration that Clodius himself forgot when he made up his quarrel with Pompey. So far as we know, the augurs in the next decade took no action on any legislation either of Caesar or of the tribunes who did his bidding. The state religion, like the constitution, was in a condition of anarchy.

The strength of popular elements within the college explains why in the records of tribunitial oratory in the late republic there is no protest against the domination of the nobility in the state religion. Such protests had been common in the early republic when plebeians were striving to break the hold of the patricians on the state cult. Livy gives eloquent versions of speeches on the subject. Similar protests were probably made by Domitius when he passed his law for popular election of priests in 104 and by Labienus and Caesar when the law was revived in 63. But after that the election not only of the *pontifex maximus* but of all the major priests in the tribal assembly resulted in the inclusion of many nobles of "popular" sympathies among the official interpreters of the state religion. At a time when Caesar was *pontifex maximus* and Pompey was a leading member of the college of augurs, when too their henchmen were constantly winning election to priesthoods, tribunitial orators would have had no occasion to declare that the *optimates* were oppressing the people through the state religion. Actually both sides were manipulating religion for their own ends.

The people, confused no doubt, and weakened in their faith, were still bound by old-time superstition. They needed a champion. If we could accept the view of Professor Farrington, the great Epicurean poet Lucretius tried to save them. Farrington thinks that Lucretius, in his passionate denunciation of religion, was seeking to free the common man from slavery to the state worship.[56] He believes that, by what amounted to a conspiracy of silence, Varro and Cicero, who knew Lucretius' poem, refrained from mentioning him in their essays because they considered Lucretius' doctrine subversive. But Lucretius did not write for the masses. He wrote, as Farrington concedes, for all mankind weighed down by superstition and fear.

> Non populi gentesque tremunt regesque superbi?

His poem on the Nature of Things was not directed to the common man at the mercy of the men who manipulated state cult to suit their own ends. If it had been, Lucretius would not have failed to show up the shocking religious abuses of his day.[57]

Caesar as dictator ended the anarchy that had taken possession of religion and politics alike. Already *pontifex maximus,* he became an augur and saw to it that both colleges were subservient. The symbols of the pontificate and the augurate on his coins, one of his chief media of propaganda, attest the importance of the official religion in his reorganization of the state. The final step was taken when Caesar was, by vote of the senate, enshrined among the official gods of the state and provided with a temple, a special priest, and festivals. The state religion, once an instrument used by the senatorial oligarchs to impose their supremacy on the people, had later, and particularly in the era of revolution, served rival groups in party politics. Now, in the control of a supreme ruler, it functioned to support a monarch numbered among the gods of the state.

CHAPTER V

THE CRIMINAL COURTS AND THE
RISE OF A NEW MAN

THE PEOPLE in centuriate or tribal assembly had once decided by their votes the fate of men charged with crimes against the state; but by a gradual development in the second century and a comprehensive reform under Sulla, standing courts (*quaestiones*) had practically replaced the judicial functions of the assemblies.[1] Public interest in the proceedings continued. A great criminal trial was a significant political event. The charges concerned offenses against the public—extortion in the provinces, embezzlement of state funds, treason against the state, malpractice in candidacy for office, acts of violence, and murder. The accused whose citizenship, rank, or property was at stake were frequently men who had held high office —ex-consuls or ex-praetors. The prosecutor was also a public figure —not, like our prosecuting attorney, an elected officer, but a man whom magistrate and jury selected for the individual case from applicants for the post. The pleaders for the defense were often men of great eminence. The witnesses usually included character witnesses of high rank, and frequently also deputations from the municipalities and the provinces. The cases were often inspired by political motives, and speeches for defense and prosecution might touch immediately on the problems of the day. The jurors were men of position selected from an official panel of senators, knights, and other high-income groups. The judge was one of the eight praetors or another specially elected officer.

The political significance of the criminal trial was enhanced by the remarkable publicity with which it was conducted. It took place in the open Forum where everyone was free to come, look on, and listen. The stage for the trial was an elevated platform; in the late seventies there were two such permanent tribunals in the Forum, one near the Lacus Curtius and the other beside the temple of Castor. To provide space for all the criminal courts—there were eight of them—other temporary platforms of wood were erected in

[1] For notes to chap. y see pp. 216–221.

the open Forum. It was these temporary structures that provided the timber used in 44 B.C. for Caesar's funeral pyre. Each platform was large enough to accommodate the presiding judge and the jury, which sometimes numbered as many as seventy. On benches below were the defendants and the witnesses.[2]

In the Forum, cases were frequently in progress on several tribunals at the same time. One man would be tried for extortion, and near by another might be up for murder and still another for embezzlement or bribery. The crowds which constantly thronged the Forum, the center of city life, could—as crowds do nowadays in Union Square or Hyde Park—drift about from one platform to another to find out what was going on. One could tell how good an orator was merely by looking at the size of the circle, the *corona* around his tribunal. The speakers often had their minds more on the crowds than on the jurors; indeed Brutus is quoted by Cicero as saying that he could not go on with his speech if his *corona* drifted away.[3] The people who came and went while the speaking was in progress could get a firsthand contact with the proceedings such as is impossible in the limited space of the American courtroom. The trial was like a great drama in which the people crowding on the steps of the tribunal made Cicero think of the audience in the theater to see a show. The very language of the law court has gone over into the theater. The cases were divided into sections known as *actiones,* and the prosecutor was known as an *actor.*

The opposing counsel and their assistants were not jurisconsults, though such men were always available for consultation, but men of public affairs. They had prepared for activity in the courts in the regular education in public speaking through which every man who desired a public career—and that meant practically the entire senatorial class—had to go. The prosecutor brought his accusation to eliminate a dangerous political rival of his own or of a friend, or to avenge a wrong done to a close relative or friend. He found in the case at the same time an opportunity to make himself known and to advance his political fortunes. Many a young man began his career with a prosecution which he undertook in his early twenties. The speakers for the defense were either old friends of the accused, who, under the obligations of Roman political society, must be ready at any moment to appear for the protection of their close associates, or they were men who by their skill in speaking were trying to acquire for themselves a circle of adherents.

The courts were a citadel of free speech. There was no such taboo against dealing with politics as was imposed at least on the new man Cicero by his candidacy for the consulship. In many of his speeches in the courts Cicero discussed political questions; in fact it was after Cicero had, in a criminal trial, made some criticisms of conditions under the "triumvirate" that Caesar decided to transfer Cicero's enemy Clodius to the plebs.'

For detailed information about the trials we are necessarily restricted to the cases in which Cicero took part, for every oration of the period which has been preserved comes from his pen. But in Cicero's history of oratory we have a catalogue of the chief speakers of his day, and the list includes every man of prominence in politics. There is Pompey, who, Cicero says, might have reached the highest pinnacle if he had not devoted himself to war, but who nevertheless had a certain range, saw situations clearly, had a fine voice and great dignity of mien. There is Crassus, restricted in training and natural gifts, but industrious and zealous, and active for many years as one of the chief patrons in the courts. His Latin was good, his choice of words not bad, his organization excellent, but he lacked spark and spoke with little emphasis. There is Cato, who, unlike others fashioned by Stoic training, achieved the heights of eloquence. There is Caesar, who of all the orators of the day is said to have spoken the most finished Latin. The catalogue could go on endlessly.

It is only through Cicero's discriminating comments that we are familiar with the activity of these political leaders in the courts. But we know the master of them all in the published version of speeches delivered in fifteen criminal trials. Cicero's court oratory was of supreme importance for his political career. It was through success in the courts that he acquired the fame and the political following that enabled him, as the only new man of his generation, to advance to the consulship. In this chapter I shall be concerned chiefly with the case by which Cicero prepared to storm "the fortress of the nobility"—the prosecution of Verres.

Already experienced in the civil courts, Cicero had appeared first in a criminal trial in the year 80 under the dictatorship of Sulla and successfully defended Sextus Roscius of Ameria, a man of the municipal aristocracy, whom one of Sulla's creatures accused of murder. Cicero is careful in his treatment of the Sullan regime; though he had not taken part in the civil war, he asserts that he and his client were favorable to the victory of the nobility. But he has the courage and the skill to show that Sulla's agents had abused the dictator's power, and he had enough support among the high nobility in Rome to procure eminent witnesses who supported his arguments. Cicero won the case.

A decade passes during which we have no important remains of Cicero's work in the criminal courts, but we know that, except for the three years of his absence from Rome, first as student of oratory in Greek lands and later as quaestor in Sicily, he was steadily occupied in the courts, and that he devoted himself particularly to the affairs of the publicans.[5]

During all this period Cicero appeared in court only for the defense. His task as a new man was to make friends and not enemies, and he was aware of the dangers to a man's career created by a prosecution. Yet, following his great models in the Roman court, the leading orators of the preceding generation, Antonius and Crassus, he apparently wished to show his powers in the grueling strain of a prosecution. It should be attempted once or at any rate not often, he advises his son many years later.[6] And in the year 70 a case came up that was made to order for Cicero, the case of Gaius Verres.

In his three years as praetorian governor of Sicily, Verres had resorted to wholesale plunder that surpassed every precedent among the Roman governors who for years had made a practice of robbing and oppressing subject people. Cicero had been quaestor in Sicily, and he knew the island well and had established himself as friend or *hospes* or patron of many Roman businessmen and leading provincials of the island. He could therefore appear in his accusation not simply as a prosecutor but as defender of the rights of his friends and clients, whom Verres had brought to ruin and misery. He could appear too as the champion of the enlightened, though ineffective, Roman laws that provided redress for allies who were wronged.

"This is the foreigners' charter of rights," he declares. "This is their strong tower, somewhat less strong now certainly than it once was, but still if our allies have any hope left to comfort their sad hearts, it must all rest on this law alone."[7]

It is tempting for one who likes Cicero to believe that a feeling for Rome's mission with allied and subject peoples and a sense of responsibility toward the Sicilians were sufficient to make Cicero assume the prosecution of a malefactor like Verres. Cicero was a Roman patriot, and he did have a feeling for Sicily and a sense of obligation to this the oldest of the Roman provinces. He speaks with obvious sincerity when he praises the land itself and Sicily's past relations with Rome. "She was the first to make our forefathers perceive how splendid a thing foreign empire is. No other nation has equaled her in loyal good will toward us ... When has she failed to pay us punctually her tribute of grain? ... Cato Sapiens called her ... the nation's storehouse, the nurse at whose breast the Roman people is fed."[8]

Cicero is conscious too of the role played in Sicily by Rome's great generals, the elder Scipio Africanus and Marcus Claudius Marcellus. When a decendant of Africanus, a bearer of the renowned name of Scipio, appeared in support of Verres, Cicero, the new man, became the defender of the great Roman whose monument Verres had stolen from the city of Segesta. "He was such a man, and so served Rome, that not one family but the whole country has the right to protect his fame. In this right I myself have a share as a citizen of the empire whose proud and glorious fame is due to him ... So, Verres, I demand of you the memorial of Scipio Africanus."[9]

But this was a crucial time in the career of Cicero, and it must be admitted that he would not have taken the case if he had not been convinced that it would further his career. His other speeches in the extortion court are all for the defense, and at least one of them is a whitewash of an obviously guilty man. In 70, Cicero, now thirty-six years old, had been for five years in the senate, and the time had come for him to seek another office. He had decided to be a candidate in that year for the plebeian aedileship.[10] He was looking toward the future, perhaps already with his eye on the consulship, which for more than two decades had been closed to new men. The case against Verres offered him great opportunities, for Verres was being defended by the leader—Cicero calls him the tyrant—of the Roman bar, Quintus Hortensius, a noble who in that year won election to the consulship. With considerable zest Cicero enters the lists to challenge Hortensius' *dominatio regnumque iudiciorum*. "However capable he may be, he will feel, when he comes to speak against me, that the trial is among other things a trial of his own capacity."[11]

The year 70 was crucial not only for Cicero but for the Roman state. The Sullan constitution, which for a decade had maintained the nobility and the senate in control of the state, had already been attacked by the young general Gnaeus Pompeius, who, with his army behind him, had forced the senate to suspend the Sullan laws and permit him to hold the consulship, for which he was ineligible because of his youth and his failure to follow a senatorial career. At the same time, Pompey had made a deal with the *populares* who were agitating for the full restoration of the legislative powers of the tribunate, the greatest threat to the supremacy of the nobility. As consul, Pompey with his colleague Crassus had immediately carried a bill to give back to the tribunes their lawmaking powers. He had also reëstablished the censorship discarded by Sulla. Strongly supported by the knights, he had been discussing in senate and public meetings[12] the need of reform of the juries, which Sulla had taken from the knights and placed entirely in the hands of senators. The courts had, like the courts of knights in the post-Gracchan period, proved venal and corrupt, and only recently shocking scandals had been created by the acquittal of men high in public life. But when Verres came to trial in August, no change had been made in jury service, and the men who sat on his case were all senators.

In this case two questions were at stake, the guilt of Verres and the reconstitution of the juries. Were senators to continue to act as arbiters of the misdeeds of their associates? At such a moment a criminal trial of a notorious plunderer was bound to have great political significance. This particular plunderer was ready to offer fabulous bribes, and the case would show whether a senatorial jury was once more to demonstrate its venality.

The political importance of the case was further increased because Verres' gold had been put at the disposal of a clique of nobles determined to curb the influence of Pompey and the *populares,* with whom he was in league. The leaders of the clique were Verres' counsel Hortensius, powerful members of the dominant family of the Caecilii Metelli, and the most aristocratic young Roman of the day, Publius Scipio Nasica. Through Verres' money this clique had just swung the elections of consuls and praetors and brought about the choice of Hortensius and Quintus Metellus as consuls for the next year and the choice of Metellus' brother, Marcus, as praetor.[13] More of Verres' money was now to purchase his acquittal, and then presumably additional funds would be available to prevent the passage of a law taking the right of jury duty from the senators.

Where did Cicero stand in the politics of the period? He was certainly opposed to Hortensius and the Metelli, but he had not yet embraced the cause of Pompey. Although in the *Verrines* he referred to Pompey in honorable terms as *clarissimus, fortissimus,*[14] he did not actually align himself with the great general until the Manilian law was proposed in 66. It is obvious from the *Verrines* that at that time Cicero distrusted the popular agitators with whom Pompey was allied, and it is not clear that he thought the restoration of the tribunate a good thing. It is perhaps significant that the office for which Cicero sued in this year was the aedileship and not the tribunate. The latter office, under its restored powers, would have provided remarkable scope for his oratory and remarkable opportunities for supporting Pompey, who was seeking the aid of tribunes. Dio is probably right in saying that Cicero decided on the aedileship because he did not wish to offend the nobility.[15] In their eyes the tribunate was associated with demagoguery.

On the reconstitution of the juries Cicero has a good deal to say in the orations, and it is significant that he is interested not in securing new jurors from a different order in the state but in having the senatorial jurors redeem their blemished reputation and thus restore the authority of the order. He speaks as a senator to his own group; his task is not to increase the unpopularity of the senate but "to help in allaying the discredit which is mine as well as yours."[16] "Today the eyes of the world are upon us, waiting to see how far the conduct of each man among us will be marked by obedience to his conscience and by observance of the law ... It is this man's case that will determine whether, with a court composed of senators, the condemnation of a very guilty and very rich man can possibly occur ... You have the power of removing and destroying the dishonor and disgrace that have for several years past attached to this order."[17]

Cicero points out that one of the jurors selected for the case, the eminent Quintus Catulus, had recently in the senate condemned the corruption of the courts.[18] Cicero had, it may be added, some reason to fear that Catulus, who was Hortensius' brother-in-law, might wish Verres' acquittal, and he is adroit in trying to align Catulus with the opponents of Verres. An acquittal will, Cicero points out, have grave consequences for the senators. "If this body of jurors shall in any way come to grief, the universal opinion will be that, for the administration of justice, we must seek not fitter men from the same order, for none such could be found" (this is a comment on the excellent men, including the most distinguished juror Catulus, who had been impaneled), "but some other order altogether"—*alium omnino ordinem.*[19]

It is apparent from many indications in the orations that Hortensius and his clique were not the only men who desired Verres' acquittal. "You must know," Cicero declares, "that there are certain persons possessed by such hatred of our order that they are already saying, openly and often, that they wish for the acquittal of Verres, thorough scoundrel as they know him to be, simply for the sake of having the senate deprived, with ignominy and shame, of its judicial rights."[20]

One may reasonably suspect that the *populares* who were allied with Pompey are referred to here, and that the plan was to give the senatorial juries enough rope to hang themselves, and then to bring in a bill that would transfer the jury to "some other order altogether," that is, the knights. These men wanted not Verres but the jurors to be convicted in the case. To quote Cicero again, "Even as you will pass your verdict upon the defendant, the Roman people will pass its verdict upon yourselves."[21] In his admonishment to the jury, Cicero—with his eye as always on the assembled multitude—even uses threats. He serves notice that, if the jurors fail to render a just verdict, he as aedile will bring Verres to trial before the people.[22]

But if the clique of nobles led by Hortensius, and also the most extreme *populares,* backed no doubt indirectly by that master of indirection, Pompey, desired for different reasons the acquittal of Verres, these two groups did not at the time represent all the elements in Roman politics. There were middle-of-the-road men ready to accept a compromise such as finally settled the controversy over the juries. They may have included the praetor Glabrio, in charge of the extortion court, the Marcelli, patrons of Sicily, who urged Cicero to take the case, and Cotta, the praetor who proposed the compromise jury law that passed.[23] I venture to suggest that the leader of the compromisers was Pompey's colleague in the consulship, Crassus, known as a middle-of-the-road man. He was the particular patron of the knights, and Cicero, as the advocate of the knights in the courts, seems to have been close to Crassus at the time.[24]

Although Cicero maintained in the speeches that the senators should redeem themselves and keep the juries in their hands, I agree with Heinze and Gelzer that Cicero was at this time associated with the middle-of-the-road men.[25] But at the same time, as a new man in politics, he stood alone. He did not need his brother's later warning not to forget that he was *novus.* He realized that the nobility wished to keep its circle closed. *Non idem licet mihi quod iis qui nobili genere nati sunt, quibus omnia populi Romani beneficia dormientibus deferuntur.* "I have not the same privileges as those men of noble birth on whom all the blessings of the Roman people are showered as they lie asleep."[26] There is, he goes on to say, hardly a member of the old families who looks with favor on the energy and industry of the new man. They treat us, he says, in a passage that shows how deeply his feelings are hurt, *quasi natura et genere disiuncti sint,* as if we and they were entirely different breeds of men.[27] Cicero reminds his audience of the new men of the past who had risen to eminence at Rome, of Cato Sapiens and Cicero's own fellow townsman Gaius Marius.

Now that we have considered the political issues in the case, let us go back and trace the progress of the trial of Verres. Preparations had been made for it months in advance. By the end of 71, deputations from all the chief cities of Sicily except Messina, which was in league with Verres, and Syracuse, which had been intimidated by him, had come to Rome to make complaints. After Cicero made known his readiness to accuse Verres, another man, a former quaestor of Verres, Quintus Caecilius, came forward also to seek the post of accuser. He was in collusion with Verres and was strongly supported by Verres' associates. It was apparently in January of 70 that the praetor of the extortion court, Glabrio, with a jury, decided by a process known as *divinatio* which of the two should act as accuser. The first of the Verrine orations that we have, the *Divinatio in Caecilium,* one of the most skillful of all Cicero's speeches, was delivered on that occasion. With much good-natured badinage directed against Caecilius' inadequacy for the task, Cicero shows that the prosecutor, under extortion laws designed to protect Rome's allies, should be the man the allies desire and not the man favored by the defendant.

Cicero was awarded the role of accuser by the court, and apparently at this time Verres tried to bribe him, but Cicero resisted. He asked for a postponement of the case for a hundred and ten days to enable him to go to Sicily for evidence. He expected to be back to carry out the prosecution in May, and then to be ready to go before the people in July as candidate for the aedileship. The publicity of a successful prosecution would be a great advantage to his candidacy.

Cicero had his difficulties in Sicily; for the ubiquitous Metelli had their agent there, another brother, Lucius, who had succeeded Verres as governor. Lucius Metellus had at first criticized his predecessor's record, but he changed sides, apparently after his brothers had decided to use Verres' funds to further their campaigns, and he put every possible obstacle in Cicero's way.[28] He tried to intimidate the senate of Syracuse, he interfered with the copying of records, and he prevented some of the witnesses from being brought to Rome. Nevertheless, Cicero, with his manifold contacts in Sicily, made a rich haul of evidence and worked with such speed and energy that he was back in Rome in fifty days instead of the allotted hundred and ten.

At Rome Cicero encountered another obstacle. Through the machinations of Verres' adherents the court schedule had been tampered with, and another case, apparently trumped up for the occasion, had been put on the docket ahead of Verres' trial which was postponed to early August.[29] That meant that Cicero had to go before the electorate as candidate for the aedileship in late July without the advantages of a successful prosecution.

First came the election of the consuls, in which Verres' funds, distributed, Cicero declares, liberally among the tribes, succeeded in effecting the election of Hortensius, Verres' attorney, and Quintus Metellus to the consulship. According to Cicero, a friend of Verres was heard to tell him in the Forum, "I hereby inform you that today's election means your acquittal."[30] Then came the election of praetors, and Marcus Metellus was not only elected but obtained by lot the presidency of the extortion court. The strategy of the defense was to have the case postponed to the following year. Quintus Metellus is said to have sent for the Sicilian witnesses and tried to intimidate them: "I am consul; one of my brothers is governing Sicily; the other is going to preside over the extortion court; many steps have been taken to secure that no harm can happen to Verres."[31]

The election of aediles came after that of consuls and praetors, and more of Verres' money was available to prevent Cicero's success. "The trial was approaching," he says, "and in this matter also those baskets of Sicilian gold were threatening me. I was deterred by concern for my election from giving my mind freely to the business of the trial; the trial prevented my devoting my whole attention to my candidature ... Verres ... flew about, this great potentate, with his amiable and popular son, canvassing the tribes and interviewing the family friends—to wit, the bribery agents—and summoning them to the fray." But Verres' agents, who had been able to control the centuriate assembly, where the men of property had a weighted vote, were not successful with the more democratic tribal assembly, which elected the aediles, and Cicero won. "The people of Rome," he says, "ensured my not being thrust out of my office by the money of a man whose wealth had failed to lure me out of my honour."[32]

The trial began less than a week after Cicero's election. It was the fifth of August, toward three in the afternoon, when Cicero appeared on the tribunal in the Forum to open the prosecution's case. In spite of all that his enemies had done, there was abundant cause for hope in the situation. Although Verres had challenged and eliminated from the jury certain good men, the jury as empaneled was made up of men of good repute. It was led by two of the most distinguished men of consular rank, Quintus Lutatius Catulus, the foremost man in Roman civil life, and Publius Servilius Vatia, one of the great generals of the period. The array of witnesses, including senators, Roman knights, and the representatives of Sicilian cities, was imposing. Moreover, so great a throng was present that the time set for the trial, which, Cicero says, Verres had purchased with his money,[33] proved an advantage for the accuser. There was far more publicity for the trial than there would have been in May, for men had come from every section of Italy to cast their ballots in the elections, to see Pompey's votive games, and to enroll themselves in the census, the first that had been taken in fifteen years—a census that doubled the citizen rolls.

Cicero began the case with greater zest because of the great throng there to see the show. He was more confident too because he was aware of the tactics of his opponents, and he was prepared to combat them. He knew they expected him to talk for days and that they had plans to make the proceedings drag along. They reckoned that the two weeks assigned to Pompey's games in August had shortened the normal court schedule. After that, since three other sets of games cut into the court calendar for the rest of the year, Hortensius thought he could push the decision over to the next year, when many of the jurors could be disqualified and when, instead of the upright Glabrio, Marcus Metellus would be judge.

And so Cicero used an unexpected device. He refrained from the lengthy exposition of Verres' crimes with which the prosecutor might be expected to open the case, and confined his initial speech, the *Actio Prima,* to a single hour of factual statements and description of the procedure to be adopted. "I am firmly resolved," he declared, "to prevent our having a change of president or jurors . . . I will not suffer the reply to our case to be made . . . when lapse of time has blurred the memory of the charges we bring. I will not permit the settlement of this case to be delayed until after the departure from Rome of these multitudes that have simultaneously assembled from all parts of Italy to attend the elections, the games, and the census . . . I hold [that] all men [should] be admitted to the knowledge of what shall here take place."[34]

Cicero states his unusual plan for the case. Refraining in the first part of the proceedings from the customary continuous oration, he will call the witnesses at once. "I shall so deal with the evidence of my witnesses as first to state each charge in full, and after supporting it by questioning, argument, and comment, then to bring forward my witnesses to that particular charge . . . Our opponents will have the same facilities as ourselves for questions, arguments, and comments."[35]

This brief, straightforward oration is the only continuous speech delivered in the case proper. Then Cicero called the witnesses, and nine days were spent interrogating them.

On the events of these nine days there is a good deal of information in the five orations of the undelivered *Actio Secunda* which Cicero wrote out later, and the material is probably reliable, for, since people would remember what had happened, Cicero would guard against undue exaggeration. On the first day, Cicero presented a list of the witnesses. Their number was legion, and in addition there was a large supply of official records and documents. Cicero mentions some thirty-five individuals by name and speaks, without giving the names, of numerous representatives of the Sicilian cities.

Always before calling the witnesses, Cicero, true to his promise, stated the charge, and we can imagine that he arranged the charges much as we see the material classified in the five orations of the *Actio Secunda*. These relate to Verres' early life and urban praetorship, his general depredations in Sicily, thefts of grain (with apologies, presumably to the public, for dealing with so dull a subject),[36] thefts of works of art, military operations, and abuses of Roman citizens.

After Cicero had cross-examined the witnesses, he provided full opportunities to Hortensius and his associates to interrogate them.

They were nonplussed by Cicero's procedure. At first, to be sure, Hortensius had something to say. In dealing with Verres' urban praetorship, Cicero, to arouse pity, brought in the young son of a deceased contractor whose work, on the temple of Castor, Verres had found faulty. The boy had lost his inheritance, and Cicero exhibited him clad in the *praetexta* of boyhood and pointed out that he no longer had the locket that freeborn children wore; presumably because of his poverty he had had to sell it. Hortensius charged that in thus exhibiting the boy Cicero was acting like a demagogue (*populariter agere*), an accusation that Cicero, dissociating himself from demagoguery, indignantly denied.[37]

Cicero expected many further interchanges like this, for the *altercatio* between the opposing counsel was a conspicuous feature of the Roman trial. But Hortensius was at a loss. In reply to one of Cicero's sallies he said that he was not skilled in solving riddles. "Not even when you have the Sphinx at your house," said Cicero, alluding caustically to a valuable ivory statue of the Sphinx that Verres had presented to his counsel.[38] As time went on Hortensius fell into silence; he had no answers.[39] Cicero, with the amazing vitality that breathes through his accounts of these days spent in hearing witnesses, went on piling up the damning evidence that he had assembled.

The evidence for the thefts of money, grain, and works of art all made a deep impression not only on the jurors but on the assembled multitude. But it was toward the end, when Cicero brought in testimony to show that Verres had flogged, tortured, and crucified Roman citizens, that feeling against Verres reached its peak. The situation was such that Glabrio, the presiding judge, once interrupted the witnesses and dissolved the court to prevent violence.[40]

The hearing of the witnesses was completed on the eve of Pompey's games, for which and for the succeeding Roman games the trial was to adjourn until the latter part of September. Verres, who after the third day had begun to feign illness, saw that he had lost and went off into exile without waiting for a verdict. There remained only the final action in fixing the fine, and Plutarch says that Cicero was bribed to make it low.[41] Plutarch may be wrong, for he is decidedly inaccurate in the account of this trial.

After the case was settled, Cicero wrote and published the five orations of the Second Act, each of them from three to five times as long as the First Act. In them he maintained the fiction that Verres was present, after having gone as far as the city gate and then come back for the rest of the trial. The Second Act is represented as taking place in the thirty-five days—September 19 to October 25—between two sets of games. These speeches rank with Cicero's most finished writing, and they are a mine of information for the Roman law courts, provincial government, the grain supply of the state, the artistic monuments of Sicily, and the development of Roman citizenship. They are at the same time political pamphlets, skillful in their appeal to nobles, particularly to the most distinguished noble, Catulus,[42] and also shrewd in their attempt to enlist the support of knights, municipal men, and people.

What were the results of this trial? The senatorial jury, either of its own accord or under pressure of public opinion, had indicated that at least it meant to condemn a wealthy man. That, as Gelzer suggests,[43] probably had its influence on the reconstitution of the juries. The senatorial order did not completely lose its right to jury duty. The jury law that was passed a few weeks later, a compromise measure, left to the senators a third of the places in the juries.[44] It provided for juries made up equally of senators, knights, and the lower-income group known as *tribuni aerarii*. Such juries served for the next two decades.

But, to turn to Cicero's career, what had he won by his months of toilsome labor in the case, his masterly handling, and his triumphant success? First of all, he seems to have obtained a concrete reward that I do not find mentioned in any biography of the orator. I think he gained the seniority rights of Verres in the Roman senate.

Ancient criminal law, both Greek and Roman, provided for the bestowal of rewards on the successful prosecutor and his assistants. It was a system that led to abuses, abundantly attested in Athenian and in Roman imperial history. But the system was not altogether bad. Where there was no public prosecutor, there was something to be said for incentives that led men to bring malefactors to justice. There were, moreover, laws to curb false accusations. At Rome, if the prosecutor lost the case, he might himself be prosecuted for *calumnia,* and his conviction would have brought him infamy and the loss of his own position.[45]

Rewards for accusers and their aides included special distinctions as well as money. Hippodamus of Miletus advocated honors for men who had benefited the state either by prowess in war or by making a discovery that was in the public interest.[46] Aristotle protested against the bestowal of honors on men who made such discoveries, holding that it might lead to intrigue and disorder.[47] The system was fully developed at Rome. Whereas in civil law financial rewards were given, political advantages and honors were customary rewards in criminal law. The rewards and also the penalties for false accusations were specified in the laws that dealt with specific crimes. The rewards included bestowal of citizenship for noncitizens, and, for citizens, enrollment in the tribe of the accused if it was better than the tribe of the accuser. For senators the rewards also included acquisition of the seniority rights of the accused.

Now Cicero had just been elected aedile, whereas Verres was of praetorian rank. If Cicero acquired Verres' place in the senate, he would still have had to be elected to the praetorship in order to advance in the state. But he would be permitted at once to appear with the *praetorii* in the senate, where a strict rule of seniority governed procedure. The presiding consul, in putting a motion, called first for the opinion of the men of consular rank and then for that of the men of praetorian rank. Often the questioning did not, for lack of time, go to the lower ranks in the senate. If Cicero took Verres' place among the *praetorii,* his influence for the future was greatly enhanced. He could begin at once to make his oratory count in the senate. Moreover, in processions of the senators at public festivals he would have the privilege of wearing the *toga praetexta* and of joining the *praetorii* instead of the men of the rank of aedile, and that would enhance his prestige.

It seems desirable to state the republican evidence for this Roman custom so little noted in Roman histories and biographies. Much but not all of it can be found in scattered references in Mommsen's monumental works.[48] From the late second century B.C. we have a fragmentary law governing the extortion courts which provides that, if the accused is convicted, the accusers who are not Roman citizens shall acquire citizenship and enrollment in the tribe of the accused.[49] In a charter of one of Caesar's colonies there is a specific provision that a member of the colony's senate who shall accuse and bring to conviction another member of the senate shall acquire that member's position of seniority in the senate.[50] This provision, like much else in the charter, seems to be based on precedents at Rome. There is, moreover, evidence for bestowals of such rewards in Rome. In Cicero's *Pro Balbo,* delivered in 56 B.C., Balbus' enrollment in the tribe of a man he had succeeded in convicting of bribery is defended as in accord with the rewards specified in the law on malpractice, and Cicero adds that such a reward is less invidious than the acquisition by a similar process of a place among the *praetorii* and the use of the *toga praetexta.*[51]

Several men acquired advancement in the senate through successful accusations. In the year 67, Gaius Papirius Carbo, an ex-tribune, accused Marcus Aurelius Cotta, an ex-consul, probably of embezzlement, and obtained a conviction. Thereupon Carbo acquired Cotta's place among the ex-consuls.[52] The case of the younger Lucius Manlius Torquatus seems to have been similar, though the evidence has never been understood. In the year 66, he with his father and Lucius Aurelius Cotta brought accusations for malpractice against the consuls elected for the following year, Publius Cornelius Sulla and Publius Autronius. The accused were convicted and the elder Torquatus and Cotta were elected consuls in their place. The young Torquatus apparently acquired the insignia and rank of P. Sulla. That is the only reasonable interpretation of a passage in Cicero's defense of Sulla, a case in which the young Cotta was again the accuser, this time on a charge of violence. "What more are you trying now to get from him? His office went to your father and the insignia of his office to you. You, adorned with his spoils (*exuviae*), come now to mutilate the man whom you have destroyed, and I, as he lies there despoiled, defend and protect him."[53] Some years later Sulla tried to rehabilitate himself by bringing suit against another senator whose place in the order he hoped to get.[54] Apparently, men convicted of malpractice in elections often made such attempts, for they were punished not by exile but simply by loss of rank,[55] and were therefore on hand to prosecute others.[56]

There are in the *Verrines* two passages that allude to the possibility that Verres' defense may bring concrete rewards for Cicero. In the first one, the orator is discussing the cogency of his evidence against Verres. "And so, gentlemen of the jury, as far as I am concerned, I have won. For what I desired was not the spoils (*spolia*) of Gaius Verres but the good name of the Roman people."[57] The other passage is at the end of the last oration in the *Actio Secunda*. Cicero considers the possibility that Verres may not be convicted and promises, as he has already done earlier in the trial, that if that happens he as aedile will bring to account before the Roman people both Verres and the men who have acquitted him. "That will be a celebrated case indeed, providing certain and easy success for myself, satisfaction and pleasure for the people. And if it is supposed that I have been hoping—though I have sought nothing of the kind —to advance myself at the expense of this one man Verres (*de uno isto voluisse crescere*), then his acquital, which can only occur if a great many men have acted like criminals, will indeed enable me to advance myself at the expense of those many (*de multis crescere*)."[58]

The *spolia* referred to in the first passage and the phrase *de uno isto voluisse crescere* are clear indications that Sulla's extortion law, under which Verres was tried, included political rewards for accusers. The same expressions, as used in Cicero's speech for Roscius delivered a decade earlier, provide further evidence for rewards in Sulla's laws. The accusers are there charged with bringing suit in order to obtain the *spolia* of Roscius.[59] Cicero, in another passage of the same oration, makes it clear that he does not mean to prosecute the accusers of Roscius. "If I wished to accuse," he says, "I should prefer to accuse others through whom I could advance (*ex quibus possem crescere*)." Cicero goes on to express scorn for such method of advancement: "The man of the greatest dignity is in my opinion the one who reaches high position through his own virtue and not the man who ascends over the misfortune and calamity of another."[60]

Verres' spoils were almost certainly available to Cicero, and one may question whether he was sufficiently strong-minded, when the time came, to refuse them. If he had done so, he would surely have stressed in later speeches his rejection of the opportunity to rise through another man's misfortune. There is perhaps an indirect reference to Cicero himself in the discussion of rewards in the *Pro Balbo*. Cicero may be speaking from personal experience when he says that acquisition, through a prosecution, of the *toga praetexta* and the praetor's place in the senate was an invidious distinction.

If, after the trial, Cicero aroused invidious comment by appearing at the games in the *toga praetexta* and by placing himself among the *praetorii* in the senate, the trial had given Cicero the means of surmounting *invidia*. For he had come out of the case the acknowledged head of the Roman bar.[61] Hortensius had been discomfited not so much by Cicero's eloquence (for the orator had relinquished the chance to demonstrate the full power of his eloquence) as by his tactics in the case, his keen cross-questioning, and his swift rejoinders. Hortensius' rule over the law courts, his *dominatio regnumque iudiciorum,* was at an end, and he gracefully acknowledged the primacy of Cicero when, in cases where they appeared later on the same side, he yielded to Cicero the privilege of delivering the peroration.

More and more it was to Cicero that senators and knights, under the frequent accusations that featured Roman politics, turned for aid, and Cicero was ready to help them. Except on a single occasion,[62] he adhered to the determination expressed in the Verrines and appeared in the future, as he had in the past, only for the defense. Cicero's eloquence as a pleader was, as his brother reminded him, a compensation for the newness of his name. "Whatever you are, you are from this," writes Quintus of Marcus' oratory.[63] Quintus goes on to point out that Marcus could ask for endorsement in his candidacies from the senators and ex-magistrates who had secured acquittal through his skill and eloquence. Marcus is urged, as he goes about soliciting votes, to have with him a retinue of the men he has defended.

Also of great importance for Cicero's future was that, through the large crowds in Rome at the time of the trial, his fame spread from one end of Italy to the other. These throngs, who took home stories of Cicero's quick wit and ready repartee, probably laid the foundations of the support from Italian municipalities on which

Cicero could count throughout his life. Men of the municipalities came in numbers to Rome to vote for Cicero when he was a candidate for praetorship and consulship, and they came in multitudes to cast their ballots for his recall from exile.

The middle-of-the-road men with whom Cicero stood in the trial of Verres, the men whom he subsequently defended when he became the first man of the Roman bar, the knights, and, among them, particularly the public contractors and the leaders of the municipalities of Italy, formed the nucleus of Cicero's backing for a political career. At the same time he had to count on the opposition of the extreme *optimates* of the right who were bent on maintaining their prestige and keeping new men out of high office.

Cicero's activity in the courts in the next few years shows his efforts to keep the friends he had made among knights and municipal men, and also to extend his influence to the circle of Pompey. In 66, because of the insistence from the knights in Asia, who had been won over by Pompey, Cicero gave his support to the law giving Pompey the command against Mithridates. In that same year he defended a prominent knight on a murder charge and, in the course of the argument, advanced the extraordinary view that, since Sulla's provisions against corruption in the courts concerned senators, the sole jurors of the time, the knights were not subject to the law and could not be prosecuted for bribery.[64] On this same question Cicero later opposed Cato in senatorial discussion.[65]

He went further in his association with Pompey and the *populares,* for he somewhat reluctantly agreed to defend Manilius, the popular and disreputable tribune who had proposed the law for Pompey's command. To Cicero's great relief the case was dropped.[66] He actually did defend, and with success, another tribune who had been in Pompey's service, Gaius Cornelius, a far better man than Manilius, but a man who by his attacks on the prerogatives of the senate had won the enmity of the clique of *optimates.*

In the trial of Cornelius five of the leading *optimates,* including Hortensius and Catulus, appeared as witnesses for the prosecution. Cicero handled them gently in the oration,[67] but he expected their opposition to his consulship, and that may be the explanation of one of the most disreputable incidents in his career. Catiline, a prospective competitor of Cicero, was accused of extortion in his province of Africa, and Cicero, thinking that a combination with Catiline might solve his own problems as a candidate, wrote Atticus that he was thinking of defending Catiline. The next comment shows that the conditions were favorable for the defense. "We have the jurors we wanted and the greatest good will on the part of the prosecutor."[58] The prosecutor, who was thus making a deal with Cicero to get Catiline off, was Cicero's future enemy, Publius Clodius Pulcher.

But Cicero changed his mind, and someone else took the case, probably with a similar deal, for Catiline was acquitted.[59] The reason for the change was apparently Cicero's hope that he could obtain the endorsement of the *optimates*. The hope was realized. The good men were determined at all costs to defeat Catiline, and they finally decided to support Cicero because he seemed the most likely to win among the candidates in the field.

Cicero's sweeping victory in all the centuries was due to the commendation of the *optimates* who brought him the votes of their great bands of clients. But Cicero had by his own energy and ability achieved the position that led the good men against their will to support a new man in his first candidacy for the consulship. It was by his career in the courts and particularly by his great prosecution that Cicero had built up the strength that impressed the *optimates*. Then it was that he made a breach in the fortress of the nobility and prepared the way for the entrance of his unknown name in the august annals of Roman consuls.

CHAPTER VI

CATO AND THE "POPULARES"

It was in the debate on the Catilinarians in 63 that the tribune-elect Marcus Porcius Cato, at thirty-two, emerged as leader of the "optimate" coalition that controlled the senate. This chapter will deal with the struggle of Cato against four men who had followed a popular course in the state, the subsequent union of three of them in a coalition rivaling that of Cato, and the success of the new coalition in gaining control of the entire state, including even the senate.[1]

"OPTIMATES" AND "POPULARES" BEFORE CATILINE'S CONSPIRACY

Until Cato, aided by his family—his brother-in-law Domitius and his future son-in-law Bibulus,—assumed leadership of the *optimates,* the coalition[2] had been dominated by old Sullans, all of them members of the plebeian nobility. The foremost man was the restorer of the Capitol, Quintus Lutatius Catulus. His close associate was the able general and *pontifex maximus,* Quintus Caecilius Metellus Pius, who died apparently in late 64. Most other members of the powerful Metelli were in the coalition, as also were the two Luculli, sons of a Caecilia Metella. Then there was Catulus' brother-in-law, the orator Hortensius, no longer after 70 the first man of the bar, but powerful nevertheless in the courts. Another leader was a consul of 67, Gaius Calpurnius Piso.[3]

The program of the coalition was simply the maintenance of the *status quo,* the preservation of what was left of the authority that Sulla had given the senate in the state. The coalition did not function as a group in election campaigns, where the old system of personal endorsements continued; it was in the senate and as an opposition group in legislative tribal assemblies that the solidarity of the clique could be observed. In the senate the *optimates* were strong enough in the sixties to maintain practically complete control over action of the body.[4] But, even with optimate tribunes to help them out, they were not sufficiently influential with the urban plebs to be a match for the *populares* in the tribal legislative assem-

---

[1] For notes to chap. vi see pp. 221–227.

bly. In that assembly, after the restoration of the tribunes' power in 70, the old struggle against the domination of a senatorial oligarchy had been actively revived.

The *optimates* had, however, gained some advantage from the disunity of the leaders who followed a popular course and made use of tribunes. There were four prominent popular leaders, Pompey, Crassus, Caesar, and Catiline, and, though they made combinations with one another from time to time, each of them was interested in his own advancement. The two considered in 63 to be most powerful, Pompey and Crassus, were open enemies, and each, to circumvent the other, was ready to unite his forces with the *optimates*.

Of the four Pompey was the man that the *optimates* hated and feared most. For a time the coalition was practically a stop-Pompey movement. He had injured them individually and had diminished their collective authority as leaders of the senate. After robbing Catulus of most of the credit for suppressing the conspiracy of Lepidus and after sharing as an equal in Metellus Pius' victories over Sertorius, Pompey took away some of Metellus Creticus' laurels in the war with the Cretan pirates and replaced Lucius Lucullus as commander in the war with Mithridates. Moreover, Pompey's whole career had been a violation of the prestige of the Sullan senate. Pompey had refrained from using revolutionary methods, but, relying on his loyal soldiers and clients, he had prevailed first upon Sulla and then upon the senate to grant him one extraordinary power after another.[5] Cicero, in his oration for Pompey's command against Mithridates, retails the list of Pompey's unparalleled distinctions and declares that there had been more departures from precedent in the career of Pompey alone than in the careers of all other great Romans added together. And Catulus and other eminent men of the senate had, Cicero stated, voted for Pompey's distinctions.[6]

But after Pompey's consulship of 70, Catulus and the other leaders were firm against Pompey. They fought hard in senate and tribal assembly against the monarchical powers conferred on him in the wars against the pirates, and continued the fight the next year when the bill was presented to send Pompey out to replace Lucullus in the war against Mithridates. They fought in vain, for

Pompey was the darling of the urban plebs and was unbeatable then in the tribal assembly. While absent in the East, Pompey continued to use tribunes to defend his interests and to interfere with the triumphs of Metellus Creticus and Lucullus. At the same time Pompey was revoking the arrangements of Lucullus in the East and was thereby undermining the authority of the senate with foreign people.[7] By 63 the war with Mithridates was almost over and Pompey, looking forward to the confirmation of his own acts by the senate, was showing signs of a desire to propitiate the *optimates*.[8]

Crassus was not properly a *popularis*. Member of the hereditary nobility, as Pompey was not, fabulously rich as a result of profits from the Sullan proscriptions, corrupt,[9] strong in clients, he was willing to use any methods to carry out his designs in politics. Sometimes he employed tribunes and profited from the lawmaking power that he had helped Pompey to restore. For that reason he could be called a *popularis*.[10] But he also depended heavily on senators whom he had bound to him by loans and bribes and by aid in candidacies and in the law courts.[11] He had strength too with the knights, in whose business ventures he was deeply involved.

Crassus' great enemy was Pompey, who had weakened Crassus' influence with the knights. Like the leading *optimates,* Crassus lost some of his military glory to Pompey, who had claimed part of the credit for the victory over Spartacus. Like Pompey, Crassus was opposed to Lucullus, whose upright reorganization of Asia had checked the exploitation of the province by the knights; but, hating Pompey and fearing the further development of his power, Crassus coöperated with the *optimates* in opposing the bills for Pompey's commands. Crassus married both his sons into old optimate families[12] and, even after he had been involved in the scandals of an abortive *coup d'état,* he got the support of the *optimates* in a scheme that was designed to cut down Pompey's power.[13] But Crassus could not persuade the good men to support two laws proposed by his tribunes to advance Crassus in rivalry with Pompey. Both these bills, one to appoint Crassus to a commission to annex Egypt and the other to set up a great agrarian commission, were defeated, no doubt because on these occasions Pompey's agents coöperated with the *optimates*. Crassus also broke with Catulus, his colleague in the censorship, when he tried to increase his own adherents by enfranchising the Transpadanes.

Caesar had in his Marian connections advantages for popular favor that neither Pompey, a Sullan general, nor Crassus, the arch-Sullan profiteer, could claim, and he exploited them by combining sponsorship of popular laws with glorification of the memory of Marius, still a great hero with the urban plebs.[14] He worked with Pompey, speaking on the Rostra for both of his great commands. But he was also working for himself. As aedile he roused the ire of Catulus, son of Marius' enemy, by restoring the gleaming trophies of Marius to the Capitol, then being rebuilt as a monument of the Catulan name. He disturbed the *optimates* too by the splendor of his games and by the number of gladiators he trained for the show in memory of his father, and later by his vigorous judgments against Sullan murderers. Report held that he had coöperated with Crassus in his revolutionary schemes against Pompey in 65, but the stories were probably products of the propaganda of the next decade.[15] Perhaps because he had obtained financial aid from Crassus, Caesar did make common cause with Crassus in supporting Catiline for the consulship of 63, and the combination was strong enough to lead to the realization of Cicero's hope that he could gain for his candidacy the commendation both of the *optimates* and of the adherents of Pompey.

In 63, Caesar returned to his alliance with Pompey's agents and worked with the tribune Titus Labienus in a whole series of popular measures. It is a sign of weakening of Pompey's power that some of the measures failed, but even so they roused public opinion against the *optimates*. The measure that was most important for Caesar's own purposes was successful. It restored to the people the right of electing public priests, thereby removing from the nobles the last of their Sullan prerogatives. Through the popular acclaim that Caesar got from this bill and through wholesale bribery Caesar was then able to defeat Catulus for the office of *pontifex maximus,* thus humiliating the foremost member of the optimate clique and raising himself to a position of primacy.[16]

Another popular move of Caesar and Labienus was an abortive

trial for *perduellio,* treason against the state, of an aged man who was accused of having, under the extreme senatorial decree, slain a tribune thirty-seven years before. This trial in the centuriate assembly, a sham from beginning to end, did not result in a condemnation. That could hardly have been secured in the centuriate assembly, where the nobles were powerful. A praetor in league with Caesar and Labienus kept the matter from coming to a vote by dissolving the assembly.[17] But the trial had served to inflame the people against the senate and against the use of the "extreme decree." Caesar could hardly have realized how important the question was to become as a result of further developments that year.

The fourth popular leader was Catiline, a man who concerned himself little or not at all with tribunitial legislation,[18] but was ready, as events showed, to move to open revolution. Member of a decayed patrician house, reportedly one of the most ruthless of Sulla's aides in his proscriptions, Catiline had been Crassus' agent in the unsuccessful *coup d'état* of 65. But he was more than a tool of Crassus. He had a large following among the debt-ridden—spendthrift youth of high rank, miserable groups in the city populace, and country people, both ruined Sullan colonists and dispossessed Marians. Whether he was the villain that Cicero and Sallust make him out to be or the savior of the lower classes, as a Marxist historian considers him to have been,[19] is hard to decide, but his involvement in Crassus' muddy schemes is against him. He had repeatedly tried to reach the consulship, and had been deterred twice by prosecutions and other obstructions. He was defeated by Cicero for the consulship of 63, and again, this time deserted by Crassus and Caesar, tried in vain for the office for 62.[20]

These four leaders had all won supporters among the senators. Pompey had lured many of them, including a few of the old nobility, to his staff in the East.[21] Crassus had numerous adherents and had shown that he could on occasion persuade the *optimates* to vote for his motions. Caesar was already strong in influence with his own patrician class—more inclined than plebeian nobles to try radical methods—and he was soon to demonstrate his influence in the senate. And Catiline had, besides his close associates among debt-

22PARTY POLITICS IN THE AGE OF CAESAR

ridden senators, certain friends even among the *optimates*.[22] Personal combinations were constantly shifting. Cicero was not unique in his sudden changes of political allies, though as a new man he attracted more attention than men of older families.[23]

CATO'S LEADERSHIP OF THE "OPTIMATES"

Catiline, after having been defeated again for the consulship in the elections for 62, turned the party of dissidents he had recruited in Rome and in disaffected Etruria into a conspiracy against the state. The senate, informed through Cicero's energetic action of the collection of arms and the gathering of hostile forces, passed the "extreme decree." The threat to private property had one immediate result. The knights, who for years had been estranged from the senate, united with the senatorial order. After the members of the conspiracy in the city had been arrested and had confessed, the senate met on the Nones of December to discuss their fate, and the knights showed their solidarity with the senate by congregating in an armed band outside the curia to await the decision.

There was reason for haste, for, in addition to the threat of Catiline's army in Etruria, there were said to be bands in the city preparing to attempt the rescue of the accused. Crassus, who could not deny his earlier association with Catiline, stayed away from the meeting, but Caesar, now praetor-elect, was there, and after all the *consulares* had urged the immediate execution of the conspirators he made an eloquent speech. While not denying the guilt of the accused, he argued effectively against using the extreme decree to put Roman citizens to death without trial, and he warned the senators that such action would rouse popular indignation. He produced a strong impression on the senators, and many of them modified their earlier vote.

It looked as if the *optimates* might lose control of the senate. Catulus protested, and Cicero, if the oration which he published three years later is reliable evidence,[24] tried to make the senate take a firm position. But it was left for one of the last men called upon, Marcus Porcius Cato, tribune-elect, to make the decisive speech which led the senate to vote overwhelmingly for immediate execution. In the version of the speech given by Sallust, Cato handles

Caesar with respect; but other writers are probably correct in declaring that Cato actually charged Caesar with complicity in the plot.[25] The knights waiting outside rushed upon Caesar when he left the senate, and Cicero intervened to save him.

Cicero, confident in the support of senate and knights, had the execution carried out. Glorying in his achievement in suppressing the conspiracy, he saw himself as the leader of all good men, as the unifying force between senate and knights, as the first man of peace, ready to stand beside Pompey, the foremost man in war. He was determined to reconcile the *optimates* and Pompey. It was perhaps out of deference to Pompey that he refused to accede to the demands of Catulus and Piso and accuse Caesar of complicity in the conspiracy. But Cicero did not get far with Pompey's agents, for they wanted Pompey recalled to rescue the state that Cicero believed he had already saved, and their strategy was to belittle Cicero and indeed to attack him for putting Roman citizens to death without trial. It was one of Pompey's tribunes, Metellus Nepos, who opened the attack on Cicero as an enemy of the people when he prevented Cicero from making the customary oration as he laid down his consulship.

Although the good men, following Catulus, hailed Cicero as the father of his country, the real hero of the famous Nones of December was not Cicero but Cato. Great-grandson of Cato the Censor and grandson of Marcus Livius Drusus, the tribune who won the battle of the nobility against Gaius Gracchus, Cato was the embodiment of old Roman virtues.

Unlike his great-grandfather, who had hated all things Greek, he had schooled his virtues under Greek teachers, Stoic philosophers who lived in his house and were constantly in his company. Cato was a practicing Stoic who, to quote Cicero, studied philosophy not to engage in disputations but in order to live by it.[26] Like the great Stoics of the Scipionic Age, Laelius the Wise and the eminent jurists, Cato, on entering upon the political career that was his heritage, rigorously applied Stoic teachings to the exercise of his duties in the state. Arriving in the senate house before anyone else, he sat there reading a roll of Stoic philosophy.[27] When he spoke in the senate he constantly interlarded his remarks with Stoic precepts.

Yet Cato had already shown himself to be not a mere doctrinaire but an efficient public servant. As quaestor, an office that most men took lightly, he had reformed and subordinated the secretariat which usually controlled the financial affairs entrusted to the quaestor, and had made himself—as he was to continue all his life—the watchdog of the treasury.[28] He took the business of empire seriously and engaged in much correspondence with governors and agents and foreign princes in distant lands.

As a practicing Stoic, Cato strove also to pursue sinners, and in the pursuit he often disregarded party or personal advantages and paid no attention to timing. In his activities he had not spared the leading *optimates*. He had attacked men who profited from the Sullan murders,[29] had had a clash with Catulus, who defended in court a man that Cato thought unworthy, and had, shortly before the Nones of December, joined in bringing an accusation against Murena, an officer of Lucullus, Cato's brother-in-law. In the course of the accusation, Cato declared that the Mithridatic War, in which Murena had won fame, had been nothing but a war with women.[30] That was a disparagement of Lucullus, who had just celebrated his belated triumph.

The curious thing about this accusation was its timing. Shocked by the barefaced bribery in the consular campaign, Cato had announced in advance that he would prosecute the victor. When one of the victors proved to be another of his brothers-in-law, Cato refrained from accusing him, but he could not be dissuaded from prosecuting Murena. It made no difference that Catiline had been defeated in the election and had gone to join his armed bands in Etruria. It made no difference that the state was now, through the "extreme decree," under martial law. Cato made the accusation, and Cicero defended Murena, treating Cato with great respect, expressing the fear that the very fact that Cato had assumed the role of accuser would be enough to convict Murena. In a spirit of banter Cicero indicated that Cato was too much under the influence of his Stoic teachers, who held that all sins were equal and every peccadillo a deadly crime. The young man would, Cicero indicated, learn with time to make some distinctions between evildoers. Murena was acquitted, and bore no grudge; in fact, as consul he intervened on one occasion in Cato's favor.[31]

In seeking the tribunate Cato had already aligned himself against the arch-enemy of the senate, Pompey. As Plutarch tells the story, Cato had had no intention of being a candidate for the office, but while en route to his country estate he chanced to meet on the road Metellus Nepos, Pompey's man, returning from the East to seek the tribunate. Cato promptly decided to become a candidate, and was enthusiastically supported by the *optimates*.[32] Both he and Nepos were elected. But it was not until after Cato's speech on the Catilinarians that the good men fully appreciated Cato's power. After that, though plenty of them probably agreed with Cicero that Cato acted more as if they were living in Plato's republic than in the dregs of Romulus,[33] the *optimates* acclaimed him as a hero and welcomed him as their standard bearer. Catulus, a disappointed old man who had only two years more to live, seems to have been ready to yield leadership to Cato.

Cato's first act in a position of leadership showed that he realized the needs of the moment. He sponsored a decree in the senate that state funds be used for an annual purchase of grain to be distributed to the populace.[34] The people were undoubtedly hungry and deeply disillusioned by the failure of Catiline's plans, and Cato's sudden popular move seems to have had some effect in winning men away from Caesar, who was trying to call to his standard the elements that had supported Catiline. It is indicative of Cato's "optimate" policy that he proposed this measure not in a popular law but in the senate. As tribune he was intent, not on rival demagogic laws such as his maternal grandfather had proposed against Gaius Gracchus, but on obstruction through the use of the veto. The only law he is known to have proposed in office limited the right to a triumph, and thus was directed against the inordinate ambition of certain men who had held high office.[35]

Cato began his fight as soon as Pompey's tribune, Nepos, abetted by Caesar, introduced a bill to recall Pompey to save the state from Catiline. Cato rushed to the public meeting, ascended the tribunal of the temple of Castor, and exercised the veto by pushing himself between Caesar and Pompey's tribune and preventing the bill from being read. Reports favorable to Cato represent him as appearing unarmed in a hostile armed gathering and silencing his opponents by the prestige of his person. But the story, as Plutarch tells it, does not make sense, and Sallust indicates that it was Caesar who, unarmed, faced an armed band. Dio may be right in saying that both were provided with armed adherents.[36]

In any case, whether from lack of armed support or of popular following, Pompey's tribune was not strong enough to prevail. There was, apparently, no effort to force Cato, like the tribune who vetoed Pompey's command against the pirates, to abandon his veto. The Pompeians doubtless knew that such an effort would have been futile with Cato. The meeting was dissolved, the senate passed the "extreme decree," and Nepos is said to have fled to Pompey.

According to one report on these rather obscure events, both the tribune and Caesar, who was praetor, were suspended from office, but Caesar was able to make his peace with the senate and gain reinstatement.[37] This was a turbulent year, filled with trials of men alleged to have been implicated in the Catilinarian conspiracy. Caesar as praetor was immune from trial, but a notorious informer charged that he had been in the plot.

The return of Pompey was now uppermost in the minds of the *optimates*. Mithridates was dead, the great war had been brought to a victorious conclusion, new provinces had been organized, and distant kings and dynasts had been brought into the orbit of the Roman state. What would Pompey do, when he came back with his loyal troops and his fresh laurels of victory? The officers in Italy had been able to overcome Catiline and his army, and there was no reason for Pompey to come back with his troops under arms, but many feared that he would. There was great relief when, on landing in Brundisium, Pompey dismissed his soldiers until his triumph some months hence, and returned to Rome with a small retinue. He was showing unmistakable signs of a desire to propitiate the nobles who controlled the senate. He wanted them to vote for the confirmation of his acts and support the rewards that his soldiers expected. Appreciating the great influence Cato had acquired, Pompey's first step was to try to win his adherence by seeking for himself and his son the hands of Cato's two nieces. Cato indignantly repudiated the offer, though, according to Plutarch, the ladies were not so unwilling.[38]

That move failed, but Pompey nevertheless courted the *opti-mates*. In his first public speech he asserted with flagrant disregard of truth that to him the authority of the senate had always had the greatest weight in public affairs.[39] But Pompey did not make any progress except with Cicero, whose achievements he eventually decided to praise, and the chief result of that connection was to produce coolness between Cicero and the good men.

In the senate Cato was the spearhead of the attacks against Pompey. Cicero's contemporary letters to Atticus can leave no doubt on that point. Just how a man of tribunitial rank gained such influence under the severe seniority rules of the Roman senate is hard to understand. Cato as a *tribunicius* belonged to the lower ranks,[40] the group scornfully referred to by Cicero as *pedarii,* footmen, whose only function in senatorial debate was normally to move in a division to the side they wished to support. It was, to be sure, possible for such men to signify their intention of speaking, and the presiding magistrate had then to continue the session or reconvene it until the man had his chance. Most senatorial freshmen kept quiet, but not so Cato. He let it be known that he wanted to speak on questions,[41] and he got his chances and showed himself not only nimble-witted and resourceful but also a master of filibustering.[42]

Cato first got through the senate a decree that condemned the wholesale bribery employed by Pompey's agents in the consular elections.[43] He was preparing himself for the far more important fight over the confirmation of Pompey's acts and the bonus for his troops. Lucullus emerged from the retirement of his villas and his fishponds to contest the settlements that violated his own agreements sponsored by a senatorial commission. When the question of Pompey's acts was put to the senate, Lucullus demanded that they be discussed not as a whole but one by one, pointing out that the senate did not have adequate information about them. That means, as Professor Broughton has pointed out,[44] that the customary senatorial commission had not been sent to the East to examine the settlements. The discussion, point by point, promised to drag along indefinitely and Pompey got nowhere.

Making no progress on the confirmation of his acts, Pompey had a tribune propose a law authorizing the use of funds brought to the treasury from the eastern victories to purchase lands for Pompey's troops and for some of the surplus city population. Cicero backed it after making amendments in the interest of private property, but the consul Metellus Celer, aided of course by Cato, put every possible obstacle in the way. In the end the tribune dragged Metellus off to prison, and when Metellus as consul summoned the senate there to him, placed his tribune's bench before the door. Metellus then ordered the wall of the prison torn down to let the senate in, and that was too much for Pompey, who called the tribunes off and let the bill drop.

Pompey had plenty of soldiers at hand by this time, and could have used force, but he had become accustomed from earlier experience to a senate that yielded to the mere suggestion of force. Inexperienced in senatorial procedure,[45] he did not know how to fight a battle against Cato's obstructionist parliamentary methods. He was completely baffled.

But Cato had also baffled Pompey's enemy, Crassus, who had been coöperating with Lucullus in opposing the confirmation of Pompey's acts.[46] For Cato had found time not only to fight Pompey's measures but to agitate against Crassus' adherents, the knights. The acquittal of Clodius, whose religious crime of invading the rites of *Bona Dea* had, at Cato's insistence, been made the occasion of a special state trial, had taken place in the previous year, and it was generally recognized that Crassus had provided the bribes that persuaded the jurors to vote for acquittal.

Cato carried a motion to investigate bribery in the courts,[47] where knights and *tribuni aerarii* were not covered by Sulla's law under which senators who accepted bribes were penalized. The knights were incensed, and not only Crassus was distressed, but also Cicero as he saw his loved concord of the orders disappearing. That was not all. The companies of public contractors, an important group among the knights, announced that they had bid too high a figure for the tax contracts in Asia, and requested the senate to make a new and more favorable contract for them. Crassus, deeply involved in the affairs of the publicans, supported them, and so did Cicero, who admitted to Atticus that the business was pretty disreputable.[48] But Cato stood out firmly and succeeded in using up so much time

talking that for months not only the matter of the publicans but all
senatorial business, including the affairs of Pompey, were at a
standstill. Both Crassus and the knights, who since the year 63 had
been close to the senate, were now completely alienated from senatorial leadership.

Just at this point Caesar came home from his governorship of
Spain with "a marvelous fair wind in his sails,"[49] and Cato, un-
wearied by his contests with Pompey and Crassus, was ready to
meet another foe of the senatorial majority. Caesar came with victories for which the senate, perhaps in the hope of delaying his
candidacy for the consulship, voted him a triumph. Caesar wanted
the triumph. Also, he was determined to be consul for the following
year, and the time was short.

Caesar was hampered by a recent law which made it necessary for
candidates to present themselves in person in the *comitium*. If he
did that, he crossed the city limits and forfeited the triumph. Hence
he sent to the senate a request that he be freed from the laws and
permitted to present himself *in absentia*. Some of the senators
wished to grant his request, but Cato took to speaking once more,
and finally used up the whole of the last day on which announcement of candidacy had to be made. Caesar did not hesitate. He
wanted the consulship more than the triumph, and he crossed the
city limits and announced himself in proper form. Caesar was a
very strong candidate and there was good prospect for his success.
But the *optimates,* doubtless with Cato in the lead, though this is
the only point on which his name does not come in, managed to
get the senate to vote undesirable assignments for the new consuls;
instead of rich overseas provinces they were given for the year succeeding their office the care of the forests and pasture lands of
Italy.[50] If the *optimates* hoped that Caesar would accordingly postpone his candidacy for office, they were wrong. He had his own
plans for the future.

The *optimates* bent all their energy on the defeat of Caesar. He
had great resources in the favor of the old Marians, and he had the
support of both Pompey and Crassus, and incidentally of their
clients and of Pompey's soldiers. He also had abundant funds for
bribery, supplied by Lucceius, with whom he had made a deal.

The *optimates,* including Cato, also supplied funds to bribe for their candidate, Cato's son-in-law, Bibulus. The result was the election of Caesar and Bibulus and the defeat of Lucceius.

THE UNION OF CATO'S ENEMIES

By this time Pompey and Crassus were both in despair over procedure in the senate, which the *optimates* controlled. Caesar, who had ties with both of them, had also been injured by the leaders of the senate. It may have been even before the consular elections that he reconciled Pompey and Crassus and entered into the deal known in modern times as the "First Triumvirate." The purpose of the deal, as Suetonius puts it in negative terms, was that nothing might happen in public affairs which was against the will of any one of the three.[51] In positive terms that meant that all three were, as far as was consistent with conflicting aims, to gain their immediate ends in the state. All three men knew that, with their enemies in control of the senate, they could achieve their ends only through the people. Thus in method if not in program they were ready to be *populares,* and Cicero calls them that in letters of 59.[52] But they called themselves *amici* or *socii,* friends in the old tradition of Roman political alliance; after the marriage of Pompey to Caesar's daughter, Pompey and Caesar were also *adfines,* relatives by marriage.

The news of the deal did not leak out at once, but it must have been known in fairly wide circles by December of 60 when Caesar's trusted agent Balbus came to Cicero to suggest that Cicero, along with Pompey and Crassus—whom Caesar would reconcile,—should serve as Caesar's adviser in his consulship.[53] Cicero later indicated that he was asked to join the group as an equal, but he may have been one of several men approached. In deciding about Balbus' proposal Cicero was, he wrote Atticus, influenced by the epic he had just written on his consulship. In it he admonished himself to keep to the course he had set himself from his youth and had established as consul, and increase the fame and glory of good men.

> Interea cursus, quos prima a parte iuventae
> Quosque adeo consul virtute animoque petisti,
> Hos retine atque auge famam laudesque bonorum.

And in refusing throughout the next year the repeated overtures of Caesar, Cicero really did live up to his own counsels. As far as his own career was concerned, he was adding to the fame and glory of the good men. Some nobles, including a *consularis* who had been considered one of the *boni,* were not so firm as Cicero.[54]

The *optimates* faced the consulship of Caesar with more confidence because Caesar's colleague Bibulus, himself a rather dull man, was evidently to be guided by his father-in-law Cato. Caesar himself started out by proposing an agrarian law—a type of legislation that in Roman tradition belonged not to a consul but to a tribune. But Caesar acted as a consul should do in trying to obtain the support of the senate in advance. He submitted to the fathers his land bill adapted from the one proposed by Pompey's tribune of the previous year, a bill to reward Pompey's soldiers and also many of the urban plebs. Cato led the opposition, insisting in true optimate style that there must be no change in the *status quo.*[55] When he began to make one of his all-day speeches, Caesar had him apprehended. As Cato was being led from the senate house, large numbers of senators followed him, and Caesar, to keep Cato from becoming a martyr, had a tribune set him free.

Then Caesar took the bill to the people. He had already made sure that the public knew about the obstructions in the senate, for it was at this time that he instituted the custom of publishing the acts of the senate. In a meeting before the people, Bibulus repeated Cato's statement against innovation.[56] Pompey and Crassus both spoke for the bill, and Pompey made it clear that his troops were at hand to aid, if necessary by force, to pass the bill. With Caesar at his side, he was no longer hesitant about the use of force which he had so far never employed in a public assembly.

Before the bill came to a vote Caesar had the Forum occupied by armed men. Three tribunes entered vetoes, and Bibulus came to the Forum and tried to speak against the bill. He was forcibly ejected, and in the struggle the fasces of his lictors, the symbol of the consul's power, were broken. Then Cato, who always entered with zest into a fight in the assembly, tried to force himself to the platform, but was also removed after a tumult. The bill was passed in violence and in defiance of the veto. It included a clause that all senators were to take oath to adhere to it. Such a clause had been inserted in the land bill of Saturninus in 100 B.C., and Metellus Numidicus had been exiled because he would not take the oath. The consul Bibulus protested the whole procedure in the senate, but the fathers were too frightened to take action. Most of the senators decided to take the oath. Metellus Celer and Cato held out for a long time, and Cato's *alter ego,* a young man called Favonius, resisted even longer than they did. In the end, to avert civil strife, they all yielded.[57] This was a compromise of principle, for it bound the senators to observe a law which could be called unconstitutional because it was passed in the midst of violence and in disregard of the veto.[58]

It was apparently at this time that Bibulus, influenced no doubt by Cato, tried a new device to deter Caesar from further legislation. He stopped going to the senate and shut himself up in his house, announcing that he was watching the heavens. That meant that no laws could be passed without doing violence to the auspices. But Caesar was no more deterred by the auspices than he had been by the veto. He continued to submit his bills to the people, acting, his enemies asserted, like a tribune.[59] There was a second land bill providing for the distribution to fathers of three children of the rich Campanian land, a major source of state revenue, a bill revising the contracts of the publicans, and another confirming Pompey's acts. With Pompey's troops at hand, the bills passed rapidly, even Lucullus, on threats from Caesar, having dropped his efforts to prevent the ratification of Pompey's settlements.

There were other laws of Caesar, and at least one of them revealed that this man, known hitherto mainly for his activity in city politics and his cultivation of the urban mob, was aware of the problems of empire. It was an excellent law controlling extortion in the provinces—a law that seems to have served in subsequent years as a check on the cupidity of provincial governors.[60] Cato ought to have supported it, for it accorded with his ideals of just rule over subject peoples. But when, as praetor of the extortion court five years later, Cato had to administer justice under this law, he avoided referring by name to the *lex Iulia* whose validity he was at that time no longer willing to question.

Meantime, Caesar's tribune Vatinius had presented a bill that gave Caesar, instead of the insignificant tasks voted by the senate, a five-year command of Cisalpine Gaul and Illyricum, with three legions and the right to name his own body of legates. The *optimates* knew that this gave Caesar a field of conquest, for Illyricum, the gateway to the always turbulent Balkans, offered opportunities for warfare and was at this very time threatened by a powerful Dacian king.[61] They probably did not realize Caesar's military genius—no one perhaps except Caesar himself suspected that,— but they did know that in a long-term command he was getting a chance to build a strong personal army; they also knew that from Cisalpine Gaul he could threaten Italy, and that in a province much of which was inhabited by men with full citizen rights, divided among nearly half the rural tribes, he would be able to maintain strong pressure on Roman elections.

The strategy of the *optimates* had failed completely. While the "popular" consul, aided by his new son-in-law Pompey and by Crassus, was showing that he could gain his ends from the people and could even coerce the senate, the optimate consul, guided by his father-in-law Cato, was in his house watching the heavens. Cato and the staunchest *optimates* even stopped going to the senate.[62] Caesar proceeded to show that he could make that body take an active part in furthering his power. When the governorship of Transalpine Gaul fell vacant, offering a more desirable field of conquest than the Danubian region, the men who were left in the senate accepted the motion of Pompey that this province should be added to Caesar's command. The question was not even taken to the people. The dynasts were perfectly willing, if the senate was acquiescent, to let it decide such a matter. Caesar, if we can trust Suetonius, did not restrain his bitter hatred and his plans for vengeance. In the senate he declared that, against the opposition and groans of his adversaries, he had reached his goal, and from it he would leap upon their heads.[63]

The compliant senate, now willing to agree to anything that Caesar proposed, put through some of his deals with foreign princes. It passed a decree recognizing Caesar's future foe, Ariovistus, king of a German tribe now settled in Gaul, as ally and friend of the

Roman people.[64] From the second century corrupt Roman nobles, bribed by foreign princes, had been in the habit of obtaining funds by sponsoring recognition of this type, and Caesar filled his coffers from the wealth of distant kings and tetrarchs. The most profitable deal, carried out not by the senate but by a law, was made with Ptolemy the Flute Player, who was restored to his throne, reportedly after paying six thousand talents to the men in power.[65]

The good men, for the rest of Caesar's consulship powerless in the senate, set to work on public opinion. The chief method adopted was the posting of edicts purporting to come from the incarcerated consul Bibulus. Cicero calls the edicts Archilochian and that makes one suspect that Cato wrote them, for Bibulus is described as dull of tongue and Cato had a pungent style; in his youth, when he was jilted, he had written iambic verses after the manner of Archilochus, though, Plutarch adds, without his obscenities. Bibulus' edicts did not lack obscenities, for they dealt with scandalous reports about Caesar. They also added details about his aedileship which implied that when he had held that office he had double-crossed Pompey. Pompey also came in for bitter attack, and he attempted in a public meeting to answer the charges. According to Cicero, he made such a pitiable spectacle that no one but Crassus could have enjoying looking at him.

The edicts had powerful influence on public opinion. Men crowded around the place where they were posted, copied them, and sent them off to the provinces. "Nothing is so popular now as hatred of the *populares*," Cicero wrote Atticus.[66] The men in power were spoken of as kings, tyrants, dynasts. Jesters dated wills in the consulship of Caesar and Julius. There were demonstrations against the "triumvirs" in the theater. A famous tragic actor recited with conscious emphasis an apposite line in a play that could be applied to Pompey the Great: *Nostra miseria tu es magnus.* The audience forced him to repeat it over and over. When Caesar came in there was no applause, but when the young Curio, at this time in league with the *optimates,* entered there was a storm of plaudits in which the knights, all rising from their seats, took an active part. Caesar was so angry that he threatened to deprive the people of their new land grants and the knights of their special seats in the theater.[67]

Demonstrations of this type, doubtless fostered by adherents of the *optimates,* forecast the power the nobles continued to wield in the electoral assemblies, where the men in power still hesitated to use violence. The dynasts managed by one means or another to eliminate most of the candidates for the consulship for the next year; they attempted to remove both a consular candidate and Cato's brother-in-law, Lucius Domitius Ahenobarbus, who was seeking the praetorship. Their method was to have a notorious informer charge that these two men and other *optimates* had entered into a plot to kill Pompey.[68] The whole matter was bungled and, after it had aroused feeling, the dynasts dropped it and let someone strangle the informer.

Perhaps through a religious device Bibulus postponed the elections until October, and Caesar, after having tried in vain to stir the people to action against Bibulus, accepted the postponement.[69] He won the consulship for his candidates, but failed to keep Domitius and other *optimates* out of the praetorship. Cicero's enemy Clodius got the tribunate, but two good men were also elected to that office.

THE REMOVAL OF CATO

When the year 58 opened, the *optimates* went back to the senate and even hoped that they could persuade one of the consuls to work with them. Their confidence was shown when two of the praetors, Domitius and Memmius, patron of the poets Lucretius and Catullus, attacked in the senate the illegalities of Caesar's consulship. Caesar was still at hand, waiting to complete his levies, and he joined with the two praetors in an altercation that lasted several days.[70] Both sides apparently published their speeches to serve as part of the mass of opposing propaganda. The contents of the propaganda will be more fully considered in the next chapter. Already there were threats of a prosecution of Caesar for his violations of vetoes, laws, and auspices. An optimate tribune threatened to bring him to trial before the people, but Caesar, about to depart, managed by threats (his soldiers were at the gates) to make all ten tribunes agree that they would not attack him while he was absent on public service.[71] It may be that even at this time Cato had made known his intention of bringing Caesar to justice.

In any case, Caesar decided to get rid of Cato and also of Cicero, who had persistently rejected all overtures. Cicero's removal was a simple matter now that Clodius was tribune, though it is indicative of the inroads the good men had made on public opinion that Clodius, before bringing in a bill against Cicero, took care to win back the fickle populace by turning the subsidized grain supply into a free dole. The good men rallied around Cicero and put on mourning when the authority of the senate was attacked in his person, but Cato counseled him, in order to avert violence, to go, as Cicero finally did, into voluntary exile.

The problem of Cato was more complicated, and Caesar and Clodius thought up an ingenious scheme to get him out of the way. The king of Cyprus, who held his throne on a claim which had already been disputed by Rome, had, unlike his brother, the king of Egypt, failed to bribe the "triumvirs" to keep him on his throne. Clodius introduced a bill to displace him and annex Cyprus to Roman domain, and named Cato as the senator to set in order the affairs of the new province. The removal of the king was a scandalous business,[72] and the appointment of Cato was, as he recognized, not so much an honor as a type of exile, but it was coupled with responsibilities to the state that Cato did not as a patriot feel he could refuse. Cato was scrupulously honest about money and he loved accounts. He was apparently moved by the opportunity of showing how upright he was and of preventing another and less scrupulous man from making money out of the commission. And so he accepted the charge.

Cato's acceptance bound him to the unconstitutionality of Caesar and particularly of Clodius, which they recognized.[73] In a public meeting Clodius read a letter from Caesar, who by this time was in Gaul. In it he congratulated Clodius on ridding his tribunate of Cato and also on taking from Cato the opportunity of protesting against extraordinary powers (since such powers had now been granted to Cato).[74] Cato knew he was involved, and although he constantly assailed Caesar's unconstitutional acts he refused in later years to go along with Cicero in declaring Clodius' tribunate invalid.[75] Such a stand would have discredited Cato's efficient and upright administration of Cyprus, authorized by a law of Clodius.

It was Cato's uncompromising resistance to three men who appealed to the people against the senate that had led to the union of the three in a coalition which had overcome the *optimates* not only among the people but in the senate and had even temporarily eliminated Cato from politics. The new group had shown itself to be a real oligarchy, not simply a group with oligarchical designs. There must have been many *optimates* who, like Cicero, blamed Cato for his stubborn opposition to all three men.[76] In swearing to observe Caesar's agrarian law and in accepting the commission to Cyprus, Cato had compromised in the end. By yielding sooner on some of the issues he might have maintained the divisions among his enemies. The creation of such divisions was henceforth to be a major objective of optimate resistance to the "triumvirs."

CHAPTER VII

"OPTIMATES" AND DYNASTS

THE BRIBERY, the violence, and the religious chicanery that characterized Roman politics in the years of Caesar's absence in Gaul have already been considered. In the brief survey of the political situation in this chapter the emphasis will be on the propaganda of the period and the effect of the propaganda in influencing public opinion and in creating rifts both among the *optimates* and within the triumvirate. In considering the propaganda, major attention will be given to Sallust's earlier letter to Caesar on the republic, a document which has not until recently been fully appreciated in its setting.

After the dynasts had shown in Caesar's consulship that they could wrest control of the senate from the *optimates* and were willing to act through the senate, it was no longer clear who the *optimates* were. Cicero, in a brochure published about six months after his restoration, tried to answer the question, and decided that *optimates* were the sound conservatives of every class, including even freedmen, the men who wished to maintain the constitution and to create *otium cum dignitate; populares,* on the other hand, were seditious men who wished violent change.[1] Forced soon afterward to become subservient to the "triumvirs," Cicero went further and pictured Caesar as a man who had returned from the storms of popular conflict to the haven of the senate house;[2] in a later speech Cicero by implication included the "triumvirs" among the *optimates.*[3] After all, since the three men now frequently worked through the senate and had the adherence of Cicero and other supposedly good men, there was a basis for the claim.

Yet there was still a citadel of *optimates* that the dynasts had been unable to storm. Within it was Cato's family and his closest associates. There was his son-in-law Bibulus, his brother-in-law Domitius, and also, for a time, his father-in-law Lucius Marcius Philippus.[4] Then there was Cato's devoted friend, the hotheaded young Marcus Favonius, like Cato a Stoic, unlike the rest of the group not a member of a noble house.[5] In Cato's absence he was

---

[1] For notes to chap. vii see pp. 227–236.

the most effective leader of the opposition, and in subsequent years he was Cato's greatest source of dependence.ᵃ

The good men were ready now to take advantage of dissensions within the "triumvirate." They combined now with Pompey and now with Crassus, but never, as a group, with the arch-foe of the constitution, Caesar. Strife between the old enemies Pompey and Crassus had broken out as soon as Caesar left for Gaul, and the *optimates* had persuaded Pompey to work with them to bring Cicero back from exile. But when, after Cicero's restoration, Pompey set out to secure another extraordinary command, they turned against him and worked with Crassus. They were unable to keep Pompey from procuring the curatorship of the grain supply, but, with Crassus' help, they did keep him from getting a military force either to administer the commission or to restore King Ptolemy to the throne of Egypt. As dissensions grew, Pompey in the senate charged Crassus with a plot against his life, and at that the *optimates* took heart; Cicero, trying at the time to steer a course between Pompey and the *optimates,* announced that he would bring up in the senate a question bearing on the validity of Caesar's consular laws; and Domitius, candidate for the consulship for the next year, made it known that he would try to take away Caesar's province of Transalpine Gaul.

At that point Caesar summoned Pompey and Crassus to a council at Luca and ended the strife between his colleagues. The three men, in a new deal that reached far beyond the original pact, divided among them the armed potential of the Roman state, agreeing to obtain for Caesar a five-year extension of his Gallic command and for Pompey and Crassus, after a joint consulship, five-year commands in Spain and Syria. During the rest of that year and the next there was a solid front in the "triumvirate" and a solid opposition in Cato's depleted party of good men. But the death in 54 of Julia, who had the devoted love both of her father Caesar and of her husband Pompey, severed the closest bond between Caesar and Pompey, and the disastrous defeat and death of Crassus on his Parthian expedition in 53 destroyed the balance of power in the three-man deal. Henceforth the good men tried to create dissension between Caesar and Pompey, and that meant an eventual alliance with Pompey, who offered the lesser threat to the constitution.

Propaganda and Public Opinion from 58 to 53 b.c.

No longer securely in control of the senate, the *optimates* again, as in Caesar's consulship, tried to work on public opinion. They ostentatiously put on mourning when the bill for Cicero's exile came up. They went down in a body to the Tiber to meet Cato on his return from Cyprus, and succeeded in having the senate pass honorary decrees that glorified his peaceful annexation of Cyprus into a kind of triumph. With Cato once more leading them, they opposed the plans for the joint consulship of Pompey and Crassus, again putting on mourning and refusing to take part in the procession to the public games.

Since proceedings of the senate were now, under a custom instituted by Caesar, made public, the good men managed to make their opposition generally known. In the senatorial minutes, Cato's opposition to the twenty-day thanksgiving for Caesar after he invaded Germany and Britain was undoubtedly included. On that occasion Cato asserted that Caesar ought to be given up to the two German tribes who, he charged, had been attacked while a truce was supposedly in force. Caesar's apologetic account of the incident in the Gallic commentaries suggests that there was something in the charge.[7] Although the senate voted the thanksgiving, the subject got a good deal of additional attention because Caesar, who had a way of losing his good sense when he dealt with Cato, wrote an angry letter to the senate assailing Cato. That letter too was doubtless reported in senatorial minutes.

The censorship of 55 provided an opportunity to remind the public of the murders with which Pompey had been charged in the wars against the Marians and Lepidus. In answering an attack made by an adherent of the *optimates* on one of his henchmen, Pompey made fun of the low birth and hoary age of the man making the charges, and asserted that he had come from the lower world to testify. "Yes," the low-born old man replied, "I did come from the shades," and he retailed a list of the men he had seen down there, men whom Pompey, *adulescentulus carnufex,* had dispatched to Hades. They included the father of Cato's nephew Brutus and the brother of Domitius Ahenobarbus.[8]

Optimate orators continued to speak in public meetings of the tyranny exercised by the men in power. One of the optimate consuls of 56 warned the people that their days of liberty were about to end. "Cry out, cry out, Quirites, while you still may," he said, "for soon you will be punished if you do."[9] The fiercest opposition was manifested in the joint consulship of Pompey and Crassus. The speeches of Cato and Favonius, apparently much more successful than the oratory of the tribune proposing the laws, roused great hostility to the award of provinces and to the levies to be raised for new wars. When the law was voted on, Cato, forcibly kept out of the assembly, climbed on the shoulders of a man in the crowd to shout an adverse omen. The bill was passed, but there was trouble in raising troops and strong feeling against the disregard of religious signs. The adverse omens reported by an optimate tribune who pursued Crassus as he departed for Syria seem to have had a bad effect on morale both at home and in the army.[10]

But such activity, though it served to keep the public aware of the new oligarchy, did not prevent the senate from passing the decree for Caesar's thanksgiving or the people from voting favorably on the laws prolonging Caesar's command in Gaul for five years and giving Pompey and Crassus their five-year commands in Spain and Syria. Too many senators had been intimidated, and the good men were still no match for the dynasts with the urban plebs, and not sufficiently fortified by Milo's armed bands to succeed in a conflict with Clodius' ruffians and the soldiers of the "triumvirs."

The optimate opposition was, however, more successful in the electoral assemblies, especially the centuriate assembly, and in the criminal courts.[11] In the elections the *optimates* could count on their clients in Italian towns and on the strength of the feeling against the dynasts. The good men had signal success in the elections for 56, bringing to the consulship Cato's father-in-law Lucius Marcius Philippus[12] and a disaffected Pompeian, Gnaeus Lentulus Marcellinus, who proved in his consulship to be a thoroughgoing optimate. They also got some good men into the praetorship.[13] There were excellent prospects for Domitius' election to the consulship of 55, and a chance that he might succeed in his threat to remove

Transalpine Gaul from Caesar's command. It was to avert that possibility that it was decided at the Council of Luca to make Pompey and Crassus consuls for the following year.

When the plan of the "triumvirs" became known, Domitius, whose courage was not equal to his ambition, was ready to withdraw, but Cato kept him in the fight. By various devices Pompey had the election postponed until the beginning of the next year when Caesar's soldiers could come down to vote and an *interrex* instead of one of the hostile consuls would conduct the election. Even so, Pompey and Crassus were afraid of the result, and on election morning their men attacked Domitius on the way to the assembly. He took to his heels,[14] but Cato stayed in the fray and was slightly wounded. Undaunted, Cato presented himself soon afterward for the praetorship and had actually been chosen by the *centuria praerogativa* when Pompey saw lightning and dissolved the assembly.[15] When he reconvened it, he had Cato kept out by force, and Vatinius was elected in his place. There was bloodshed too at the election of aediles. This year was the only time in Pompey's career that he actually used violence while an assembly was in progress, and the good men probably did not let the people forget it.[16]

An attempt to break the hold of the *optimates* on the elections was made by Crassus. As consul he sponsored a law forbidding clubs within the tribes. But the law produced no effect.[17] It is indicative of the strength of public opinion against the consuls that, when they held the election for the next year, Pompey and Crassus did not again attempt to decide the issue by violence, but allowed Domitius to get his consulship and Cato his praetorship. After that, Pompey countered the strength of the *optimates* by the encouragement of anarchy, and as a result the next two years opened without consuls in office. At the same time, Pompey, remaining in Italy and administering Spain through legates, did everything he could, as he journeyed about making levies, to build up his own party in the Italian cities.[18]

In the courts the *optimates* constantly brought suit against the minions of the dynasts,[19] and the jurors were sufficiently favorable to enable them to get a good many convictions. Even when the accused were acquitted, the courts, thronged with people, served as a sounding board for charges against the men in power. Pompey as consul tried to obtain more favorable jurors by a law that provided for their selection, not from the rank and file of senators, knights, and tribal representatives from whom since the year 70 the jurors had been drawn, but from the richest men in each group.[20] We do not know how the law was administered, but actually it seems to have strengthened the *optimates* in the courts. The trials were especially numerous in 54,[21] when Cato as praetor of the extortion court administered Caesar's law of 59 but declined to refer to it, under Caesar's name, as the *lex Iulia.*[22]

Cicero could no longer plead in the courts for the good men and their henchmen. He was forced after the Council of Luca to follow the bidding of the dynasts and to defend their adherents, including some of his bitterest enemies. But other orators took his place. The most effective, until Caesar won him over, was the man known as a poet, Calvus, the head of the Attic School of the plain style in oratory; in prosecution after prosecution he assailed Caesar's ex-tribune Vatinius, and, though he never succeeded in getting a conviction, his speeches made a deep impression.[23] In general the optimate orators, representing the opposition, seem to have produced more effect than the counsel for the defense.

There was also a good deal of written propaganda against the "triumvirs." The edicts of Bibulus and the orations of Domitius and Memmius were in circulation. The elder Curio published in the form of orations virulent indictments of Caesar, and a historian presented events of the previous decade in a fashion that was highly unfavorable to Caesar.[24] The most telling attacks came from two gifted poets who, for personal, not ideological, reasons, were opposed to the men in power. The poets were Calvus, whose speeches against Caesar's follower Vatinius have already been mentioned, and his friend, the brilliant Gaius Valerius Catullus. Their biting iambics provided the opposition with priceless slogans. Most of the verses in which Calvus assailed Pompey and Caesar are lost,[25] but those of Catullus are preserved. He was the son of a prominent man of Verona, one of the chief cities of Caesar's Cisalpine Gaul, and he had personal knowledge of the man who was his chief target, Caesar's engineer Mamurra, pictured as a rapacious and licentious creature. Many of the verses are too scurrilous to quote, but here are a few of the less offensive lines with F. A. Wright's lively translations:[26]

> Quis hoc potest videre, quis potest pati
> Nisi impudicus et vorax et aleo,
> Mamurram habere quod comata Gallia
> Habebat ante et ultima Britannia?
> . . .
> Eone nomine, imperator unice,
> Fuisti in ultima occidentis insula

> "If he were not a glutton devoid of all shame
> And a gambler, who could endure this game,
> That Mamurra should swallow the treasures of Gaul
> And sweep up the riches of Britain withal?
> . . .
> Was this then the reason, O general rare,
> That you to the far western isle did repair?"

In the closing line Caesar and Pompey are lumped together as dynasts who had destroyed the state:

> Socer generque, perdidistis omnia.

The lines are perhaps untranslatable in English, but here is Wright's version:

> "O was it for this, little father and son,
> That you squandered our treasure and left Rome undone?"

Caesar showed his wrath over these verses but Catullus kept on:

> Irascere iterum meis iambis
> inmerentibus, unice imperator.

> "Again my verse beneath the ban will fall
> Of our unique and only general."

Caesar made overtures to Catullus, but at first he was repulsed:

> Nil nimium studeo, Caesar, tibi velle placere
> nec scire utrum sis albus an ater homo.

> "Your favors, dear sir, I can quite well forego;
> And I don't care if you are a white man or no."

But in the end Caesar succeeded in winning over the two poets.[27] He wrote of his own accord to Calvus and they became reconciled. He approached Catullus through the young man's father, with whom Caesar was on terms of hospitality, and, when Catullus offered apologies, invited him to dinner. Catullus died before he could celebrate the new friendship, and his invectives remain, as Caesar realized, an indelible blot on Caesar's name.[28]

The cases of Catullus and Calvus are indicative of the inroads the "triumvirs" and particularly Caesar were making in the optimate ranks. He was building up a great personal party. How skillful, urbane, and charming Caesar was we know from Cicero's correspondence. Caesar tried in every way to make the orator's enslavement as pleasant as possible, taking Cicero's brother Quintus as his legate and treating Quintus with great distinction. To Marcus, Caesar not only made generous loans, but, by appointing the orator one of the curators of the great buildings he was constructing for the populace at Rome, he provided opportunities for handsome profits from public contracts. Other men were being won over by favors, by the steady stream of Gallic gold that Caesar was pouring into Rome, and even by marriage alliances. Caesar actually made inroads into the house of Cato. Lucius Marcius Philippus, father-in-law of Cato, became the husband of Caesar's niece Atia, and after that he was, if not a partisan, at least benevolently neutral toward Caesar. Among the new adherents won by Caesar were Domitius Calvinus, one of the men who as tribune vetoed Caesar's first agrarian law, and Gaius Memmius, whose speeches against Caesar, delivered in his praetorship, were in circulation. Even Domitius Ahenobarbus, in the very center of the Catonian stronghold, was caught dealing with the enemy; as consul he made an infamous pact with his old allies, Memmius and Calvinus, candidates for the consulship for the following year.[29]

The good men were thus losing adherents to the "triumvirs." At the same time they themselves were trying to drive a wedge between Pompey and Caesar. They still distrusted Pompey, but they realized that hope of survival rested on attaching Pompey to themselves. In the published propaganda it was repeatedly suggested that Caesar had, in dealings with Crassus in 65, double-crossed Pompey.

Caesar was said to have been in the plot for an unsuccessful *coup d'état* at the beginning of 65; indeed it was even charged that he was to have been made master of horse under Crassus as dictator; he was credited with sharing in Crassus' scheme to build up a force against Pompey in Spain; Caesar was even assigned the major role in the design to annex Egypt to Rome. The stories are reported only by Suetonius, who was well read in the propaganda against Caesar, and who quotes as authorities Bibulus' edicts, Curio's speeches, and two anti-Caesarian historians. I agree with Strasburger that the charges are the invention of propaganda against Caesar.[30]

Pompey's well-known jealousy made the propaganda effective. Even before the death of Julia he had shown an unwillingness to read in the senate the dispatches that described Caesar's remarkable victories. The good men might sooner have won over Pompey if after Julia's death they had been willing to make him dictator. He was seeking the office in order to rid the state of an anarchy which he was fostering. But the good men were not ready for that step, and, chiefly because of Cato's opposition, the proposal of a dictatorship for Pompey made by his cousin, a tribune of 53, did not pass. In that year until well into July no magistrates except plebeian officers were chosen. The courts too were paralyzed, for there was no urban praetor to select the jurors. Then came the news of Crassus' defeat and death on his Parthian expedition. Not only was the three-man deal at an end; Roman arms were in disgrace and the eastern provinces were in peril. It was apparently at this time that the senate passed the decree of martial law, commissioning Pompey as proconsul to defend the state.[31] He might have seized the dictatorship, but he had had enough of direct action by violence, and since the good men, and Cato particularly, were unwilling to consent to a dictatorship, he settled affairs sufficiently to permit the election of regular magistrates for the rest of the year.

Pompey's Sole Consulship

To understand the propaganda of the year 51 it is necessary to consider the events of Pompey's sole consulship. Bribery and violence continued rampant in late 53 and early 52, increased because the old enemies Milo and Clodius were seeking respectively consulship and praetorship, each determined to keep the other out of office. The year 52 also opened with only plebeian officers elected. The brawls in the streets prevented the choice even of an *interrex*. Finally things came to a head on January 18 when Milo with armed bands encountered Clodius, also with an armed guard, on the Appian Way and slew him. Clodius' body was taken by his followers to Rome, exhibited with its wounds on the Rostra, and then carried to the senate house, which went up in flames as Clodius' funeral pyre. Murder and arson were the order of the day.

Again the senate passed the extreme decree and again Pompey was commissioned to quell the disturbance. A levy of all the men of military age in Italy was ordered. Again people talked of a dictatorship, and finally such remnants of the good men as had not already allied themselves with Caesar or Pompey saw that something had to be done and that Pompey would have to be their agent. They still could not make up their minds to offer him the dictatorship. Instead they decided to appoint him sole consul, and the proposal was made in the senate by Bibulus and seconded by Cato.

The office the good men offered to Pompey was completely unconstitutional. Pompey was ineligible for the consulship and was at the time holding proconsular power, not, under the laws, to be combined with the consulship. Moreover, a consul without a colleague was a contradiction of the meaning of the office. A *consul solus* was in effect a dictator, and Pompey, like the old-time dictator, was commissioned to complete a specific task—to set the state in order.[82] Here was the most extraordinary office of Pompey's extraordinary career, and, like the awards of power he had received in the seventies, it was given to him by the senate. Cato and Bibulus, like Catulus and the Sullan leaders, had contributed to Pompey's unparalleled powers.

With the full coöperation of the *optimates,* Pompey set about the reform of the state, demonstrating the energy and the organizing ability that had characterized his military career. He sponsored a law against violence and another against malpractice in candidacy. There were special courts for the trials and a limited panel of three hundred and sixty jurors, selected by Pompey from the men of highest repute among senators, knights, and *tribuni aerarii*. Cato was on the panel. The courts were under elective presidents chosen from men of consular rank, and Domitius was selected to head the court on violence. The accused were to be defended by only one counsel, whose time allowance would be limited, and there were to be no character witnesses—conditions that sounded the death knell of republican court oratory and court intrigue.[33] Pompey was at hand with armed men to keep order. In the trials Milo, defended in vain by Cicero, was condemned, as also were the worst of the Clodian offenders.[34]

The law on malpractice was made retroactive and therefore applicable to Caesar's contest for the consulship. But Pompey, in spite of his new alliance, did not at once break his bonds with Caesar. Although Vercingetorix had taken advantage of revolution in Rome to organize the great Gallic rebellion, Caesar was lingering in his Cisalpine province to see that affairs in Rome were properly settled. And he managed to bring pressure on Pompey to look out for his interests. Caesar's great concern was to make sure that he could move from his proconsulship directly into the consulship, so that he would not be accused in the courts. Cato had vowed that he would accuse Caesar, and Cato could be depended on to keep his vows. And so Caesar devised a law to safeguard his interests, a law permitting him to seek the consulship *in absentia*. It was proposed with Pompey's strong support by all ten tribunes, and thus purported to represent the united will of the people. Cato made one of his all-day speeches against the bill, but nevertheless it passed.[35] For the moment Caesar's future seemed secure.

But during the rest of the year Pompey was not so friendly to Caesar; the news of the serious reverses suffered by Caesar in the early part of the Gallic revolt may have had some influence on Pompey's policy. He decided not to accept Caesar's proposal of a new marriage alliance between their houses, but instead married the widow of Crassus' son, daughter of the noblest man of Rome, Metellus Scipio, a man who had been in Crassus' orbit, a personal enemy of Cato.

Not only did Pompey refuse a marriage connection with Caesar; with the coöperation of the *optimates* he made arrangements which strengthened his own position and weakened Caesar's. Pompey's command in Spain and Caesar's in Gaul were apparently to have expired together before the end of the year 50.[36] The senate proceeded to lengthen Pompey's command in Spain by several years, and that meant that he would still have an army when Caesar had to give his up.

Moreover, Pompey sponsored a law which changed radically the conditions under which Caesar had been granted his governorship of Gaul. Governors had hitherto been appointed from consuls and praetors in office, and the old governor could stay on until his successor arrived at the end of the year. Thus Caesar expected, in accordance with the law of the ten tribunes, to be elected to the consulship *in absentia,* I believe for the year 49, and to stay with his army in his province until the end of the year and then move from the immunity of his proconsular office into the immunity of the consulship.

Pompey's new law, from which he himself, *suarum legum auctor idem ac subversor,*[37] was exempt by action of the senate, provided another method of selecting provincial governors. They were to be chosen not from the magistrates of the year but from the ex-consuls and ex-praetors who had not held provinces. There were a number of such men, including Cicero and Bibulus, who under this law had to go off to govern Cilicia and Syria, and Domitius, who still had his eye on Transalpine Gaul. Such men, unlike the magistrates hitherto appointed to governorships, could take the Gauls over at any time of the year. And that meant that Caesar, even if he were elected *in absentia,* would have an interval between laying down his army command and entering upon his consulship. In that interval he would surely be prosecuted, and he could be brought before the special courts that Pompey had set up, with jurors that Pompey had selected. Pompey and the *optimates* had apparently set a trap for Caesar.[38]

Pompey's third consulship was a preliminary alliance with the *optimates,* but the alliance was not yet complete. Pompey had not completely broken with Caesar and he still distrusted Cato. Pompey, as well as Caesar's agents, probably contributed to the defeat of Cato for the consulship of 51.[39] Pompey could hardly have wished to see the stern Cato in office, and was doubtless the more opposed because his new father-in-law Metellus Scipio was Cato's bitter enemy. Cato, according to his admirers, bore his defeat with Stoic resignation, and declined to be a candidate again, holding that the people had rejected him in an election carried out in order. At the end of the year he clashed with Pompey. When Pompey, in violation of his own laws, tried to appear as character witness for one of his adherents, Cato as juror stopped his ears.

<h2 style="text-align:center">CICERO AND SALLUST ON THE REFORM OF THE STATE</h2>

Cicero's dialogue on the Republic, written from an optimate point of view, was published at the time of Cicero's departure for his provincial governorship of Cilicia in May of 51. Sallust's earlier letter to Caesar, presenting the view of an adherent of Caesar, has now been dated in the same year. Both works present programs for the revival of the body politic described as in a state of decline, and both are related to the conditions of the period. Sallust's letter, a political pamphlet, is a direct reflection of those conditions, while Cicero's more general discussion of the old Roman republic has indirect bearing on problems of the moment.

Pompey had withdrawn from the city, returning to his cultivation of Italy, and had left the good men in control of the senate. The control, as things turned out, was not so secure as many believed it was, for Metellus Scipio and other partisans of Pompey were in the senate, and Caesar also had his supporters. But there can be no doubt that the good men were feeling a freedom they had not enjoyed for many years. Even Cicero shared in it. Before Pompey left Rome, Cicero had, for the first time since the trial of Verres, assumed the role of prosecutor. The accused was an adherent of Pompey, a tribune of 51; this was the trial in which Cato as juror declined to listen to Pompey as a character witness. Cicero also clashed with Pompey at the trial and delighted in the acclaim he received from good men.[40] He felt that once more he was accepted as an optimate.[41]

It was a sign of Cicero's new freedom that he decided to publish the dialogue on the Republic on which he had been working for three years. Cicero had undertaken it, as he had the *De Oratore,* to fill his time and comfort himself for his ignominious state of servitude. He had toyed with the idea of setting the scene in his own time and making himself the major spokesman, but, no doubt because of his vulnerable position, he put his views into the mouth of Scipio Aemilianus and set the dramatic date of the dialogue at the beginning of the era of revolution, just after the death of Tiberius Gracchus. That too was a time when the state needed regeneration. Cicero waited to issue the dialogue, doubtless in revised form, until he felt that he belonged once more with the good men.[42]

The *Republic,* designed as a Roman counterpart to Plato's *Republic,* deals with the ideal constitution and the ideal citizen. The constitution recommended is not a utopian state, such as had never existed among men, but the state that "our ancestors left to us,"[43] the pre-Gracchan constitution of Rome that had excited Polybius' admiration because it combined the best elements of monarchy, aristocracy, and democracy. The last two books on the ideal citizen are almost entirely lost, but a line of Ennius attributing Roman power to ancient *mores* and heroic men gives the theme:

Moribus antiquis res stat Romana virisque.

"The *mores* themselves have perished for lack of heroic men," Cicero declares.[44] Obviously men of the stature of the old Romans must rise to renew the state.[45] Probably Cicero thought that he himself among others might measure up to the ideal.[46]

It can hardly be doubted that Cicero's proposal for the reform of the state, more definitely stated in his *Laws,*[47] represented the ideal of Cato's party of *optimates.* They had fought consistently for the *status quo,* but what they longed for was the pre-Gracchan (or the Sullan) constitution, when the authority of the senate had been predominant in the conduct of public affairs. Cato's party was now spoken of as a *factio,* and the emphasis Cicero places on that word in the dialogue is significant. *Illa factio,* he calls it once.[48] A *factio* is defined as a depraved aristocracy which has assumed oligarchical power, a group like the thirty tyrants of Athens or the second decemviral college at Rome.[49] Cicero was, I think, subtly defending the Roman *optimates* from the charge that they were an oligarchy, and at the same time urging them to prove themselves true *optimates.*

Sallust had been tribune the year before and had made vigorous speeches against the good men. *Factio* is a favorite word of his. His speeches are lost, but we can gain some idea of their content from the pamphlet he addressed to Caesar. It has usually been dated a year or two later, but Carlsson has shown, to my mind conclusively, that it belongs to the year 51.[50] The pamphlet is a document of major importance for the political strife of this period.

Sallust starts out with the assumption that Pompey's reform of the state in the previous year had put the *factio* in control, and he recommends to Caesar a series of counterreforms. First of all, Sallust considers the people. They are described as a poverty-stricken inert multitude, sunk in slavery. They are not now capable of taking an active part in public affairs. To awaken them to liberty Sallust proposes that the people be revived by the admission of new citizens, and that old and new citizens be sent out together in colonies. He obviously has the Transpadanes in mind when he speaks of new citizens. He concedes that Caesar will, like the tribune (of 91 B.C.) Marcus Livius Drusus, be accused of establishing a *regnum* if he makes extensive awards of citizenship, but he advises the course since it will benefit the state as well as Caesar.

Another essential reform is the diminution of the power of money among the people. Two measures, according to Sallust, would accomplish this, the inclusion of poorer men among the jurors and the removal of distinctions among the classes in the centuriate assembly. Jurors should, Sallust holds, be chosen not from the highest income groups but from the entire first class. That would apparently mean that the minimum census for jurors would be about one-sixth of the sum required by the jury law then in operation.[51] It may be noted that Sallust's suggestions, while obliterating the advantages of the first class in the centuriate assembly, would have conciliated the men of that class by giving them jury duty. These two proposals of Sallust were aimed at the two chief sources of optimate strength, the juries and the centuriate assembly. In these fields, as we have seen, Pompey and Crassus had, by laws in their joint consulship, tried to lessen the influence of the *optimates*.[52]

Sallust does not mention the tribal assembly, perhaps because he saw no need of reform in this body in which Caesar, unchecked by the *factio,* had won his great political successes. Caesar at the time was courting favor with the tribal assembly by having a splendid marble structure built to serve as a permanent voting place for the tribes.

Then Sallust considers the senate, and it is significant that, in spite of his career as a *popularis* and his assumption that Caesar represents the people, Sallust regards the senate as the bulwark of the state. It is, Sallust says, from men who through their own merits have gained riches, honor, and public office, that concern for the welfare of the state is to be expected.[53] Sallust seeks to abolish not the influence of wealth in the senate but the power wielded by the *factio.* That, he believes, can be accomplished by increasing the size of the senate (which, incidentally, would mean the opening of office to more new men) and the institution of a secret ballot. Under that method men would no longer be constrained to vote according to the wishes of the overlords.

It is evident that Sallust is aware of the charge that Caesar would establish a *regnum,* but that is not what he expects. The letter ends with an impassioned plea to Caesar to restore the republic, to bring back liberty which has been overthrown.

Throughout the letter it is clear that the nobles in the *factio* are the men charged with overthrowing liberty and the republic. Pompey comes in for criticism only as the person who "either through perverseness or because he wanted nothing so much as to injure you has sunk so low that he has put weapons in the hands of enemies."[54] The enemies (*hostes*) are the common enemies of Caesar and Pompey, the men in the *factio.*[55] His pen dipped in venom, Sallust describes them as tyrants over the state. They are a small group, but they control the treasury and they put their own men in office. They hold the people in slavery, plundering and pillaging and, as in a captive city, employing license instead of laws. They also have control of the courts, and in their condemnations they have, Sallust says in an exaggerated statement, gone far beyond Sulla in their cruelty.

"To Marcus Cato and Lucius Domitius and the other men of the same *factio,*" Sallust declares, "have been offered up, like sacrificial victims, forty [older] men of senatorial rank and also many promis-

ing young men."[56] Yet even so they are not satiated. They go on de-
priving "some of rank and others of citizenship."[57] Sallust is
speaking here of the activity of the *factio* in the courts, and the
statement, which has not been understood, refers, I think, to the
trials which continued to be held under Pompey's laws on malpractice and violence. The penalty imposed for malpractice was loss
of rank; for violence it was loss of citizenship.

Sallust goes on to suggest that an attack on Caesar in the courts
is in prospect. "To bring you low these cowardly men would, if they
could, give their lives ... They would rather imperil liberty by
your downfall than through you have the empire of the Roman
people, now great, become the greatest." A threat to try Caesar
under Pompey's law on malpractice seems to be in Sallust's mind.[58]

Sallust pictures the oligarchy in control of the state as a lazy group
(*inertissimi*),[59] able to talk but not to act. He mentions by name the
arch-enemies, and they are Cato and his circle, Bibulus, Domitius,
Favonius, and a certain Lucius Postumius whom we know from
a chance allusion in Cicero's letters as a close associate of Cato.[60]

"Marcus Bibulus' courage and strength of mind burst forth
(*erupit*) in his consulship. He is dull of tongue, by nature evil rather
than shrewd. Would that man show daring whose supreme office,
the consulship, was a supreme disgrace? Is there great force in
Lucius Domitius? No part of his body is free from iniquity and
crime—his lying tongue, his bloody hands, his running feet ...
There is only one of them, Marcus Cato, whose natural endowment
—adroit, ready of word, shrewd (*versutum, loquax, callidum*)—I
do not scorn. All this is acquired by Greek training. But virtue,
vigilance, industry do not exist among the Greeks. Do you suppose
that through precepts of men who in indolence have lost their
liberty a government can be maintained? The rest of the *factio* are
utterly indolent nobles who, like an inscription, have nothing to
offer except a good name. Men like Lucius Postumius and Marcus
Favonius are like the supercargo of a big ship. When they arrive
safe they are useful, but if something goes wrong they are the ones
to be thrown overboard because they have the least value."

Thus Sallust with bitter hatred wrote in 51 his sketch of the *factio*
to which, in his view, Pompey had consigned the state. There is

malice even in the picture of Cato, who is made out to be a man of words rather than action, a shrewd politician rather than a man of principle, a man dependent, as Cicero had long since suggested he was, on the precepts of the indolent Greeks.[61]

The general view is that Sallust in this document reveals the announced, if not the real, program of Caesar, but one may doubt that this was so. It may be questioned whether Caesar at this time had a specific program beyond the maintenance of his own position. When he was in control of the state he followed Sallust's advice in the creation of new citizens and in the increase of the senate, but he disregarded the rest. He actually raised rather than lowered the census requirement for jurors. The letter belongs to a well-known literary type, the letter of advice to statesman or ruler,[62] and Sallust, though he was influenced by some of the programs set forth by popular orators, is probably to be believed when he claims the suggestions as his own. The letter seems to be a product of his tortuous mind rather than of Caesar's clear thinking. One may doubt whether Sallust, with all his gifts, was an effective propagandist either as a tribunitial orator or as a pamphleteer.

Caesar's Propaganda and the Gallic Succession

Very different from the angry letter of Sallust is Caesar's contribution to the propaganda of this period, his seven books on the Gallic War, completed and revised, if not written in full, in the winter of 52–51, and probably published in 51.[63] In them Pompey is mentioned in complimentary terms more than once. His generosity in lending Caesar a legion is praised, as is also the *virtus* he showed in setting the city in order after the death of Clodius.[64] There is not a word about the power Pompey put into the hands of the nobility. The nobles come in for only one unfavorable comment, and that is in a passage in the first book where Caesar quotes Ariovistus as saying that messages to him from many nobles and leaders of Rome make it clear that he would gain their favor and friendship if he should bring about Caesar's death.[65] The whole work, written with amazing subtlety and skill, is an apology for the Gallic proconsulship, an apology that is strengthened by the appeal made to men's pride in the victory of Roman arms and the expansion of Roman power. It is an answer to the charges that his enemies and notably Cato had made against Caesar.

The Gallic commentaries show how Caesar was countering the accusations of his opponents. He was continuing also to counter with Gallic gold. Members of the *factio* proved to be less powerful than Sallust had thought they would be. Their diminished effectiveness may have been partly the result of the temporary eclipse of Cato, who in the years 51 and 50, either voluntarily or under constraint, stepped into the background.[66] The chief leader was Marcus Marcellus. As consul in 51 he did everything he could against Caesar. He attacked Caesar's grants of citizenship among the Transpadanes and had a citizen of Caesar's new colony, Novum Comum, flogged. He made persistent efforts to deal with the question of the succession to the Gallic provinces; if he could appoint a governor to take over during the year 50, he would deprive Caesar of the privilege accorded him by the law of 52 under which Caesar would be elected to the consulship while he was still holding his army.

Pompey, occupied in various sections of Italy and supposedly about to depart for Spain, was rarely in the vicinity of Rome. At one time he seemed, by his vague statement that everyone should obey the authority of the senate, to agree with Marcellus' plans. The senators themselves were, however, less compliant. They failed to go to meetings, and in the summer Marcellus could not get a quorum. Gallic gold was having its effect. And finally Pompey, forced in a showdown to state his opinion, made it clear that he was not yet ready for a definite break with Caesar. He declared that he was not willing to have the question of the Gallic succession discussed until after March first of the following year. And so the senate desisted for that year after passing on September 29 a decree, vetoed by Caesar's tribunes, that on March first of 50 the assignment of the Gallic provinces should be the first order of business. Caesar for the moment had won.

When March of 50 came the *optimates* failed again to make progress, for Caesar by that time had acquired, reportedly for a handsome sum, the aid of the brilliant tribune Gaius Scribonius Curio, a man on whom the *optimates* had been counting in their opposition to Caesar.[67] Caelius writes to Cicero of Curio's sudden shift. "In the most fickle manner he has deserted to the people and begun to speak for Caesar."[08] Curio proved to be the most effective propagandist Caesar had ever had,[09] and in later years his change of allegiance was regarded as the act that had turned the scales of history.[70] He appeared as a *popularis,* presenting agrarian and grain laws. He proved to be a remarkable demagogic orator.[71] Curio kept pointing out the danger to the state because Pompey as well as Caesar had an army. Playing upon the dread of civil war, still vivid in the memories of many of his listeners, Curio argued that both should lay down their commands. When it became evident that Pompey was now working with the *optimates* against Caesar, Curio became outspoken against Pompey, and recounted the illegalities and the violence of his second consulship.[72]

With the senate Curio was not less successful. By constant use of the veto he blocked action on the chief issue of the year, the succession to the Gallic provinces. By his persuasiveness he constantly won adherents.[73] The deep impression that Curio made on the senate was apparent in a meeting held just before he laid down his office on December 9. The consul, Gaius Marcellus, cousin of the consul of 51, and firmly with the *optimates* in spite of his marriage with Caesar's great-niece, had won a favorable vote on two measures, first that Caesar should give up his command and second that Pompey should retain his. Then Curio suddenly put the vote on a motion that both should lay down their commands. It carried by the staggering majority of 370 to 22.

After that vote, in conflict with the vote Marcellus himself had just obtained, the consul took things into his own hands. Accompanied by the consuls-elect, he went to Pompey outside the wall, placed a sword in his hands, and invested him with the command of the two legions taken from Caesar for the Parthian War and with the task of defending the state, obviously against Caesar. That was practically a declaration of war, a declaration of the consul without the authority of the senate. Pompey accepted the commission, and set forth to Campania to take command of the legions and to levy more troops.

The proponents of peace and conciliation were still numerous. Cicero, on his way back from Cilicia, writes to Atticus in mid-

December from Formiae: "The good men are not, as is believed, in agreement. What Roman knights and senators I have seen, men who criticize sharply everything else, but also this journey of Pompey!" and later, "So far I have found practically no one who doesn't think we ought to concede to Caesar's demands rather than fight it out."[74] But the senate stiffened, perhaps because, as Caesar suggests,[75] it was intimidated by Pompey's armed forces. When, at the beginning of January, it voted that Caesar should give up his army, Curio's successor in the tribunate, Mark Antony, and another tribune vetoed the senate's action, and, after several days of hot discussion, were warned by the consul to withdraw before the formal declaration of martial law was made. The tribunes left the senate house just before the senate made that declaration through the "extreme decree." That decree regularized the action already taken by Marcellus in investing Pompey with the defense of the state against Caesar; it charged with the task not only Pompey but the consuls and the other proconsuls—including Cicero, still holding his *imperium,* and Domitius, appointed by the senate to Caesar's province of Transalpine Gaul.

The tribunes fled to Caesar, who was at Ravenna. Caesar, hoping that an accord could be reached, had only one of his ten legions in Cisalpine Gaul. Apparently after he received the news of Pompey's commission to defend the state he sent for two of the other legions which were in Transalpine Gaul.[76] Caesar did not wait for his reinforcements to come. He moved the legion and some detachments of Gallic cavalry across the Rubicon, the boundary of Italy proper, to Ariminum. He was thus invading Italy with an armed force. An act of war had been committed against the senate with which Pompey was now allied, or, as Caesar would have it, against the clique of *optimates,* the men who had once been united against Pompey, had then become the common enemies of Pompey and Caesar, and had latterly bent all their energies to bring Caesar to justice. Now, strengthened by Pompey's soldiers, they had disregarded the vetoes of Caesar's tribunes, had invoked martial law against him, and had robbed Caesar of the immunity that in his view was guaranteed by a law of the people. How important the threat of a trial was in determining Caesar to resist by arms is indicated by the words he uttered when he gazed upon the bodies of his enemies on the field of Pharsalus: "They would have it so. After my great achievements, I, Gaius Caesar, should have been condemned by my enemies if I had not appealed to my army."[77]

The *optimates* had succeeded in their efforts to detach Pompey from Caesar, and they were now in alliance with Pompey. It was an unholy alliance, unholy for Pompey because, in his jealousy, his unwillingness to brook an equal, he had gone back on an ally whose unconstitutional deeds he had aided and abetted. It was unholy for the *optimates* too, the upholders of the old constitution; for in defying the man they considered the greater threat, they were depending on a leader who, while giving lip service to the constitution, had held himself above all laws. No wonder Cicero kept telling Atticus that there were no good men left. But Caesar knew better than that. There was one man in the senate whom he hated and feared more than all the rest. Perhaps Caesar realized more fully than the senators the power of moral leadership that Cato could wield. Cato had joined with his optimate colleagues in entrusting the defense of the state to Pompey. Yet in his selfless devotion to the state he was in a position of isolation, a leader, as Seneca later pictures him,[78] of a third party of which the other member was the *Res Publica*.

CHAPTER VIII

CATONISM AND CAESARISM

MY SUBJECT in this chapter is the ideal of the republic which became associated with Cato's name, the conflict between that ideal and Caesarism, and the manner in which Augustus resolved that conflict by laying claim to the republicanism of Cato. To understand that conflict it will be necessary to consider the attempt of Caesar, later successfully carried through by Augustus, to break the old combinations of nobles and clients and organize all the citizens of Rome into a single "party," or, more correctly, into a group of clients, united in loyalty to the ruler. Throughout the discussion I am under constant obligation to Anton von Premerstein and Ronald Syme, a German and a British scholar who in the 'thirties independently interpreted the political struggles of the period in the light of the rise of National Socialism.[1]

Party divisions in the Civil War and the persistence of the divisions into the Augustan Age have been fully discussed by Syme. They will be touched on briefly here. It should be stated at the outset that, except for a brief flare-up after the death of Caesar, the old political intrigues, the heated and often violent struggles in public meetings, assemblies, and law courts were practically ended at Rome after Caesar crossed the Rubicon. Henceforth party conflict was mainly in the hands of trained soldiers, men who had taken an oath of allegiance to their commander and were fighting to bring about his victory and the bonus he had promised them. Although the Civil War was technically a war between Caesar and the senate, actually it was fought by the personal armies of Pompey and Caesar.

It had been expected that the good men, combining their influence with Pompey's in the Italian towns,[2] would be able to recruit a considerable army, but they were slow about the business of recruiting, they lost to Caesar many of the troops they had gathered, and they were soon barred by Caesar's swift march down the Adriatic from access to their supporters. Most of the men who fought on the senatorial side in the final contest were in Pompey's service.

---

[1] For notes to chap. viii see pp. 236–240.

After he was cut off from Italy and had lost most of his army in Spain, the troops consisted in large part of foreign soldiers supplied by client princes under obligation to Pompey. The party of Pompey, pictured by Caesar as a barbarian horde, was fighting against the party of Caesar.

Ideologies, which hardly affected the armies, were emphasized by the leaders of both sides at the begining of the war. The senatorials, with Cato once more taking a prominent part in the discussions, declared that they were saving the state from the tyranny of Caesar, and Caesar asserted that he was freeing the state from the domination of an oligarchy. Both sides claimed thus to be preserving the *res publica*. From Cicero's letters it is clear that at first he was conscious of Caesar's defiance of the senate. When Pompey and the consuls ordered all senators and knights to leave Rome with them and declared that they would consider as enemies any who failed to do so, public opinion among the senators was strong enough to make most of them not actually committed to Caesar go along. Even Caesar's father-in-law went with the others.

Caesar in his constant communications to the senate stressed particularly his *dignitas,* a word that Syme renders "rank, prestige and honor,"[3] but he managed to relate his *dignitas* to the cause of the people that he was championing. Caesar's position had been guaranteed by the law of the ten tribunes passed in 52, the law that granted Caesar the privilege of standing for the consulship *in absentia.*[4] This privilege, this *beneficium populi,* the oligarchs had, according to Caesar, taken from him. Caesar and the people were one, and, as he quotes his conversation with Lentulus, he was liberating both, *se et populum Romanum,* from the *factio paucorum,* the tyranny of an oligarchy.[5] Caesarism meant the identification of the Roman people with Caesar.

But in spite of the emphasis on ideologies at the beginning of the war, personal considerations that were always paramount in Roman politics proved for most men to be the decisive factor. Caesar's father-in-law and other prominent senators eventually adopted the course of neutrality that Caesar was ready to approve. Among them was even Gaius Marcellus, the consul of the previous year who had commissioned Pompey to defend the state against Caesar. He was married to Caesar's great-niece, and Caesar brought pressure.[6] It was almost certainly a personal tie with Pompey that led Caesar's best general, Titus Labienus, to desert Caesar for Pompey.[7] It was the debt to Pompey, who had brought him back from exile, that decided Cicero, after long months of considering a neutral course, to depart for Pompey's camp.[8] Cicero had no illusions about the republicanism of Pompey. Both Pompey and Caesar were seeking a tyranny, he declares, and rings the changes over and over again on that idea.[9] Although perhaps a majority of the senators not too old to travel decided in the end to follow Pompey to the East, most of the knights and the landowners of Italy stayed out of the conflict. They were interested mainly in peace and the protection of their possessions and were reassured when Caesar showed an unexpectedly high regard for private property.

As time went on, the rival propaganda stressed personal interests rather than ideologies. The senatorials talked about low morale among Caesar's troops, spreading abroad reports that came before the war broke out and that were apparently confirmed by Labienus after he left Caesar. The leading men of the senate, notably Pompey, also dealt in threats, hints of proscription for the men who failed to align themselves with the senatorials. Pompey, according to Cicero, was turning into a Sulla.

Caesar's propaganda was far more effective because he had success to back it up and also because he had experienced agents to carry it out. The speed of Caesar's movements down the Adriatic, the success of his maneuvers as contrasted with the inefficiency of Pompey, and the favor shown Caesar by the municipalities were all stressed.

But the great stock in trade of the Caesarians was Caesar's policy of mercy, what Cicero calls his *insidiosa clementia* as contrasted with the *iracundia* of the senatorials.[10] As Caesar captured one detachment of enemy troops after another, he consistently followed the same course. He enrolled the troops under military oath in his own army and let the leaders go free. The policy may have originated from a natural abhorrence of cruelty in civil strife, an abhorrence born of the terrible examples he remembered in Marian and Sullan days. But the great publicity Caesar gave to the policy shows that he was trying to gain adherents, especially to add members of the upper class to his party. This is from a letter sent to his agents Oppius and Balbus, dutifully circulated by these gentlemen: "Let this be the new thing in our victory that we fortify ourselves by mercy and generosity."[11] And later Caesar writes to Cicero: "I am not moved by the fact that those whom I have let off free are said to have gone away to make war on me anew, I like nothing better than to be like myself and to let them be like themselves."[12] It was shrewd propaganda, based on the personal traditions of Roman politics, for Caesar had conferred a favor on the men he set free, and he could arouse sympathy by convicting them of ingratitude.[13]

In the rival camps during the war, Caesar on the one side had complete control, but Pompey on the other was hampered by his eminent associates who considered themselves his equals. It was not Pompey's party, Pompey was a member of the party; *non Magni partes sed Magnum in partibus esse,* Lucan says.[14] Pompey could not command; he had to beg Domitius not to make a stand against Caesar at Corfinium, and he begged in vain and was helpless while Domitius lost an army.

Cato, according to the legend that grew up about his activity in the war, was in favor of giving Pompey at once the supreme command that was eventually conferred.[15] But for the early weeks of the conflict we can check Cato's course from Cicero's letters, and it is clear that at that time Cato was one of the troublemakers. Appointed to take charge of Sicily and the levies there and in southern Italy, Cato was slow in leaving to assume his task. He wanted to have a share in the exchange of communications with Caesar. Perhaps too he was afraid, as others were, that Caesar would succeed in his efforts to detach Pompey from the good men.[16] Cicero wished Cato would go,[17] for Caesar would have been easier to deal with if Cato had been eliminated from senatorial councils. Cato was willing to make some concessions, but the negotiations broke down on his unalterable condition that Caesar should first withdraw to his province. Cato then went off to Sicily, but too late to save the army from Caesar's forces; to avert needless bloodshed among the inhabitants he abandoned the island without a struggle.

In the senatorial camp in Macedonia, Cato seems to have stayed aside from the quarrels that were going on according to the regular traditions of the Roman senate. Marcus Marcellus and Cicero became disgusted and withdrew into inactivity. Domitius, Lentulus, and Scipio vied with one another for Caesar's office of *pontifex maximus*. Cato, meanwhile, was concerned with the good name of the senate. In the senatorial council he sponsored a decree that no allied city should be plundered, thus emphasizing, as he had done all his life, Rome's responsibility to subject peoples. By another decree, that no Roman citizen should be put to death except on the field of battle,[18] he tried to introduce to the senatorial side something of Caesar's clemency. Both decrees were needed to check the cupidity and cruelty of his senatorial colleagues.

In military affairs Cato claimed no prominent position, insisting that as a man of praetorian rank he was inferior to his consular associates. Pompey, according to Plutarch, was afraid to give him an important command for fear that, in the event of victory, he himself might be eliminated by Cato.[19] In the end Pompey placed Cato in charge of the port and lines of communication at Dyrrachium.

It was at Dyrrachium that Cato and Cicero received from Labienus the news of the disaster, of the death of Domitius and the flight of Pompey. There was a heated meeting soon afterward in Corcyra, in which Cato is said to have urged Cicero to take the supreme command, and, when Cicero declared his intention of withdrawing from the war, Pompey's son was, according to Plutarch, kept by Cato from murdering Cicero.[20] The survivors of the senatorial army split up. Cicero, Cato's nephew Brutus, the able soldier Cassius, and eventually Favonius returned to Italy to enjoy the mercy of the dictator. Brutus and Cassius actually took service under Caesar. Cato managed to salvage fifteen cohorts, and he, Scipio, and Labienus, after learning of the death of Pompey, made their way to Africa.

The struggle that took place in Africa was the final contest of the Roman republicans against Caesar. The subsequent war with Pompey's sons and Labienus in Spain was simply a contest with the party of Pompey. In Africa the great dependence was upon the alliance with King Juba of Numidia. It was thus, as the Caesarians pointed out, another alliance of Romans with a barbarian.

Cato, while yielding the supreme command to his old enemy Scipio, who outranked him, seems to have had a major part in the effective preparations for the war. Once more in the final contest he was not on the field of battle. He was in charge of the port city of Utica when the news came of Caesar's decisive victory at Thapsus. Cato's first aim was to hold Utica, but Caesarian sympathies, long evident in the inhabitants, were now openly expressed. He strove, as we know not only from his panegyrists but from the Caesarian who wrote a history of this war, to save the lives of the Uticenses, threatened by the cruelty of the fugitives from battle.[21] He concerned himself too for his comrades in arms, both those who wished to continue the fight in Spain and those who were ready to return to make peace with the victor.

But for Cato there was no place with the party of Pompey, and no return. When his arrangements were all completed, he dined and retired to his chamber. After reading the great discourse of the condemned Socrates on the immortality of the soul, Cato stabbed himself. The scene of his death is described in one of the finest passages Plutarch wrote.[22] As Pope put it in the prologue to the rather frigid tragedy that Addison wrote on Cato, he is in that scene

A brave man struggling in the storms of fate
And greatly falling with a falling state.

The hostile population of Utica appreciated Cato's greatness and honored him with a public funeral.

Cato had chosen to die with the republic. Henceforth the men who revered his memory were republicans rather than *optimates*. Let us pause for a moment to consider Cato's conception of the republic whose personification he became. *Res Publica* meant *res populi*,[23] public possession of and public responsibility for Roman government. The public that counted was Cato's own class, the hereditary nobility who as magistrates and senators represented the people. Cato committed suicide because Roman government had now become the responsibility of one man. The state was *res unius, res ad unum redacta;* it was the private possession of a monarch.

Cato had set forth his views on public responsibility in countless speeches: short, pithy speeches, or, if he needed to upbraid the

senate and people or to use up time in a filibuster, endless ha-
rangues.[24] The speeches are lost; most of them he did not leave in
written form. The only one known in antiquity was the speech on
the Catilinarians of which Sallust has given us an eloquent version.[25]
Fortunately, besides Sallust, Cicero, directly or indirectly, tells us
a good deal about Cato's speeches.[26]

Cato's cure for the ills of his day was apparently much like Cicero's
in the *Republic* and the *Laws,* a return to the constitution of pre-
Gracchan days when men like his great-grandfather had guided
the state with a virtue that, in Cato's nostalgic view, accorded with
the Stoic ideal set forth by his Greek teachers. He spoke constantly
of abstractions such as *virtus, constantia, severitas, innocentia, con-
tinentia.*[27] He was not unaware of the great problems of his time.
Better than any of his optimate colleagues except Lucullus he understood the responsibilities of empire, and better than Lucullus
he knew the corroding effects of empire on the body politic. It was,
as Cato saw it, Rome's destiny to pacify and dominate the world,
but he insisted on a rule of justice and of self-restraint in dealing
with allies and conquered people. He was unwilling to vote on a
triumph until he had looked at the record and found out whether
the victorious general had conducted himself with fairness toward
his foes.

Cato's attitude on imperial rule comes out in the correspondence
between him and Cicero in the year 50.[28] Cicero had heard Cato
declaim on the subject in the senate, and when he wanted a thanksgiving for minor successes in Cilicia he wrote to Cato to stress with
justifiable pride the uprightness of his rule. Cato answered in a
priceless letter, the only thing we have from his pen, explaining
why he had not voted with the majority for the thanksgiving but
instead had proposed a congratulatory endorsement of Cicero. The
letter is crammed with Cato's abstractions. "I did what I could
conscientiously do in my speech and vote," Cato writes. "I praised
your upright and wise defense of the province, the preservation of
King Ariobarzanes and his kingdom, the restoration of the allies
to a ready acceptance of our rule. As for the thanksgiving that was
decreed, I am glad of it if, in a matter that was in no wise left to
chance but was secured for the republic by your remarkable pru-

dence and self-control, you prefer to have us thank the gods rather than give the credit to you. But if you think a thanksgiving is a forerunner of a triumph and that is why you prefer to have thanks given to chance rather than to you, [I remind you that] a triumph does not always follow a thanksgiving and that it is a much more splendid thing than a triumph to have the senate decide that a province was held and preserved rather by the mercy and incorruptibility of the commander than by the strength of a military force or the favor of the gods. That was what I expressed in my motion."[29]

Cicero paid tribute to Cato when he replied, "If I don't say all men but many men were Catos in our state, where the marvel is that one Cato has arisen, what triumphal chariot or what laurel could I compare with praise from you?"[30] Immediately afterward, as Caesar took pains to point out to Cicero,[31] Cato proved that he was not the figure of perfection his admirers made him out to be. Cato voted for a thanksgiving for the hardly more important successes of his son-in-law Bibulus. For members of his family Cato could relax his sternness. Nor was he as completely uncompromising as he was later made out to be. Years before, he had yielded to Caesar and Clodius and involved himself in their unconstitutionality, and he was ready to make some concessions to Caesar even in 49.

Yet he was a great man and a patriot in an age of corruption and decay. He was not a great statesman. He failed in life to achieve the identification with the state that his admirers accorded him after his death. He was a resourceful obstructionist, but he lacked constructive ideas. When he compromised, it was too late. He saw the problems of his day but he did not know how to meet them. Like so many good men of our own time, he was almost without hope. He knew the selfishness and greed of his optimate colleagues, and he was fully alive to the perils of the alliance with Pompey. Seneca says he looked forward to death if Caesar won and voluntary exile if Pompey were victorious.[32] The story goes that after the Civil War began he refused as a sign of mourning to shave his beard or cut his hair, and would not put on a garland at banquets.[33] The story, like many other details of his conduct during the Civil War, may be apocryphal, but there can be no doubt that Cato consciously went into the war as a doomed man in a doomed state.

We return to the events immediately following the death of Cato. At Rome, among the old nobles who had been pardoned and were living under Caesar's dictatorship, the story of Cato's death made far more impression than the news of Caesar's victory in Africa. The nobles were still permitted under Caesar's mild rule to talk and write with relative freedom, and some of them were talking and writing of the republic, of the old days of public responsibility for the body politic. And Cato's unconquered soul speedily became identical with the republic and liberty.

Cicero felt frankly envious of Cato's fame and wished that he had had the courage to die in like manner. At Brutus' request he wrote a laudation of Cato, a book that was the foundation of the Cato legend that went down into the empire. It is an irreparable loss that the book was not preserved. Cicero approached the problem with some trepidation, for he knew that if he gave Cato the praise he deserved, the Caesarians, with whom Cicero was then associating, would not like it, since, he tells Atticus, Cato "foresaw that everything that has happened would take place, and he fought to prevent it from happening and died to keep from witnessing its accomplishment."[34] One cannot doubt that in his *Cato* Cicero was as outspoken about the conditions under which he was living as he was in his history of oratory written a few months earlier. In that work he praised the good fortune of Hortensius, who died without seeing the Forum denuded of the law courts, and spoke of the night that had fallen on the republic.[35] Brutus and other men in Rome also wrote laudations of Cato.

It was Cicero's *Cato* that prompted Caesar, while he was still absent on the Spanish campaign, to compose a pamphlet in reply, an *Anticato*. Perhaps because he was conscious of the justice of Cato's indictments, Caesar had hated Cato for years and had been unable to view Cato's acts with the generosity that he showed to other foes in civil life. Caesar's *Anticato* is lost, but we can see his attitude in the commentaries on the Civil War where he explains Cato's opposition on the ground of long-standing personal enmity and indignation over his defeat for the consulship.[36]

The *Anticato* was couched in oratorical form, divided into two parts.[37] I believe that it was presented, as Roman political pamphlets often were, as a speech for the prosecution, divided, as such speeches regularly were, into two acts. Thus Caesar, whom the living Cato had vowed to bring to trial, was himself accusing his dead enemy. We do not know what was the charge under which Cato was arraigned. Perhaps it was *maiestas,* treason against the state, a crime with which Cato may have threatened to charge Caesar. The work was designed to conciliate Cicero, whose literary art received the most extravagant praise, and to prove the falsity of the ideal of Catonism that was now taking form in the minds of the republicans. Caesar's work apparently followed the worst traditions of Roman invective oratory as we know it from some of Cicero's coarsest speeches. It dealt with Cato's private life and particularly with his fondness for wine. Cato's friends, who had enjoyed with him long evenings of philosophical conversation, conceded that he did like wine, but Caesar made him out a sot. Caesar also accused Cato of avarice. That was given as the motive for his divorce of his wife so that she could marry Hortensius and his subsequent remarriage with her when Hortensious left her a rich widow. There may even have been charges of gross immorality.[38] In treating Cato's public life, Caesar, as Cicero tells us, either denied the facts set forth by Cicero or objected to the motives assigned or tried to show that the acts which were extolled were not praiseworthy.[39] Caesar's vicious and unjust attack served only to build up Cato's reputation. It contributed to the revival of republicanism at Rome.[40]

To that revival Caesar also contributed by the policy he followed when, six months before his death, he came home from his victory over the Pompeians in Spain. Men had been hoping that, after the Civil War had ended, Caesar would restore the constitution and make the laws and the courts function again. When, before Caesar left for Spain, he had pardoned Marcus Marcellus, the bitterest of his enemies still alive after Cato died, Cicero took Caesar's *clementia,* now turned into kingly munificence, as a promise of republicanism, and exhorted him in a warmly laudatory speech to reëstablish the constitution.

Sallust, a partisan of Caesar, understood the situation better than

Cicero did, and in another pamphlet, addressed to Caesar a few months before the speech for Marcellus, he has not a word to say about the old popular program or about the reorganization of the constitution that he had recommended a few years before. Instead he counsels an absolute ruler on certain social reforms that would improve the condition of the state.⁴¹

As time went on, Cicero became less and less hopeful. He saw for instance the statue set up to Caesar, "the unconquered god," in the temple of Quirinus, perhaps a subtle piece of rival propaganda against the image of Cato's unconquered soul forming in the minds of the nobles. But Brutus apparently went on hoping. Just before Caesar's return from Spain, Brutus wrote to Cicero that Caesar was becoming converted to the good men, that is, was becoming an optimate.⁴² Cicero was very skeptical by this time.

There proved to be reason for the skepticism, for Caesar on his return did not settle down to put the state in order. In view of the brief time he spent in the city (not more than sixteen months between 49 and his death in 44), he accomplished wonders in the reforms he carried out in Rome and Italy, and in provincial organization. He demonstrated, as already he had done in Gaul, that he was a great administrator and that he had the welfare of the state at heart. But he had neither time for republican government nor interest in it. He was embarking on further wars, planning for a great Parthian expedition, and his idea was to leave behind him, not the old disorders of courts and assemblies and of senatorial wrangling, but a stable government responsible to him alone.

Caesar was completely disillusioned about old forms. As early as 49 he had had his difficulties with a tribune (a Caecilius Metellus, the last free representative of that old family) who had barred the way to the treasury and had, to the wrath of the people, been pushed away from the door so that Caesar could take possession of state funds. After that, Caesar, when he was in Rome, functioned only as a dictator, an office which the tribunes could not touch.⁴³ Even so, tribunes continued to have a nuisance value.

Caesar was showing a constantly increasing scorn for republican institutions. The republic, he was quoted as saying, was but a name without substance or form.⁴⁴ It seemed at times that it was only to make a mockery of the constitution that Caesar maintained the assemblies and the senate. He called the assemblies only to have them vote in the affirmative on laws constructed in his offices[45] and to elect the candidates he had commended. He nominated the consuls and half the other offices, leaving the people free to choose the others—that is the way the annoying tribunes got in. His scorn of the constitution was shown by an event of the last day of 45, two and a half months before his death. Word came that a consul in office had suddenly died, and Caesar hastily called the centuriate assembly and had it elect on his commendation a man to serve part of a day. "This may seem amusing to you," Cicero writes to a friend. "You weren't here. If you had seen it you couldn't have kept back the tears."[46]

In the senate, too, Caesar was showing the same contempt toward republican institutions. Cicero, now one of the elder *consulares,* got letters from foreign princes he had never heard of, thanking him for voting them honors of which he knew nothing.[47] The senate, controlled by Caesar's henchmen, whom he had added to it in large numbers, was as subservient as the assemblies. Only in plumbing the depths of servile flattery did the senators take the initiative, as they voted Caesar every distinction that Rome had ever devised for her great men and invented new and un-Roman honors that placed him among the gods in heaven.

Caesar was a monarch, and, while making sport of the old constitution, he was concerned, as every monarch must be, to establish a firm basis in popular support. Before setting out for the Parthian War he took steps to reward his adherents, increase their numbers, and unite them in loyalty to him. He depended first of all on his soldiers, and he rewarded them generously with cash bonuses and sent out in colonies, with ample grants of land, those who had served him longest. He settled them in units according to their old formations, sometimes with their centurions as magistrates of the colony. Thus they could easily be called out at need to serve him again. He had already enfranchised the populous Transpadane region, thus increasing by perhaps as much as fifty per cent the citizen rolls and making the new citizens his personal clients. He restored the old Marian families to office and recalled the men exiled by the courts and disgraced by the censors. He enlarged the senate from about 600 to 900 members, bringing new men into the ranks of office holders. Many of them came from sections of Italy enfranchised in the Social War but since then debarred from any share in office.[48] He was thus uniting Rome and Italy; by taking in also men from across the Po and even from across the Alps he brought the provinces closer to the central regime. All these men were under personal obligation to Caesar for their advancement.

And Caesar took a further step, the significance of which was first understood by Premerstein. Caesar attempted to bind to himself in a kind of superclientele all the senators and citizens alike. The step was not taken until the last months, perhaps the last weeks, of Caesar's life. The servile senate made the proposals. It voted that Caesar should be dictator for life, that his person should be sacrosanct like that of a tribune, that he should be called the father of his country, and (this is the detail that concerns us particularly) that all citizens should take oath by his Genius, his attendant spirit. Suetonius and Appian are specific about the oath, and they indicate that everyone, and not merely the senators, as has been generally assumed, took it.[49] There probably was not time before Caesar's death to administer the oath universally, but the senators had certainly taken it.

The oath, according to Appian, pledged men to guard Caesar and Caesar's body with all their strength and invoked a curse on any man who did not offer Caesar such protection. It was thus much like the oath the Italians took to Livius Drusus, and also like the oaths of allegiance later taken to the emperors. The senators who had sworn the oath were a bodyguard for Caesar, who refused in the city to have his person protected by a military guard. Even the conspirators took the oath, if we can credit Appian's version (very different from Shakespeare's) of the speech Brutus made just after Caesar's murder. In it Brutus defended himself and his associates against the charge of perjury. That charge was also made against them in Antony's funeral oration; according to Appian (here again Shakespeare's version is different), he read the text of the oath.[50] By this oath, actually taken or to be taken by all the Romans, Caesar was accepted as the patron or rather the *pater* of the whole state and the old relationship of *fides,* the tie that bound patron and client or father and son, united him with all the citizens.

Caesar, I believe, wished to cement the union by having himself declared king. The divine honors that he accepted, the temple, the priest, the name Divus Julius, and the festivals that marked the rule of the Hellenistic monarchs, all point in that direction.[51] But Caesar was still sensitive enough to public opinion to refuse the crown offered him by Mark Antony a month before the assassination. The title was relatively unimportant. Already, as dictator for life, he was all-powerful.

It was in his acceptance of that title that Caesar particularly outraged Roman sentiment. When the senators brought him the decree, as he was seated in his golden chair before the new temple of Venus, the mother of his house, Caesar failed to rise to thank the fathers. He was, as Premerstein points out, the patron, the master, receiving his clients. The incident is given by some ancient writers as the motive of Caesar's murder.

The time was ripe for liberation. In republican circles, as we know from Cicero's letters, for months there had been vague talk of tyrannicide. The natural leader was Marcus Brutus. He was Cato's nephew, he revered Cato's memory, and he had lately divorced his wife and married his cousin, Cato's daughter, widow of Bibulus. More than that, he was the descendant of the Brutus who drove out the last king of Rome and on his mother's side of Ahala, famous slayer of a would-be tyrant of the early republic. As we have seen, Brutus was slow in making up his mind about Caesar's intentions, but the events of the months following Caesar's return from Spain convinced him. Undoubtedly he was influenced by his far more dynamic brother-in-law Cassius, and probably too by his wife, Cato's daughter.[52] He and Cassius became the leaders in a plot to slay the tyrant. The group, some sixty senators, mainly men pardoned by Caesar, associated in a loose organization with no oath binding them, determined to carry out the deed; and with them were several of Caesar's longtime adherents. Although some of the men were actuated by personal motives, there can be no doubt that republican sentiment, roused by Cato's death and strengthened by Caesar's contemptuous attitude toward the constitution, inspired the majority. It was as liberators, restorers of the republic, that they slew Caesar in the senate house.

The weakness of the conspirators' organization became evident after the assassination. They failed in a political struggle to bring back republican government, and they went off to gather an army and fight under the symbol of Libertas against Caesar's successors. Caesar's adopted son Octavian and Mark Antony pursued the republican liberators, calling them parricides, murderers of a patron, of the father of his country, violators of a sacred oath, perjurors. And such propaganda was remarkably effective, especially with the city populace. Even before the victory of Antony and Octavian it turned the murdered Caesar from a tyrant into a martyr, enshrined as a god in the cult of the state.

In fourteen years of civil strife against the liberators, against Pompey's son, and finally against his old ally Mark Antony, Caesar's adopted son Octavian, later called Augustus, was concerned with building a party for himself. With Antony and Lepidus he began by eliminating his enemies through brutal proscriptions of senators, with Cicero heading the list, and of knights. No policy of mercy for them. The nucleus of Octavian's party, in a state where arms had replaced civil intrigue, was provided by the legions and the veterans of Caesar who could be called out in their old units. To these soldier clients, after his break with Antony in 32, Octavian added all the inhabitants of Italy. Of their own accord, he tells us in his account of his achievements, "all Italy took an oath of allegiance to me, and demanded me as *dux* in the war that I won at Actium."[53] The oath was the renewal of the oath instituted but probably not universally administered in the last days of Caesar.

After that, to quote Premerstein,[54] who, as he was watching the growth of Nazism, saw the situation clearly: "There was only one party in the entire state, the party of order and the fatherland, and only one leader, overtopping all the little *principes,* the *princeps* Octavian." Horace reflects the development when he later addresses Augustus as *maxime principum.*[55] All the citizens were now Octavian's clients. The word *partes,* of which the modern derivative, party, has been used for groups identifying themselves with the entire state, was discarded; it became indeed a synonym of sedition. Octavian's following was *tota Italia.*

This organization of all the citizens as his clients was carried further by Augustus in his later years when he established his own version of the ruler cult, the worship not of his person but of his attendant spirit, his Genius.[56] Augustus, aided by armed forces near the city and by the organization of an efficient police force such as the old republic had never had, used the cult to bring order to the troublesome urban plebs. At the crossroads he set up altars to his Genius and his household god. There men came to express to him the loyalty they had once given to patrons among the nobility, to take oath by his name and to exercise in celebrations in his honor the energies they had once employed in rioting and violence. A similar policy was adopted in Italy, and a slightly different one in the empire, which also was bound with remarkable efficiency to the person and the house of Augustus.

The voluntary character that Augustus claims for this new patron-client relationship followed the traditions of republican clientage.[57] There was no senatorial decree such as had provided for the oath to Caesar. Men acted *sua sponte, consensu universorum.* There were doubtless efficient gauleiters to whip up the "spontaneity" that Augustus emphasized.[58] But the new clientele was in accord with the republicanism that Augustus was cultivating. The republic had become more and more popular in the years when Antony in the East had been assuming the role of the Hellenistic king, and it was common talk that Antony was the successor of the tyranny of Caesar.

Augustus took account of the republican sentiment when he reorganized the state. *Non regno tamen neque dictatura sed principis nomine constitutam rem publicam.*[59] It was in the senate, where republican sentiment was strongest, that Augustus in 27 b.c. staged his restoration of the republic. As he puts it: "After having by universal consent secured complete control I transferred public responsibility from my power to the control of the senate and the Roman people. In recognition of this act I was by senatorial decree given the name Augustus.... After that I surpassed all men in prestige, but of power I had no more than the men who were my colleagues in office."[60] Not a word to indicate the military force on which this prestige rested.

Augustus built up the senate to support his republicanism, seeking out and endowing the heirs of old noble families, many of them sons of men he had murdered in his cruel proscriptions. Most of them accepted him and served him faithfully.

Under the rule of this new-style republican, Cato, the symbol of the old republic, became a hero and received the homage of the nobles and the poets and the historians of the new regime. And with this cult of Cato went almost a conspiracy of silence against the mighty Julius, the tyrant who had overthrown the republic.[61] The tradition, especially as it passed down to Seneca and Lucan in the reign of Nero, has been studied in two very interesting papers by Professor Alexander.[62]

It is in Sallust and under Nero in Lucan's epic on the Civil War that we find Cato and Caesar considered together. A few years after the death of Caesar, Sallust, who had retired to private life, wrote his history of the Catilinarians, the occasion of the first conflict between Cato and Caesar. Sallust by this time was far removed from the popular conflicts in which he had once been involved. Looking back on the political strife he had known, he holds that the old leaders of the *factio* and of the popular parties had in general been pursuing their own ends in a corrupt state, a state singularly lacking in the type of man that had made Rome great. But in his time there had been, Sallust decides, two men of surpassing virtue, Caesar and Cato, and Sallust makes a fascinating comparison of the two. They are not yet, as in Lucan, examples of vice and virtue, of tyranny and liberty. Augustus had not yet, to paraphrase Professor Alexander, assassinated Caesar's memory.[63]

Sallust emphasizes Caesar's openhandedness (with just a hint of demagoguery), his mercy, and his energy. The picture of Cato is more interesting. Already he is integrity, sternness, and steadfastness incarnate, the Cato of legend. Cato the party man (and he was a party man), whose character Sallust had described in malevolent terms a few years before, is forgotten. In fact Cato is definitely excluded from party strife. He did not vie *divitiis cum divite neque factione cum factioso,* "he wished to be rather than to seem to be a good man."[64]

The development of the Cato legend, as Syme and Alexander

have pointed out, is clearly seen in the great court writers. Vergil in the *Aeneid* represents Cato as the lawgiver of the good in the lower world, and Horace puts him, glorious for his death, in a procession of republican heroes.[65] In the ode celebrating the history of the Civil War to be written by the liberty-loving Pollio, Horace represents the whole world subdued (by the great Julius who is not mentioned)

> praeter atrocem animum Catonis.[66]

Horace has Cato in mind (and Caesar too) in his famous picture of the just man who is unmoved in his firm purpose by the face of the threatening tyrant (*voltus instantis tyranni*).

> Si fractus illabatur orbis,
> Impavidum ferient ruinae.[67]

Livy's attitude toward Cato is clear from the statement, quoted from a lost book, that no one increased Cato's fame by praise or diminished it by vituperation.[68]

And what of Caesar in the same writers? Vergil in his epic glorifying the Julian house has only one definite allusion to the man who lifted the fame of that house above other noble families. And in that passage, an unfinished line, there is an implied rebuke to Caesar for making war on his country.[69] Livy questioned whether the birth of Caesar was a blessing to the Roman state.[70] In general the poets, if they speak of Caesar, concern themselves with the impiety of his murderers and the translation of his soul to heaven where the Julian star brings blessing to Rome and to Caesar's son and heir. Vergil in the *Georgics* writes magnificently of the omens preceding Caesar's death,

> impiaque aeternam timuerunt saecula noctem,[71]

and in the *Eclogues* he celebrates Caesar's apotheosis and the star that brings fertility to the lands. Horace's only references to Caesar in the odes are an allusion to the gleaming Julian star and a description of Augustus as Caesar's avenger.[72] And Ovid, writing much later in Augustus' long reign, in a spirit of flattery rather than conviction, explains that Caesar had to be translated to the heavens to prevent his great son from having a mortal father.[73]

This emphasis on the impiety of the men who murdered Caesar and on the apotheosis of Caesar became the official attitude of

Augustus. He built a great temple of Divus Julius and another of Mars the Avenger to record the punishment of his father's murderers, and he affixed the star to every statue of Caesar. Caesar as he had been in life was forgotten. Augustus, the restorer of the republic, was the architect of the new order. Caesarism was not the frank monarchy of Julius. It was still monarchy, but it was veiled now in republicanism—in Catonism, if you like.

Augustus showed his attitude toward Cato when he said to a man who had maligned Cato that anyone who objected to a change in the state was both a good citizen and a good man.[74] Augustus by that time had reason to object to changes in the state. Yet there is reason to believe that in the end Augustus felt that there was danger to his new order in the glorification of Cato. It was, I believe, late in his life that he wrote an answer to the laudation of Cato written by Brutus.[75]

What prompted Augustus to deal with Cato? One may conjecture that it was the succession of plots against his regime, and particularly the plots that were led by members of the old noble houses whose prestige he had revived. The best known of these conspiracies, that associated with the emperor's daughter Julia, had in it an Antonius, a Scipio, a Gracchus, and a Claudius Pulcher, bearers, all of them, of great noble names. By that time Augustus' republicanism had worn thin. He had ceased fostering the revival of ancient houses and was giving the consulship to new men.[76] He may have decided that the cult of Cato was leading to the formation of a rival party of genuine republicans and that it ought to be checked.

But the general attitude toward Cato and Caesar had been fixed in the early years of Augustus, and that attitude, as Professor Alexander was the first to show, went down into the empire. Caesar was often forgotten. Augustus, not Caesar, headed the list of emperors by whom men swore in the official oath of the state. Augustus, not Caesar, acquired a legend. At the same time the Cato legend continued to flourish, and, even when under Nero the republicanism of the *princeps* was frankly a sham, it was respectable to follow the lead of the great Augustan writers and praise Cato. Cato represented the republic and liberty. At the same time he was the exemplar, the almost too perfect exemplar of virtue, the ideal of Stoicism to which so many men of the upper classes turned in the grim days of Julio-Claudians.[77] In that guise we see him in the writings of Seneca during the days when Seneca was serving Nero.

Cato also helped some men to maintain independence in days of servility and to die as he had died. Thus Seneca, after he was discarded by Nero and was anticipating his own end, became preoccupied particularly with Cato's death. Seneca died, when the time came, in a manner that was worthy of his great example. Cato also inspired another and a far greater man, Thrasea Paetus. Nero's determination to bring about Paetus' death is described by Tacitus as an attempt to destroy virtue itself.[78] Paetus wrote a life of Cato, a major source of Plutarch's splendid and inaccurate biography.

It is in the epic on the Civil War written by Seneca's nephew Lucan, the work of a man who had not the courage to die as Cato did, that, as my colleague Professor Marti has shown,[79] Cato and Caesar are presented as contrasting personifications of the Stoic idea of virtue and vice, of liberty and tyranny. Lucan met his ignominious death under Nero before he had time to deal in his unfinished epic with the magnificent scene of Cato's death. He would doubtless, as Professor Alexander has argued, have treated the subject in ample proportions.[80] In the poem as it has come down to us Cato is the figure produced by the legend to which his death gave rise, the saint of the republicans and the Stoics. On him, if the day of liberty ever dawns, Lucan predicts that the allegiance now given to the Caesars will be bestowed.

> Ecce parens verus patriae, dignissimus aris,
> Roma, tuis, per quem numquam iurare pudebit,
> Et quem, si steteris umquam cervice soluta,
> Nunc olim factura deum es.[81]

"Behold the true father of his country, the man really worthy of your altars, O Rome, the man by whose name it will never shame you to take oath. And if the day ever comes when your neck is freed from the oath, it is Cato you will make a god."

It is thus for Cato that Lucan claims the altars, the oaths of loyalty, the godhead that the Romans, now all clients of the emperor, were giving to the Caesars.

There was not a real party of Cato, for under a rule based on military force it took trained soldiers to make a party. Such parties were organized from time to time by the commanders of the praetorian guard or of the provincial armies. The most distinguished nobles were not appointed by suspicious emperors to military commands. Instead of a party there was a cult of Cato, *sanctus Cato,* maintained, without opposition, in the houses of senators and nobles. They are new nobles with strange names that Cato would not have recognized, men who had acquired public office through the policy of Caesar and his successors who drew into the senate representatives of Italy and the provinces. These new nobles looked back to the "Age of Cato,"[82] when Roman magistrates and Roman *consulares,* as representatives of the republic, had had prestige and power, and they honored Cato because he had ended his life rather than see such prestige and power die. The image of Cato helped the best of the nobles like Thrasea Paetus to maintain dignified independence in the midst of servility. When the time came it helped them to meet death courageously.

But the cult of Cato did not reach down to the lower class. Many of that class, if the day of liberty, of which Lucan sang, had dawned, would hardly have known his name. They were as happy as they had been in the time of Cato; if they were provincials, they were happier, for Caesarism, as organized by the master administrator Augustus, succeeded even at its worst in checking the rival exploitation of subject people which Cato, unique in his class, had been powerless to curb. It brought for a time to the one world of Rome something of the ideal of just government of the conquered that the great Augustan poet had expressed for Rome, an ideal that Cato and Caesar shared. The people, citizens and subject races alike, were no longer divided into clients of various noble houses who governed the *res publica* for them. They were all clients and worshipers of the reigning Caesar and all the deified Caesars, beginning not with Julius but with Augustus. They were little concerned when the new parties, the armies, substituted a new Caesar. For unlike the nobles, they had not exchanged liberty for slavery. They had passed from the domination of an oligarchy to the domination of a monarch.

NOTES

[1] For the voluminous bibliography on Sallust in the prewar years see Kurfess' detailed reports in Bursian's *Jahresbericht* 252 (1936) 1–88; 269 (1940) 1–69. Further work on Sallust continued in Germany during World War II. See bibliography cited by Franz Lämmle, "Sallusts Stellung zu Cato, Caesar, Cicero," *Museum Helveticum* 3 (1946) 94 ff. On the *Jugurtha* see Kurt von Fritz, *TAPhA* 74 (1943) 134 ff.

[2] The two letters (available in Kurfess' text, Leipzig, 1930) are preserved in cod. Vat. lat. 3864 of the ninth-tenth century. The manuscript also contains Caesar's *Gallic Wars,* four books of Pliny's *Letters,* and speeches and letters excerpted from Sallust's *Catiline, Jugurtha,* and *Histories.* The two letters, headed *ad Caesarem senem de re publica,* follow the letters from Sallust's other works, without explicit indication of authorship. They are nowhere mentioned in antiquity. The general view was that the letters were *suasoriae* produced under the empire in imitation of Sallust's style, but R. v. Pöhlmann (*Sitzber. bayer. Ak. d. Wiss.,* phil.-hist. Kl. 1904, 3 ff.) and later Eduard Meyer (*Caesars Monarchie und das Principat des Pompeius,* 2d ed., 1919 [1st ed., 1918] 563 ff.) provided strong support for accepting them as the work of Sallust. For the extensive recent bibliography see Kurfess' reports cited in n. 1 above and E. Clift, *Latin Pseudepigrapha* (Baltimore, 1945) 107 ff. The most important study of the second letter (the earlier of the two) is that of Gunnar Carlsson, "Eine Denkschrift an Caesar über den Staat," *Skrifter utg. av. Vetenskaps-societeten i Lund* 19 (1936). In classical scholarship of the last twenty-five years there has been almost unanimous agreement that the works were written by Sallust, but skepticism on the subject has been expressed by several scholars. Cf. Hugh Last, *CQ* 17 (1923) 87 ff., 151 ff., and also for his present views, *Mélanges offerts à J. Marouzeau* (Paris, 1948) 357; M. L. W. Laistner, *The Greater Roman Historians* (Berkeley, 1947) 46 f., 169 f.; K. Latte, *JRS* 27 (1937) 300 f.; E. Fränkel, *Deutsche Literatur-Zeitung* 57.1 (1936) 884. Ronald Syme (*The Roman Revolution,* Oxford [1939] 52 n. 3, 248, and 460) and E. T. Salmon (*CPh* 32 [1937] 72 ff.) leave the question open, though Salmon is convinced of the genuineness of the first (the later) letter. In accepting the letters as works of Sallust, I am influenced by the indirect evidence of the manuscript, by the style, by the echoes in the letters of Plato and Xenophon, both favorites of Sallust (cf. L.A. Post, *CW* 21 [1927] 19 ff.), and by Dio's statement (43.9.3) that Sallust had written treatises condemning corruption. But my strongest reason for believing that we have here the work of Sallust is that a late rhetorician could hardly have had the understanding that the writer of the letters has of the party conflicts of the period. How would such a man have thought of putting Lucius Postumius into the *factio* of nobles

(*R.P.* 2.9.4; see Cic. *Att.* 7.15.2 for this little-known adherent of Cato)? I accept, as Kurfess is inclined to do, Carlsson's dating of *R.P.* 2 in 51; Meyer placed it in 49, and Gelzer and others in 50. Carlsson has shown how the letter fits into the conditions of 51, and I shall discuss it more fully in chapter vii. On the date see note 50 there. I also accept the *Invectio in Ciceronem* as the work of Sallust. See Clift, *op. cit.* 92 ff.

[3] Cicero's letters will have to be used with greater caution if one accepts the view presented by Professor Jérôme Carcopino, *Les Secrets de la corres-pondance de Cicéron* (2 vols., Paris, 1947), esp. 2.459 ff. The general opinion has been that the letters to Atticus were not published until the reign of Nero, but Carcopino argues that the entire correspondence of Cicero was edited and brought out in or shortly after 33 B.C. The publication, according to Carco-pino, was designed to serve as propaganda for Octavian, and much was there-fore suppressed. Carcopino's view deserves the most careful consideration, but it does not, in my opinion, invalidate any use I have made of Cicero's cor-respondence in this book.

[4] Appian, *B.C.* 1.2; cf. Vell. 2.3.3. See nn. 10, 16, 34 below.

[5] See M. Gelzer, *Die Nobilität der römischen Republik,* Berlin, 1912. As Gelzer shows, only men of equestrian rank were in practice eligible for public office. Cf. Cic. *Sest.* 97: maximorum ordinum homines quibus patet curia.

[6] I accept Gelzer's definition (*op. cit.* 22 ff.) of *nobiles* as descendants of men who had held consulship, military tribunate with consular powers, or dictator-ship. See also A. Afzelius, *Classica et Medievalia* 1 (1938) 40 ff. and 7 (1945) 150 ff.

[7] See Münzer, *Römische Adelsparteien und Adelsfamilien* (Stuttgart, 1920) *passim.* This book is referred to hereafter as *RA.* For a convenient sum-mary of the evidence see Syme, *The Roman Revolution* (hereafter *RR*) 83 ff.

[8] See Gelzer, *op. cit.* 40. Münzer s.v. "Norbanus" (5) *RE* would apparently add to the list C. Norbanus, consul in 83, but it is noteworthy that Cicero, who is fond of drawing parallels between himself and other new men, no-where mentions Norbanus as a *novus homo.*

[9] See n. 36 to chap. iii, below.

[10] The decay of the Roman state after the fall of Carthage (see n. 16 below) is Sallust's constant theme in his historical works. The corruption of empire is graphically described in the *Jugurtha,* with the constantly recurring words *omnia Romae venalia.* See also Jugurtha's reported exclamation on leaving Rome (35.10): O urbem venalem et mature perituram si emptorem invenerit. Funds of foreign princes and provincials were a major source of the vast for-tunes spent on bribery in the late republic.

[11] *The American Commonwealth* (rev. ed., New York, 1914) 2.5.

[12] Polybius (cf. 6.11.2) professes to describe the Roman constitution at the beginning of the Second Punic War, but obviously includes in his account much that he had observed more than half a century later. In what seems to

be a revision of his original text he emphasizes cycles in political development and the prospect of a decline at Rome, but the view that he wrote or rewrote the account of the constitution in the sixth book after the time of the Gracchi seems to me untenable. See K. Svoboda, *Philol.* 72 (1913) 465 ff.; F. Taeger, *Die Archaeologie des Polybios* (Stuttgart, 1922) 115; E. Kornemann, *Philol.* 86 (1931) 169 ff. According to the view of these scholars, the revision of Book Six took place before 146.

[13] The personal character of Roman political relationships has been illuminated by the studies of Fustel de Coulanges and Gelzer. See the former's posthumous work "Le Patronat et la 'commendatio' dans la société romaine," in *Les Origines du système féodal* (Paris, 1890) 205–247 (*Histoire des institutions politiques de l'ancienne France,* Vol. 5). This discussion was brought to the general attention of classical scholars by Gelzer (*op. cit.* 49), who has elaborated on the subject in a long series of subsequent investigations. See, for instance, *Neue Jahrbücher* 45 (1920) 1 ff. and in the *Real-Encyclopädie* the biographies of Lucullus (s.v. "Licinius" 104), Crassus (s.v. "Licinius" 68), Catiline (s.v. "Sergius" 23), and Cicero (s.v. "Tullius" 29). Further material can be found in Gelzer's *Caesar, der Politiker und Staatsmann,* a biography first published in 1921, which appeared in a third and much enlarged edition in Munich in 1941. This new edition has much more on Caesar's political alliances than was to be found in the earlier book. See the detailed review by Syme, *JRS* 34 (1944) 92–103. Depending on Gelzer's results, Münzer has made important contributions, especially on the political relationships of the period from 366 to Sulla, and Syme in his investigations of the times of Caesar and Augustus has presented a new view of the personal associations that carried over from republic to empire.

[14] *Societas, coniunctio, necessitudo, familiaritas* are variants of *amicitia.* See chap. ii above for further discussion.

[15] Cic. *Fam.* 5.8.5.

[16] Sallust, eager to show the corruption of his own times, has painted a far too idyllic picture of Roman politics in the period before the destruction of Carthage. See *Iug.* 41.2: Neque gloriae neque dominationis certamen; cf. *Catil.* 10; *Hist.* frg. 11 Maurenbrecher. See Gelzer, *Nobilität* 103 ff.; Münzer, *RA, passim.* The general view is that Sallust, in dating Roman decline from the fall of Carthage, is following Poseidonius. Cf. W. Schur, *Sallust als Historiker* (Stuttgart, 1934) 61 ff. and *Klio* 29 (1936) 60 ff. Against this view see Gelzer, *Philol.* 86 (1931) 274 ff. Compare Kurfess' reports (see n. 1) for further bibliography. See also n. 34.

[17] *Comm. Pet.* 53. See n. 83 to chap. iii, below.

[18] See the important analyses of these words by Hermann Strasburger, s.v. "Optimates," *RE.* For *factio,* except for omission of the occurrences in Sallust's *De Re Publica* 2 (see n. 22 below) full citations are available in Wulff's article "Factio" in the *Thesaurus Linguae Latinae.* See also "Factiosus."

[19] Festus (Paulus) p. 76 L: Factio et factiosus initio honesta vocabula erant unde adhuc factiones histrionum et quadrigariorum dicuntur. modo autem nomine factionis seditio et arma vocantur. I leave out of consideration the technical usage of *testamenti factio*. Early examples of the word in a bad sense are to be found in a fragment of a speech of the elder Cato (frg. 156 Malcovati) and in *Auctor ad Herennium* 1.8. For *factiones* in the law courts, bands of accusers, see Cic. *Brut.* 164; *Q.F.* 3.1.15. Cf. n. 38 to chap. ii, below.

[20] Sall. *Iug.* 31.14–15: Quos omnis eadem cupere, eadem odisse, eadem metuere in unum coegit. Sed haec inter bonos amicitia, inter malos factio est. For the idea that *amicitia* could exist only among good men see Cic. *Lael.* 18 and 65. On the general meaning of *factio* as a long-term grouping as contrasted with *coitio,* a combination for a special occasion, see Gelzer, *Nobilität* 102 ff.

[21] Frg. 52 Malcovati: C. Gracchus contra Q. Aelium Tuberonem: utrum inimicorum meorum factio an magis sollicitudo te impulit ut in me industriior sis quam in te.

[22] *Factio* occurs six times in Sall. *R.P.* 2, in 2.4; 4.2; 8.6; 9.4; 10.8; 11.6. Cf. *factiosus,* 3.3 and 6.4. In every instance except the one quoted in n. 33 below, *factio* refers to Caesar's enemies in the senate. See chap. vii above.

[23] Cic. *Rep.* 3.23. On the possibility that Cicero is answering Sallust's use of the word in his tribunitial orations see chap. vii.

[24] *C.D.* 2.21: Iniusti optimates quorum consensum dixit esse factionem. Cf. Cic. *Rep.* 1.68: Quos <tyrannos> si boni oppresserunt, ut saepe fit, recreatur civitas; sin audaces, fit illa factio, genus aliud tyrannorum, eademque oritur etiam ex illo saepe optimatium praeclaro statu, cum ipsos principes aliqua pravitas de via deflexit. Cf. also 2.44.

[25] I believe that the word came into general currency with that meaning after the tribunate of Sallust. Cicero's failure to employ it before that date for political groupings indicates that it was not in common use. See n. 35 below.

[26] See Roscoe's edition, London, 1847, 5.376 (from "Thoughts on Various Subjects").

[27] M. Ostrogorskij, *Democracy and the Organization of Political Parties* (New York, 1902) 2.572 ff.; Robert Michels, *Political Parties: A Sociological Study of the Oligarchical Tendencies of Modern Democracy* (New York, 1915). The theory of Michels is quoted with approval in the article "Partito," published in 1935 in the *Enciclopedia Italiana.*

[28] The commonest Greek word for party is στάσις, which is often used with a genitive personal name to show a personal grouping. Μερίς, which would correspond to *partes,* is comparatively rare. The Greek terminology is not particularly significant for purposes of this study, since Plutarch, Appian, and Dio wrote a century and a half to three centuries after the period under consideration. They were obviously influenced in their language by Greek historians who were describing Greek party struggles. For their terminology see Strasburger, *op. cit.* 789 f.

[29] See Post and Salmon, *op. cit.*; cf. Egermann, *Sitzber. Ak. Wiss. Wien,* phil.-hist. Kl. (1932) 214.3.

[30] *Factio* occurs thirteen times and *factiosus* seven times in the *Catiline, Jugurtha,* and *Histories.* (For occurrences in *R.P.* 2 see n. 22 above.) The words are used for the conspiracy of Catiline (*Catil.* 32.2), for a citizen of Lepcis in Africa (*Iug.* 77.1), for a general tendency toward factionalism (*Catil.* 18.4; 51.32 and 40, both from Caesar's speech). The other instances are either specific references to the clique of nobles who were enemies of Marius and of the *populares* of the seventies and sixties, or come from general discussions of *factio* and *partes.* For the latter use see *Iug.* 41, where *factio* represents a band of nobles with oligarchical designs, while *partes* represents a "popular" grouping. See discussion below. Sallust nowhere speaks of *factio paucorum,* but in his discussions and in his versions of the speeches of popular tribunes contantly refers to *pauci.*

[31] *B.C.* 1.22.5. Caesar is echoed by Augustus, *Res Gestae* 1.2: Rem publicam [do]minatione factionis oppressam in libertatem vindica[vi]. See W. Weber, *Princeps* (Stuttgart, 1936) 1.141, with notes.

[32] *B.G.* 8.50.2. Contendebat ... contra factionem et potentiam paucorum.

[33] Sall. *R.P.* 2.10.8: Quippe apud illos <maiores nostros> una res publica erat, ei omnes consulebant, factio contra hostes parabatur.

[34] There are 44 occurrences of the word in Livy. Of these 14 refer to Rome, the rest to other communities, chiefly Carthage and the Greek city-states. Most of those applying to Rome concern factions of the nobles, and particularly of patricians opposed to plebeians, but the word is also used of a popular group, the *forensis factio* supporting the aedile Cn. Flavius in 304 (9.46.10 and 13; cf. 2.48.4). The word is used for Roman politics in Books 31–45 only in a reference to the *factio* opposed to the elder Scipio Africanus (38.55.3). Livy's avoidance of the word for Roman affairs in these books may indicate that he was under the influence of the view set forth by Sallust in the *prooemium* of the *Histories,* namely, that Roman politics was in an ideal condition in the period between the Second and Third Punic Wars. On Sallust see Schur, *Sallust als Historiker* 90 ff. If the language of the *Periochae* can be taken to represent Livy, he may have used the word again in the period of revolution. See *Per.* 77 and 84 for the *factio* of Marius and Sulpicius and of Carbo.

[35] Caesar employs *factio* for Roman politics only in the passage quoted in the text (see n. 31), but he uses it eight times for party groupings in Gaul. Hirtius employs it only once (see n. 32 above). The other writers of the supplements to Caesar's commentaries do not use *factio.* See Merguet, *Lexikon zu den Schriften Cäsars und seiner Fortsetzer,* s.v. "factio." Nepos uses the word for Greek parties. See the *Thesaurus.*

[36] Cic. *Att.* 7.9.4 (late 50 B.C.). Cicero imagines that he is addressing Caesar. Tenuisti provinciam per annos decem non tibi a senatu sed a te ipso per vim et per factionem datos.

[87] The *Thesaurus* article on *partes* has not been published. I have collected the material in Sallust and have made use of Merguet's lexicons of Caesar and of Cicero's orations and philosophical works; also of Oldfather, Canter, and Abbott's *Index Verborum Ciceronis Epistularum* (Urbana, 1938). Full material from Livy has not been collected.

[88] Cic. *Rep.* 1.31. See Sall. *Iug.* 41.5: Omnia in duas partes abstracta sunt (between senate and people); Sall. *R.P.* 2.5.1: In duas partes ego civitatem divisam arbitror, sicut a maioribus accepi, in patres et plebem; Caes. *B.C.* 1.35. The Massilienses are quoted as saying: divisum esse populum [Romanum] in partes duas, neque sui iudici neque suarum esse virium discernere utra pars iustiorem habeat causam; principes vero esse earum partium Cn. Pompeium et C. Caesarem. Occasionally there is a suggestion that there are more than two parties. See Sall. *Hist.* 1.13 M, *omnium partium decus,* and *Catil.* 37.10.

[89] Strasburger, *op. cit.* 786 ff., lays too much stress on what he calls the abstract meaning of *partes;* he considers the word to be frequently a synonym of *causa.* Adjectives like *bonae, optimae, malae, perditae,* applied to *partes,* might seem to support this view, but even in such cases the reference is often to persons. The association of *partes* with individuals is stronger in Cicero than Strasburger indicates. For *partes* as personal groupings there is evidence, not cited by Strasburger, in the supplements to Caesar's commentaries. See n. 41.

[40] The *partes* of Marius and Sulla are alluded to indirectly in *Quinct.* 69; *Rosc. Am.* 16 and 137; *Verr.* II.1.35, and the rival *partes* of the Gracchan period in *Catil.* 4.13. Cf. also *Manil.* 10: *alterius partis periculum, Sertorianae atque Hispaniensis.* On Caesar's party see *Phil.* 5.32; 13.39 and 47; *Fam.* 10.33.1; *ad M. Brut.* 2.4.5. With Cicero's quibbling over the meaning of *partes* in *Phil.* 13.38 ff., on which Strasburger comments, compare *Phil.* 2.70: *ad ipsas tuas partes redeo, id est ad civile bellum.* Cicero there and in *Phil.* 13 distinguishes between *partes* and *seditio.* Under the empire, when *partes* were not permitted in civil life, *partes* became practically synonymous with *seditio;* see Tac. *Ann.* 16.7 and 22. The meaning of *factio* had a similar development; see note 19.

[41] Caesar uses *partes* rarely for political divisions, see *B.C.* 1.35 (cf. note 38). It is a favorite word with the writer of the *Bellum Hispaniense,* and always refers to the party of the Pompeians; cf. *Pompeianarum partium* chaps. 35 (twice), 37; see also 20, 26, 32. It is used of personal parties in the *Bellum Alexandrinum* and the *Bellum Africum: Bell. Alex.* 7, *in parte Caesaris; Bell. Afr.* 87, *suis partibus* (of Cato), and *Caesaris partibus* (cf. 88, of Cato, *quamquam oderant partium gratia*).

[42] See, however, Sall. *R.P.* 2.4.1: L. Sulla ... supplicio hostium partis suas muniri intellegebat. Compare also *Invectio in Ciceronem* 3, *modo harum modo illarum partium,* and 4. Here, the *partes* are not necessarily personal,

though the emphasis on Cicero's sudden support of Caesar and Crassus is striking.

⁴³ *Catil.* 37–38; *Iug.* 41; *Hist.* 1.6–13 M. On the arrangement of these fragments of the *Historiae* see F. Klingner, *Hermes* 63 (1928) 165 ff.

⁴⁴ *Iug.* 43.1: Metello ... quamquam advorso populi partium; *Iug.* 41.1: Ceterum mos partium popularium et factionum ac deinde omnium malarum artium paucis ante annis Romae ortus est. Before *factionum* the word *senatus* or *senatores* occurs in all the good MSS except N (Pal. 889). Gruter (see Jordan's note, 3d ed., Berlin, 1887) bracketed both *popularium* and *senatus* as glosses and Ahlberg in his edition (Leipzig, Teubner, 1919) follows Gruter and leaves the words out of the text. I am inclined to follow Jordan and bracket *senatus* but retain *popularium*. Strasburger fails to notice the manuscript reading here. The only place in which he finds *partes populares* is Livy 3.39.9 (on plebeian magistrates): cuius illi partis essent rogitare. populares? quid enim eos per populum egisse? optimates? In *Catil.* 37.10 Sallust, as Strasburger notes, avoids using *partes populares* by employing the circumlocution *quicumque aliarum atque senatus partium erant.* For other occurrences of *partes* see *Iug.* 40.2–3; 73.4. In *R.P.* 2.2.4, where the word *partes* does not occur, Caesar is mentioned as a supporter of the plebs against the *factio nobilitatis. Factio* is specifically associated with the people only in Val. Max. 4.1.13, *populari factione,* and in Livy's allusion to *forensis factio* cited in note 34.

⁴⁵ *Iug.* 41.6: Ceterum nobilitas factione magis pollebat, plebis vis soluta atque dispersa in multitudine minus poterat. See the whole of 41–42, *Catil.* 37–38, and *Hist.* 1.1–13 M.

⁴⁶ *Sest.* 96; cf. 97 ff. Cicero is answering a question of the prosecutor, who asks him to define *natio optimatium.* See n. 1 to chap. vii, below. The definition, adjusted to Cicero's personal situation (Strasburger, *op. cit.* 774), includes under *optimus quisque* men of all ranks, *municipales, rustici,* and even *libertini.* See n. 52.

⁴⁷ *Att.* 8.1.3; 8.11.7; 8.16; 9.1; 9.5.3.

⁴⁸ *Leg. Agr.* 1.23; 2.7–10, 43 (for Cicero's claim to be *popularis* see 1.23 and 2.9); *pro Rabir. perd.* 11–15; *in Catil.* 4.9. The language of these orations of 63 and of the speeches delivered after Cicero's return from exile show how much talk there was of *populares* at Rome.

⁴⁹ *Optimates* does not occur in any work of Sallust except the *Invectio in Ciceronem.* Cf. sec. 4 (on Cicero's change of allegiance): quos tyrannos appellabas, eorum potentiae faves, qui tibi ante optimates, eosdem dementes ac furiosos vocas. But Sallust (like Cicero in 49 B.C.) is fond of suggesting that the so-called *boni* (or *probi*) are not good. See *Hist.* 1.12 M.; *Iug.* 31.15–16; 85.9; *Catil.* 54.6; *esse quam videri bonus malebat* (of Cato). For Caesar as *bonus* see *R.P.* 1.1.6. *Popularis* in a political sense occurs in Sallust only in *Iug.* 41.1. See n. 44 above.

[50] See his description, *History of Rome,* Dickson's translation (rev. ed., New York, 1900) 3.303: "Both parties contended alike for shadows and numbered in their ranks none but enthusiasts or hypocrites. Both were equally affected by political corruption, and both were in fact equally worthless. Both were necessarily tied down to the *status quo,* for neither on the one side nor on the other was there found any political idea—to say nothing of any political plan—reaching beyond the existing state of things; and accordingly the two parties were so entirely in agreement that they met at every step as respected both means and ends, and a change of party was a change of political tactics more than of political sentiments."

[51] That is true of Strasburger, s.v. "Optimates," *RE.* After all, Sallust provides excellent evidence for the division, as also do the Greek writers who deal with the period. Appian is particularly important, for he had an excellent Roman source for the beginning of the *Civil Wars.* Strasburger has tried to trace back to eighteenth-century British historians the attribution of a two-party system to Rome, and has seen in it a reflection of the British two-party system. But he could have found a similar division in Sallust, Plutarch, Appian, and Dio, or in later times in Machiavelli. See *Discorsi sopra la prima Deca di Tito Livio,* Bk. 1, esp. sec. 4. W. Wachsmuth, who in 1853 published his *Geschichte der politischen Parteiungen alter und neuer Zeit* (3 vols., Braunschweig), wrote without any apparent bias derived from parties of his day. His work, the only general treatment of parties in ancient and modern times that I know, is, at least for the ancient world, excellent. His chapter headings for the discussion of the period of revolution (I, 231–369) reveal his emphasis: "Die Parteikämpfe der Demagogie gegen die Nobilität bis zur Sullas Dictatur" and "Parteien der grossen mit monarchischer Tendenz, Demagogie und bewaffnete Banden gegen den Senat."

[52] Since the third edition of Gelzer's *Caesar* may not be available, I quote his comment on *optimates* and *populares* there (p. 24): "Es ist charakteristisch für die römischen Verhältnisse, dass beiderlei Bezeichnungen nur für Politiker, niemals aber für ihre Anhänger, die sie bei den Abstimmungskämpfen der Volksversammlung gegeneinander aufboten, gebraucht wurden, und wenn man in Rom nunmehr von zwei Parteien spricht, so handelte es sich dabei um die Frage, ob die politischen Entscheidungen wie bisher vom Senat ausgehen sollten oder ob sie nicht, wie das staatsrechtlich immer möglich gewesen war, in weiterm Umfang auf die Volksversammlung zu übertragen seien. Dem entsprechend würden die 'Populären' am zutreffendsten als 'Demagogen' wiedergegeben." Strasburger, s.v. "Optimates," *RE,* promised in the article "Populares" to give a full list of the men designated as *populares* in ancient sources. The article has not been published and I have not made a full collection of the material. But as far as I have been able to observe, all the men whom Cicero refers to as *populares* are either members of the senate or men of the senatorial class; it is of tribunes of the plebs (particu-

larly of the famous tribunes opposed to the senate from the time of the Gracchi) and of leaders like Caesar, Pompey, and Crassus that Cicero most often uses the word. *Pro Sestio* 96 ff. might seem to be in conflict with this view (see note 46 above and the corresponding passage in my text), but there Cicero is engaging in special pleading.

[53] Sall. *Catil.* 38 (Rolfe's translation, Loeb text); cf. *Hist.* 1.12 M.

[54] In *R.P.* 2 Sallust makes it clear that he still thinks of Caesar in 51 as a proponent of the plebs. Cf. especially 2.2.4. For the identification of Caesar with the people at this period see Caelius, apud Cic. *Fam.* 8.6.5. (of Curio in February 50): transfugit ad populum et pro Caesare loqui coepit. See n. 44 above.

[55] See Gelzer, *Caesar,* 3d ed., 24; Syme, *JRS* 34 (1944) 93.

[56] Sall. *Catil.* 38; cf. Cic. *Leg.* 3.26.

[57] *Leg.* 3.26: Sapientis autem civis fuit causam nec perniciosam et ita popularem, ut non posset obsisti, perniciose populari civi non relinquere. In the *De Provinciis consularibus* 38, Caesar is represented as returning from his *cursus popularis* to the *curia;* that is, he is turning into an optimate. Nemo umquam hic potuit esse princeps qui maluerit esse popularis. Sed homines aut propter indignitatem suam diffisi ipsi sibi, aut propter reliquorum obtrectationem ab huius ordinis coniunctione depulsi, saepe ex hoc portu se in illos fluctus prope necessario contulerunt; qui si ex illa iactatione cursuque populari bene gesta re publica referunt aspectum in curiam atque huic amplissimae dignitati esse commendati volunt, non modo non repellendi sunt verum etiam expetendi. Cf. also Cic. *Har. resp.* 40 ff. and Gelzer's comments, s.v. "Tullius" (29), *RE* 946.

[58] *Verr.* I.151; cf. *Cluent.* 138; *Off.* 2.73; *Leg.* 1.19; *Fin.* 2.17. See particularly Q. Cicero, *Comm. Pet.* 5: si quid locuti populariter videamur.

[59] *Att.* 2.1.6. See *TAPhA* 73 (1942) 22.

[60] *Apud* Cic. *Fam.* 8.14.1 (on Domitius' defeat for the augurate in 50): Magna illa comitia fuerunt, et plane studia ex partium sensu apparuerunt; perpauci necessitudinem secuti officium praestiterunt. On the relative importance of personal relationships and programs in electoral and legislative assemblies see chap. iii.

[61] On Tiberius as the agent of nobles whose designs were blocked in the senate see Münzer, *RA* 257 ff. For the fact that both senate and people were divided see Cic. *Rep.* 1.31: duo senatus et duo paene iam populi.

[62] See Plaumann, "Das sogenannte Senatus Consultum Ultimum," *Klio* 13 (1913) 321 ff. Plaumann is not convincing in his attempt to show that the decree was first used after the death of Tiberius Gracchus. In his list of such decrees passed under the republic Plaumann omits the instance in 53 pointed out by Meyer, *op. cit.* 210 n. 3.

[63] *Ann.* 12.60. The subject under discussion is the juries: cum Semproniis rogationibus equester ordo in possessione iudiciorum locaretur aut rursum

Serviliae leges senatui iudicia redderent, Mariusque et Sulla olim de eo vel praecipue bellarent.

[64] I have discussed the evidence in *CPh* 36 (1941) 121 n. 32.

[65] *Hist.* 3.48.8: *ex factione media.*

[66] *Ibid.* 3.48.6 and 23.

[67] Cinna is known rather for his *regnum* or *dominatus* than for his activity as a *popularis*. According to Strasburger, *op. cit.* 786, he is never spoken of as *popularis* in ancient sources. See also Harold Bennett's excellent dissertation, *Cinna and His Times* (Menasha, Wis., 1923) 68.

[68] Plut. *Pomp.* 47.3.

[69] *C.* 2.1.4–5.

NOTES TO CHAPTER II
Nobles, Clients, and Personal Armies
(Pages 25–49)

[1] Throughout this chapter, I am constantly under obligation to Gelzer's *Nobilität;* for a more general treatment, which follows Gelzer, see W. Kroll, *Die Kultur der ciceronischen Zeit* (Leipzig, 1933) 1.1–80.

[2] Sall. *Iug.* 63.6–7 (of Marius): Consulatum nobilitas inter se per manus tradidit. novos nemo tam clarus neque tam egregius factis erat quin indignus eo honore et <is> quasi pollutus haberetur. Compare the similar statement on Cicero, Sall. *Catil.* 23.6. On new men see Gelzer, *op. cit.* 1–42, especially 40–42. For more recent bibliography and a discussion of the varying meaning of *novus homo* see Strasburger in *RE*. I have in general employed the term, as Cicero often does, for men of equestrian family who advanced all the way to the consulship.

[3] 6.54.2 (Paton's translation, Loeb text).

[4] *Pis.* 1; *Planc.* 51. Cf. Sall. *Iug.* 4.5.

[5] *Iug.* 4.7–8; cf. 73.7.

[6] On the patrician families see Mommsen, *Röm. Forschungen* (Berlin, 1864) 1.71–127; for the patrician houses surviving in the late republic see 122.

[7] *Mur.* 16. See Gelzer, *op. cit.* 25; on the patriciate in the time of Caesar see Syme, *RR* 68 f.

[8] For the family tree of the Caecilii Metelli see Syme, *RR* table 1. For the kinsmen of Cato see table 11. Numerous genealogical tables are to be found in Münzer, *RA* (see n. 7 to chap. i, above), and in the biographical articles in *RE*.

[9] *De Off.* 1.71–73, with the succeeding discussion of the duties of the statesman. The *De Officiis* was written in 44 after the death of Caesar. For an earlier statement of Cicero on the duty of taking part in public affairs see *Rep.* 1.1–12.

[10] Lucretius 2.11–13. This passage and the next are quoted in the translation of William Ellery Leonard.

[11] 3.995–1002.

[12] Tac. *Dial.* 34; Quintil. *Inst. Or.* 12.6.1.

[13] 6.19.2.

[14] Suet. *Aug.* 89.

[15] For the house of the man of politics (and therefore of his son) see *Off.* 1.138. The emphasis on decorum in the passage that follows is important; on the unseemliness of certain trades and professions see 150–151.

[16] On the age at which various offices could be held see Mommsen, *Römisches Staatsrecht* (3d ed., Leipzig, 1887) 1.563–572.

[17] On extravagant aedileships see Cic. *Off.* 2.57. The passage that follows deals with all manner of liberality in public life.

[18] Suet. *Iul.* 9. In Cicero's law on malpractice (passed in 63) candidates were forbidden to give such shows unless provision for them had been made in a will. See Mommsen, *Römisches Strafrecht* (Leipzig, 1899) 870 n. 5.

[19] Provincial governors regularly had *legati* under them; men entrusted with special commands might have a considerable number. Pompey had twenty-five in his war against the pirates, and Caesar about a dozen in Gaul, all of whom were provided with *imperium (legati pro praetore)*. See Drumann-Groebe, *Geschichte Roms* (Leipzig, 1899–1929) 4.420 ff.; 3.700 f.; cf. Mommsen, *Staatsrecht,* 3d ed., 2.696 ff. Caesar is conspicuous among men who eventually pursued a military career because, except for brief absences in Further Spain as quaestor and praetorian governor, he remained in the city during the entire interval between his quaestorship and his consulship. He held two special offices in the city in this period, that of road commissioner and that of *iudex quaestionis*. According to Plutarch, *Caes.* 5, he was curator of the Via Appia and spent large sums in repairing the road. On the political value of such a task for the candidate see Cic. *Att.* 1.1.2. The roads over which men traveled to vote were doubtless placarded with notices publicizing the benefactions of road commissioners.

[20] The candidate himself should not, according to Cicero (*Mur.* 43–46), have his mind on a prosecution since it would divert him from the campaign. But there were always friends who could act for him. Such trials were particularly numerous in the year 54.

[21] Under this charge (*ambitus*) the successful candidates for the consulship of 65 were prosecuted through the agency of their defeated competitors and were condemned. The defeated men then obtained the consulship.

[22] Pompey and Crassus are the only men who attained a second consulship in the interval between the dictatorships of Sulla and Caesar. Cicero hoped for a second consulship after the death of Caesar.

[23] The censorship was suspended by Sulla and revived by Pompey in 70. The five sets of censors chosen after that date (65, 64, 61, 55, and 50) did not complete the *lustrum*. For Cicero's desire for the censorship see *Att.* 4.2.6.

[24] See Sall. *Iug.* 31.10 (from the speech of the tribune C. Memmius): Sed incedunt <pauci nobiles> per ora vostra magnifici, sacerdotia et consulatus,

pars triumphos suos ostentantes. On the priesthoods see chap. iv. Since the *lustrum* was completed only in 69, in our period, one of the greatest distinctions of the nobles, the honor of being *princeps senatus,* the first man on the census rolls, fell into disuse. That honor was regularly bestowed on a patrician, and, in every instance that we know, on a member of the *gentes maiores,* the Aemilii, Claudii, Cornelii, Fabii, and Valerii. It is probable that in the censorship of 70–69 it was conferred on Mamercus Aemilius Livianus, consul of 77 (Val. Max. 7.7.6), who seems not to have lived long after 69. On his career see Münzer, *RA* 312 f. On the *princeps senatus* see Mommsen, *Röm. Forsch.* 1.92–94.

[25] For the evidence see Drumann-Groebe, *Geschichte Roms* 5.209 ff., esp. 213 n. 5.

[26] *Serm.* 1.6.34–37.

> Sic qui promittit civis, urbem sibi curae,
> Imperium fore et Italiam, delubra deorum,
> Quo patre sit natus, num ignota matre inhonestus
> Omnis mortalis curare et quaerere cogit.

[27] Compare the numerous comments on the selection of Tullia's third husband in Cicero's correspondence of 51–50.

[28] Plut. *Cato Min.* 52; cf. 25. Hortensius was not, as is sometimes asserted, childless, but he and Cato would be more closely bound together if they had children by the same mother. See Lucan, *Phars.* 2.332–333: sanguine matris permixtura domos. Thus Pompey and M. Aemilius Scaurus were considered to be united because they had children by the same mother. Cf. Ascon. pp. 19–20 C.

[29] On adoptions as a method of uniting families see Münzer, *RA* 103 f. and *passim.*

[30] *Rep.* 2.1. See also the *Somnium Scipionis* in Bk. 6, *passim.*

[31] See Münzer, *RA* 314 ff. and *Hermes* 71 (1936) 222 ff.

[32] *Phars.* 8.73.

[33] Cicero's *De Amicitia,* a discussion put into the mouth of C. Laelius, whose friendship with Scipio Aemilianus was renowned, has significant material on friendship between men in politics.

[34] Ascon. *In Scaur.,* pp. 20, 28 C.

[35] *Fam.* 3.10.10 (to Appius Claudius, whose daughter had married Pompey's son): Qua denique ille facilitate, qua humanitate tulit contentionem meam pro Milone adversantem interdum actionibus suis?

[36] *Att.* 9.2A.2. Cicero was not unaware that Pompey had deserted him when the bill for exile came up (*Att.* 8.3.3), and the Caesarians kept reminding Cicero of it to keep him from feeling obligation. See the letter of Mark Antony, *Att.* 10.8A.2 (of Pompey): *ut beneficium daret prius iniuriam fecit.*

[37] Cic. *Cael.* 26; cf. L. Mitteis, *Römisches Privatrecht* (Leipzig, 1908) 1.390 f. See Pfaff s.v. "Sodalicium" and Ziebarth s.v. "Sodales" in *RE;* De Robertis,

Il Diritto Associativo Romano (Bari, 1938). The *lex repetundarum* (*CIL* 1.2[2d ed.] 583, secs. 20 and 25) provides that a man who was a *cognatus, adfinis,* or *sodalis,* or a member of the same *collegium* as the accused should be ineligible for jury duty on the case.

[38] *Comm. Pet.* 19: Nam hoc biennio quattuor sodalitates hominum ad ambitionem gratiosissimorum tibi obligasti C. Fundani Q. Galli C. *Corneli* C. Orcivi. Horum in causis ad te deferendis quid tibi eorum sodales receperint et confirmarint scio, nam interfui. *Factio* seems to be used in the same sense in Cic. *ad Q. Fr.* 3.1.15. *Gabinium tres adhuc factiones postulant;* cf. *Brut.* 164. See Mommsen, *De Collegiis et Sodaliciis Romanorum* (Kiel, 1843) 41 f.

[39] See G. M. Calhoun, *Athenian Clubs in Politics and Litigation* (Austin, Texas, 1913).

[40] See the evidence for the trials under the *lex Varia* of 90, G. Niccolini, *I Fasti dei Tribuni della plebe* (Milan, 1934) 222 ff.

[41] Cicero constantly uses *coniurare, coniuratio* of the conspiracy. See the story in Sallust, *Catil.* 22, for which however Sallust does not vouch. Premerstein, "Vom Werden und Wesen des Prinzipats," *Abh. bayer. Akad. der Wiss.,* phil.-hist. Abt., N.F. 15 (1937) 31 f., holds that, while the Athenian clubs (ἑταιρεῖαι and συνωμοσίαι) were associations of equals, the Roman *coniuratio* was usually made up of inferiors who swore allegiance to a leader. The evidence for the conspiracy of Catiline does not support his view. Certainly Lentulus, an ex-consul who boasted of his destiny, and probably Cethegus asserted leadership for themselves.

[42] Cf. Q. Cicero, *Comm. Pet.* 33 on the equestrian centuries; 6 on noble youths. See nn. 33, 36, 38 to chap. iii below.

[43] *CIL* 1.2, 2d ed., 1764, with references cited there. Cf. *ILS* 6093 ff. See also Münzer, *RA* 51 n. 1. On *hospitium* see Gelzer, *Nobilität* 52 ff., where he discusses *hospites* in association with the whole group of adherents in the *fides* of a noble.

[44] *Rosc. Am.* 15, J. H. Freese's translation, Loeb text.

[45] *Ibid.* 16. On Roscius' association with Roman nobles see 15, 77, 119, 149. On the relations of hospitality between M. Livius Drusus and Q. Pompaedius Silo, leader of the Italians, see Plutarch, *Cato Min.* 2.1.

[46] *Leg.* 3.36.

[47] Cf. Cic. *Phil.* 3.15–16. See Tac. *Ann.* 4.3 on the scorn felt for Livilla and her *municipalis adulter,* Sejanus.

[48] Sall. *Catil.* 31.7; Cic. *Sulla* 22–25.

[49] See Cicero's letters to Cato from Cilicia, *Fam.* 15.3 and 4. Cf. Plut. *Cato Min.* 19.2.

[50] See Max Radin, *Marcus Brutus* (Oxford Univ. Press, 1939) 81 ff.

[51] Cic. *Fam.* 13.45, W. G. Williams' translation, Loeb text. Cf. also 43, 44, 47. See Münzer s.v. "Egnatius" (35) *RE.*

[52] *Fam.* 13.13, W. G. Williams' translation.

[53] Cic. *ad Q. Fr.* 3.1.10.

[54] There was no hard-and-fast distinction between *amici, hospites,* and *clientes* (see however Gell. 5.13). Seneca (*de Benef.* 6.34) notes that it was an old custom for kings to divide their friends into groups: Apud nos primi omnium *C.* Gracchus et mox Livius Drusus instituerunt segregare turbam suam et alios in secretum recipere, alios cum pluribus, alios universos. See Fustel de Coulanges, *op. cit.* (in n. 13 to chap. i, above) 211 ff.

[55] Dion. Hal. 2.9–11, E. Cary's translation, Loeb text. See M. Pohlenz, "Eine politische Tendenzschrift aus Caesars Zeit," *Hermes* 59 (1924) 157–189.

[56] *Fides* between friends and inferiors is discussed by Gelzer, *op. cit.* 52 ff., and by R. Heinze, *Hermes* 64 (1929) 140–166 (reprinted in Heinze, *Vom Geist des Römertums* [Leipzig and Berlin, 1938] 25–58).

[57] Cic. *Mur.* 71–72.

[58] *Comm. Pet.* 34–38.

[59] *R.P.* 2.5.4–5:Ita paulatim populus qui dominus erat <ac> cunctis gentibus imperitabat, dilapsus est et pro communi imperio privatim sibi quisque servitutem peperit. Sallust is concerned with adherents of the *factio* of nobles, but the statement is equally applicable to the followers of the demagogic leaders.

[60] Cic. *Pis.* 8, and Ascon. *ad loc.* p. 7 C; cf. M. Cary, *CAH* 9.484. For the complete evidence see Kornemann, s.v. "Collegium," *RE* 405 ff.; De Robertis, *op. cit.* (in n. 37 above) 74 ff.

[61] Cic. *ad Q Fr.* 2.3.5 (in February, 56). On the interpretation of this passage see De Robertis, *op. cit.* 100 ff. Cf. n. 101 to chap. iii, below.

[62] See Syme, *op. cit.* 73 ff.; *JRS* 34 (1944) 93; Premerstein, *op. cit.* (in n. 41 above) 16 ff.

[63] See Cic. *Flacc., passim.*

[64] Plut. *Crass.* 7. Crassus is quoted as saying that no man was really rich who could not support an army out of his revenues. Cf. Cic. *Parad.* 45; *Off.* 1.25; Plut. *Crass.* 2.7; Pliny, *N.H.* 33.134.

[65] *CIL* 1.2, 2d ed., 709, with *addenda* on p. 714 (*ILS* 8888). On the elder Pompey's influence on his son's career see Gelzer, *Abh. preuss. Ak. Wiss., phil.-hist. Kl.* 1941, 14.1–33.

[66] See Syme, *JRS* 28 (1938) 113 ff.

[67] Diodorus 37.11D (17B). See the discussion of Premerstein, *op. cit.* (in n. 41 above) 27 ff. Premerstein, though believing that an oath was taken on this occasion, did not accept Diodorus' version as the genuine text of the oath. But see the illuminating study of Carl Koch, *Gestirnverehrung im alten Italien* (Frankfurt, 1933) 89 ff. Through a newly discovered calendar fragment from Ostia (*CIL* 14, Suppl. 4547) it was possible for Koch to identify τὸν γενάρχην Ἥλιον of Diodorus' text with Sol Indiges and to show that there was an ancient cult of the god at Rome. Koch's investigation has provided evidence for believing that Diodorus' version is a translation of the oath actually taken.

⁶⁸ Sall. *R.P.* 2.6.4–5.

⁶⁹ See the *denarius* struck by Drusus' *hospes,* Q. Pompaedius Silo. On the reverse is represented a youth about to sacrifice a pig; eight warriors point their swords toward the victim. See H. A. Grueber, *Coins of the Roman Republic in the British Museum* (London, 1910) 2.329.

⁷⁰ See Ascon. p. 3 C; Suet. *Iul.* 8; Dio 37.9.3; cf. Plut. *Crass.* 13.2. On Caesar's colony at Novum Comum and the attendant enfranchisements see T. Rice Holmes, *The Roman Republic* (Oxford, 1923) 1.326; 2.317–320.

⁷¹ *R.P.* 2.6. Sallust does not specifically mention the Transpadanes, but there can be no doubt that he has them in mind.

⁷² All soldiers, on entering military service, took the regular military oath. Premerstein, *op. cit.* 44 ff., 73 ff., distinguishes between it and the oath of fealty to the emperor taken by the soldiers. The latter oath, he believes, established a relationship like the old Roman bond between patron and client.

⁷³ See L. R. Taylor, *CPh* 36 (1941) 113 ff.; *TAPhA* 73 (1942) 1 ff.

⁷⁴ *R.P.* 2.11.3: Quippe cum illis maiorum virtus partam reliquerit gloriam dignitatem clientelas. Cf. *Iug.* 85.4.

NOTES TO CHAPTER III

DELIVERING THE VOTE

(Pages 50–75)

¹ Marsh, *A History of the Roman World from 146 to 30* B.C. (London, 1935) 18 ff. and *passim;* Appendix 2, 370 ff.; Last's review of Marsh, *AJPh* 58 (1937) 467–474.

² The most comprehensive discussion of the tribes is still that of Mommsen, *Römisches Staatsrecht* 3 (1887) 161–198. The two studies of Kubitschek are useful: *De Romanarum tribuum origine ac propagatione* (Vienna, 1882) and *Imperium Romanum tributim discriptum* (Vienna, 1889). The article "Tribus" published in *RE* in 1939 had not been completed at the time of Kubitschek's death. It is concerned mainly with polemic and adds little new material.

³ See Beloch, *Römische Geschichte* (Berlin and Leipzig, 1926) map II at end.

⁴ Appian, *B.C.* 1.49, 53 and 55; Vell. 2.20: Cum ita civitas Italiae data esset, ut in octo tribus contribuerentur novi cives, ne potentia eorum et multitudo veterum civium dignitatem frangeret plusque possent recepti in beneficium quam auctores beneficii, Cinna in omnibus tribubus eos se distributurum pollicitus est. See Mommsen, *op. cit.* 3.179, n. 1; Beloch, *op. cit.* 578 ff.

⁵ Asconius (p. 52 C) speaks of rural tribes *quae propriae ingenuorum sunt.* (There were also many *ingenui* in the urban tribes.) Cicero (*Leg. Agr.* 2.79) indicates that a property qualification for the rural tribesman was still commonly assumed: ante rusticis detur ager qui habent quam urbanis quibus ista agri spes et iucunditas ostenditur.

[6] See Kubitschek, *Imperium Romanum tributim discriptum* 270–272. Caesar's tribe, the Fabia, was divided into as many sections. Some tribes, like the Velina of the Picene region, seem to have remained fairly unified geographical districts. It has generally been believed that the rural tribes were unequal in the number of voters they included, but Cavaignac has argued that after the Social War an effort was made to equalize the number of voters in them. See *Rev. Belge* 9 (1930) 815 ff.

[7] On Sulla's object in abolishing the censorship see T. Frank, *Economic Survey of the Roman Empire* 1 (Baltimore, 1933) 255. On the popular demand for the censorship see Cic. *Div. in Caec.* 8 (delivered in January, 70): Etiam censorium nomen quod asperius antea populo videri solebat, id nunc poscitur, id iam populare et plausibile factum est.

[8] On the Pompeian sympathies of the censors of 70 (both of whom were later Pompey's legates in the war against the pirates) see Syme, *RR* 66.

[9] Cic. *Verr.* I.54.

[10] Pompey had great strength in the tribe of Picenum, the Velina (see Cichorius, *Römische Studien* [Leipzig and Berlin, 1922] 158); he probably had considerable influence also in his own tribe, the Clustumina, in which much of Umbria was registered. But it may be doubted whether he was powerful enough to compete with the *optimates* in other tribes. In the censorship of 70–69 he may have given particular attention to the enrollment of the people in the Gallic cities south of the Po in whose status his father had been interested. See Ascon. p. 3 C; Pliny, *N.H.* 3.138. Cf. R. Gardner, *CAH* 9.195–196. Recent enrollment of many men from this region may explain Cicero's words in a letter of 65 (*Att.* 1.1.2): *quoniam videtur in suffragiis multum posse Gallia.* The use of *videtur* suggests a new situation. Pompey was able later, in a time of disorder at Rome, to summon men to help him both from Picenum and from Gallia (that is, the country south of the Po). Cf. Cic. *ad Q. Fr.* 2.3.4.

[11] "Roman Census Statistics," *CPh.* 19 (1924) 329 ff. Mommsen's view (*op. cit.,* 3d ed., 2.368) was that after the Social War new citizens could register in their home communities without coming to Rome; but if that had been so, the numbers registered would surely have been larger.

[12] Of course such rural tribesmen must have been much courted for their votes. Last (*op. cit.* in n. 1 above) seems to think that they were fairly numerous, but Cicero, *Sest.* 109 (see n. 63 below) is against that view. Some suggestion of relative numbers of poor men in rural and urban tribes may perhaps be had from a fragmentary imperial inscription which gives by tribes the numbers added to the list of men receiving free grain. See *CIL* 6.10211 (Dessau, *ILS* 6046). The figures are as follows: for the urban tribes, Palatina 4191, Suburana 4068, Esquilina 1777, Collina 457; for the two rural tribes listed on the broken stone, Romilia 68, Voltinia 85. On the interpretation of these figures see, however, Mommsen, *op. cit.* 3.446 n. 3.

[13] See Lengle s.v. "Tribuni aerarii,"*RE*. They were the old paymasters of the army and there is some reason to believe that in the late republic they had a census rating of 300,000 sesterces. On their service in juries see chap. v.

[14] Patrician Manlii (*ILS* 4942), Aemilii, and at least one branch of the Cornelii (Cichorius, *op. cit.* 147 f.) were registered in the Palatina. The Claudii Pulchri were also in that tribe. See the inscription of Mytilene, *Inscriptiones Gr. ad Res Rom. Pert.* 4.33c, where the name of an Appius Claudius in this tribe can be supplied. Cf. Mommsen, *Sitzber. preuss. Ak.* 1895, 894 n. It has not been noticed that Cicero provides evidence that Clodius belonged to the Palatina. Cf. *Dom.* 49: *ita repellebantur ut etiam Palatinam tuam perderent.* The names of other senators in this tribe are known under the empire. In the bodyguard of Cn. Pompeius Strabo (*ILS* 8888; for full text see *CIL* 1.2, 2d ed., 709 and the *addenda* on p. 714) was a man whose name is lost but who belonged to another urban tribe, the Suburana (or Succusana). P. Sestius, the tribune of 57 defended by Cicero in 56, belonged to the Collina. See Münzer s.v. "Sestius" (6) *RE;* for senators in the Collina under the empire see Wissowa, *RE*. No senators are known in the fourth urban tribe, the Esquilina.

[15] See Mommsen, *op. cit.* 3.189. The *lex Plautia* of 89 provided for jury lists of fifteen men from each tribe; in order to make up the lists, which had to be composed of men having a residence in Rome, it was necessary to go outside the classes of senators and knights. The jury law of 70, providing for a panel that included *tribuni aerarii,* men of lower census than the knights, was apparently based on the precedents of the *lex Plautia.* The *tribuni aerarii* seem to have been directly related to the tribes, and it may be that they were selected for jury duty in such a way as to counteract any inequalities in the tribal distribution of the senators and knights available for jury service.

[16] For the evidence see Mommsen, *op. cit.* 3.532 ff.

[17] Cf. Greenidge, *The Legal Procedure of Cicero's Time* (Oxford, 1901) 454.

[18] See the text of the senatorial decrees, listed by O'Brien Moore s.v. "Senatus consultum," *RE,* Suppl. 6. See also the important inscriptions cited in notes 14 above and 19 below. The tribes of many prominent men, Catulus, Cato, and Crassus, for instance, are not known.

[19] See the document concerned with the land of Pergamum which goes back to an original of 129 B.C. It is known in fragmentary copies from Adramyttium (*IGR* 4.262) and Smyrna. Cf. Passerini, *Athenaeum* 23 (1937) 252–283. As Passerini points out (263 f.), the men in this list seem to belong to the consul's *consilium.* It is probable that all members of the *consilium* were drawn from the senate.

[20] This may explain why members of the same family, the Memmii for instance, sometimes appear in different tribes. On the shifts made by some censors in tribes see Livy 40.51.9.

[21] *Comm. Pet.* 18.

[22] Cic. *Balb.* 53–57. See nn. 48–51 to chap. v, below.

[23] Service in the legions seems regularly to have required a rural tribe. See Mommsen, *op. cit.* 3.451, 784. The land bonus often given to veterans put them in the property-owning classes of the rural tribes.

[24] It was the view of Mommsen (*op. cit.*, 3d ed., 2.402 ff.) that certain citizens were, as punishment, removed completely from the tribes and placed in a special class known as the *aerarii*. Fraccaro (*Athenaeum* 21 [1933] 150–172) has argued convincingly that after 304 B.C. the phrase *tribu movere*, frequently used in censorial action, denotes removal from a rural to an urban tribe; along with such a degradation in tribe often went inclusion in the *aerarii*, which, in Fraccaro's view, may have meant subjection to a heavier *tributum* than was required of the ordinary citizen. See also Last, *JRS* 35 (1945) 40 ff.

[25] See Mommsen, *op. cit.* 3.434–444; cf. Bloch, *Histoire romaine* (Paris, 1936) 2.1.100 ff.

[26] Cic. *Flacc.* 17 and 66. Cf. M. E. Park, *The Plebs in Cicero's Day* (Cambridge, Mass., 1921). See my paper "Foreign Groups in Roman Politics of the Late Republic," to be published shortly in *Latomus*.

[27] On the disorderly character of the urban tribes see Cic. *Sest.* 114: Palatinam denique per quam omnes illae pestes vexare rem publicam dicebantur. The reference is to Vatinius' failure in his candidacy for the aedileship to carry the Palatina, tribe of his coadjutor, Clodius. On the Collina as a source for Clodius' disorderly bands see Cic. *Mil.* 25: Convocabat tribus, se interponebat, Collinam novam dilectu perditissimorum civium conscribebat. The exact meaning of the passage has been disputed. I think it means that Clodius, already provided with private armed forces from the Collina, was gathering a new band from the same tribe.

[28] The tribunes were P. Sulpicius Rufus in 88 (Livy *Per.* 77), C. Cornelius in 67, and C. Manilius in 66 (Ascon. pp. 45 and 64 f. C; *Dio* 36.42). Clodius planned to propose the measure in his praetorship (Cic. *Mil.* 87 and 89; Ascon. *In Milon.* p. 52 C; *Schol. Bob.* p. 173 Stangl). See Mommsen, *op. cit.* 3.439 f.; E. Meyer, *Caesars Monarchie*, 2d ed., 212 n. 6.

[29] See J. A. O. Larsen, *CPh* 40 (1945) 65 ff.

[30] Suet. *Aug.* 46.

[31] Botsford's valuable book *The Roman Assemblies* (New York, 1909), one of the most important productions of American classical scholarship, gives a full bibliography up to the date of its publication. The more recent discussions have, like the earlier ones, been concerned rather with the origin of the assemblies and the third-century reform of the centuriate assembly than with the actual working of the assemblies in the late republic. The most detailed discussion of the functioning of the assemblies in the period under consideration in this study is to be found in Marsh, *op. cit.*, in the articles of Cavaignac cited in the notes of this chapter and in L. Homo, *Roman Political Institutions*

(London, New York, 1930). Homo's discussion depends on a good many unproved suppositions.

[32] *Rep.* 2.39: <Servius Tullius> relicuum populum distribuit in quinque classes senioresque a iuniobus divisit easque ita disparavit ut suffragia non in multitudinis sed in locupletium potestate essent, curavitque, quod semper in re publica tenendum est, ne plurimum valeant plurimi. See also *Leg.* 3.44 and compare my discussion (pp. 60–62) of the bill for Cicero's recall submitted to the centuriate assembly.

[33] The centuries had originally been independent of the tribes, but after the reform, which took place between 241 and 219, they became divisions of the tribes. Certain nontribal groups persisted in the centuriate assembly. There were the eighteen centuries of *equites equo publico,* men of the officer class, many of whom in our period were sons of senators, and there were several supernumerary centuries of *fabri, accensi, proletarii,* etc. See Botsford, *op. cit.* 201 ff.; G. de Sanctis, *Storia dei Romani* 3.1 (Turin, 1916) 353 ff.

[34] See Livy 1.43.8; Dion. Hal. 4.18.2; Cic. *Rep.* 2.40. Dionysius says that in his day (the time of Augustus) this century was larger than the five classes together. Mommsen, *op. cit.* 3.285 f., identifies this century with the *accensi.* But see Botsford, *op. cit.* 207 n. 12.

[35] If we accept Cicero, *Rep.* 2.39–40 as a description of the voting arrangements in the days of Scipio Aemilianus (and also of Cicero), the first class represented a large proportion of the total vote. According to the statement there, the entire vote was 193; to obtain a majority only eight centuries of the second class had to vote after the seventy centuries of the first class, the century of *fabri,* and the eighteen centuries of *equites equo publico* had cast their ballots. Cicero, *Phil.* 2.82–83 seems to me to indicate that the description does refer to Cicero's own time. In favor of that view see Mommsen, *op. cit.* 3.274 ff., and Niccolini, *Atti Soc. Ligust. di Scienze e Lettere,* N.S. 4 (1925) 38–96; against it see Botsford, *op. cit.* 211 ff., and de Sanctis, *loc. cit.* No explanation of the voting arrangements is satisfactory. Cavaignac, who accepts 193 as the total vote, has an ingenious scheme. See *Journal des Savants* 9 (1911) 247 ff. and *Rev. Phil.* 8 (1934) 72 ff.

[36] The property qualification of the first class is variously given as 100,000, 110,000, 120,000, 125,000 asses (presumably sextantal asses), that is, from forty to fifty thousand sesterces. Polybius (6.23.15) seems to indicate that it was 10,000 drachmae, which in his day would be somewhat more than forty thousand sesterces. Mattingly's view (*JRS* 27 [1937] 99 ff.) is that the qualification was 50,000 sesterces in the second century and that it was raised to 100,000 in 89 B.C. The view of Belot that after the Second Punic War the census of the knights was required for the first class has been widely accepted in France. See for instance Cavaignac, *Rev. Phil.* 8 (1934) 73. It was effectively disproved by Botsford, *op. cit.* 91 ff., and by de Sanctis, *op. cit.* 3.1.369 ff. They do not cite the most conclusive evidence against the view, that of Sallust, *R.P.*

204   PARTY POLITICS IN THE AGE OF CAESAR

2.7.11–12, perhaps because they do not accept the attribution of the work to Sallust. In proposing that the whole first class should be eligible for jury duty Sallust makes it clear that the range of wealth among the jurors (the lowest of whom in his day, the *tribuni aerarii*, had a census rating slightly below that of the knights) would be greatly increased if his proposal were carried out. The passage indicates that the census rating of the first class was considerably below that of the knights. See n. 51 to chap. vii, below.

[37] There is no reason to suppress (as A. C. Clark does in the Oxford text) the repetition of *renuntiatur* in Cic. *Phil.* 2.82: prima classis vocatur, renuntiatur.

[38] Before the third-century reform, the centuries of knights (at that time largely senators and senators' sons) voted first as *praerogativae,* and had great influence on the outcome. After the reform, when a century of the first class served as the *praerogativa,* the centuries of knights voted after the first class. Where we have information on the identity of the *praerogativa* (Livy 24.7.12; 26.22.2; 27.6.3) the century chosen is designated by a tribal name and is taken from the *iuniores.* It is possible that the *praerogativa* was always selected from the men of military age. There is no evidence for the view of Mommsen *op. cit.* 3.293 that only the rural tribes were eligible for the lot of the *praerogativa.* It would be interesting to know who voted in the first class of the urban tribes. Perhaps it was a small group of senators and knights (see n. 14 above). If so, the richer men had even more influence here than they had in the rural tribes.

[39] On the *praerogativa* as the *omen* of the election see Cic. *Mur.* 38; *Div.* 1.103; 2.83, with Pease's notes in his edition, published in *University of Illinois Studies in Language and Literature* 6 (1920) and 8 (1923).

[40] *Planc.* 49: Una centuria praerogativa tantum habet auctoritatis ut nemo umquam prior eam tulerit quin renuntiatus sit aut eis ipsis comitiis consul aut certe in illum annum. The words *in illum annum* are not clear, and the text may be wrong. Accounts of elections during the Second Punic War, valuable for showing the importance of the *praerogativa,* prove that the statement as it stands is not literally true. On three occasions, after the choice of the *praerogativa* was announced, speakers intervened to make the people change their vote. Once it was the presiding magistrate (Livy 24.7–9) who urged the people to make a wiser choice in time of peril. On another occasion (Livy 26.22) a man who had been designated consul by the *praerogativa* objected that because of weak eyesight he could not undertake the duties of high office in a crucial period. On both occasions the *praerogativa* voted again, and more wisely. On a third (Livy 27.6), tribunes intervened without effect on the final outcome. There are no other known cases of interruption through speeches after the *praerogativa* had voted.

[41] Plut. *Cato Min.* 42.

[42] Cic. *ad Q. Fr.* 2.14.4.

⁴³ Ascon. p. 94 C; see Cicero's letters of congratulation to the consuls of 50, of whom one was elected by unanimous vote and the other apparently was not (*Fam.* 15.7; 15.12.1).

⁴⁴ Sall. *R.P.* 2.8.1: Sed magistratibus creandis haud mihi quidem apsurde placet lex, quam C. Gracchus in tribunatu promulgaverat, ut ex confusis quinque classibus sorte centuriae vocarentur. Ita coaequatur (ms. *coaequantur*) dignitate pecunia, virtute anteire alius alium properabit. On the interpretation of *pecunia* as an ablative, parallel in construction with *dignitate,* see Carlsson, *op. cit.* (in n. 2 to chap. i, above) 93, n. 38.

⁴⁵ Cic. *Mur.* 47 (referring to a proposal of Servius Sulpicius Rufus, who was defeated for the consulship of 62): Confusionem suffragiorum flagitasti, †praerogationum legis Maniliae, aequationem gratiae, dignitatis, suffragiorum. Graviter homines honesti atque in suis vicinitatibus et municipiis gratiosi tulerunt a tali viro esse pugnatum ut omnes et dignitatis et gratiae gradus tollerentur. *Praerogationum* is a corruption in which, as A. C. Clark suggests in his apparatus, Oxford text, a reference to *praerogativa* is probably to be found. Perhaps the correct reading is *praerogationem,* though I know no parallel for the use of this rare word in this sense. Presumably C. Manilius, popular tribune of 66, had proposed a bill of this type. As Carlsson has pointed out (*op. cit.* 92 ff.), Servius Sulpicius was consul in 51, the year in which he dates Sallust's *De Re Publica* 2.

⁴⁶ Q. Cicero, *Comm. Pet.* 29: Omnis centurias multis et variis amicitiis cura ut confirmatas habeas.

⁴⁷ *Pis.* 3: Me cuncta Italia . . . priorem consulem declaravit. See n. 71 below. On crowds in Rome at the *comitia* see *Verr.* I.54; *Sest.* 125; *Sulla* 24. On soldiers and veterans who might come from widely scattered regions see Plut. *Cic.* 14; Cic. *Mur.* 37–38 (where the *urbana suffragatio* is contrasted with the soldier's vote). On Caesar's soldiers at the *comitia* see note 106.

⁴⁸ Cic. *Mur.* 42.

⁴⁹ *Att.* 1.1.2. Cicero's plan was to go to Gaul as legate for the governor, C. Calpurnius Piso. From *Phil.* 2.76 it appears that he actually went. The passage deals with Antony's canvass for his own consulship in that region.

⁵⁰ See Kubitschek, *Imperium Romanum* 93, for the list of tribes in Aemilia and Liguria. To these should be added at least two and perhaps three additional tribes of northern Etruria (*Regio* VII) that were in Caesar's province. The name *Gallia togata* indicates that this province was largely made up of citizens.

⁵¹ *B.G.* 8.50; cf. 52. Labienus was placed in charge of this province *quo maiore commendatione* (manuscript variant, *maior et commendatior*) *conciliaretur ad consulatus petitionem.*

⁵² *Comm. Pet.* 30–31.

⁵³ On municipalities see *Comm. Pet.* 3, 17, 18, 24, 30, 31, 32, 50; on the urban plebs, 29–30, 51.

[54] *Comm. Pet.* 50: ex municipiis multitudo eorum quos tua causa venisse appareat.

[55] On the order of elections, the dates, and the independent schedule of the elections for plebian officers see Mommsen, *op. cit.*, 3d ed., 1.580 ff.

[56] Cic. *Planc.* 7. Cicero insists that the superior *dignitas* of Plancius' defeated opponent is not the decisive factor in a minor election: his levioribus comitiis diligentia et gratia petitorum honos paritur, non eis ornamentis quae esse in te videmus. See also 9. This oration and the *Pro Murena* are filled with material on the Roman election. On the throngs from Plancius' own tribe and from the neighborhood who came to his *comitia* (as also to Cicero's) see *Planc.* 21–22.

[57] In this period the only essential difference between the *concilium plebis*, where tribunes proposed their laws, and the *comitia tributa,* where consuls and praetors usually proposed theirs, was that a tribune presided over the *concilium plebis* and a consul or a praetor over the *comitia tributa.*

[58] The supremacy of the tribal assembly in matters of legislation may date from the *lex Hortensia* of 287, when *plebiscita* of the *concilium plebis* were made binding on the whole state. The centuriate assembly was still called for declarations of war and to pass the censorial law (apparently a mere formality, cf. Botsford, *op. cit.* 237). It must have acted on such laws when censors were chosen in 70, 65, 64, 61, and 55. In theory it alone could decide on the life of a citizen and it was summoned for the appeal of C. Rabirius, condemned for *perduellio* in 63. See n. 17 to chap. vi, below. Sulla as consul in 88 tried to destroy the influence of the tribal assembly by requiring that all legislation should be submitted to the centuries. See Appian, *B.C.* 1.59. Sulla's law was later revoked and he did not renew it as dictator, contenting himself instead with the removal of the tribune's legislative powers. Caesar as dictator submitted at least one law to the centuries (Cic. *Phil.* 1.19), and the senate also used the centuriate assembly after Caesar's death (Appian, *B.C.* 3.30). See Ludwig Lange, *Römische Alterthümer* 2 (3d ed., Berlin, 1879) 605 ff.

[59] A provision of the *leges Aelia et Fufia* passed about 150 to regulate *obnuntiatio* (see n. 22 to chap. iv, below) was that no law might be proposed in the *trinum nundinum* between the announcement of the *comitia* and the formal election. Cf. Cic. *Sest.* 56; *Schol. Bob.* p. 148 Stangl. On suspensions from these laws see Cic. *Att.* 1.16.13; 4.16.5. Cicero himself may have been freed from them in 63 to propose his law on *ambitus.* See *Vatin.* 37. Cf. Lange, *op. cit.* 3.245. Certainly C. Piso received a dispensation when he proposed his law on *ambitus* in 67. C. Cornelius, tribune of that year, was apparently attacking such senatorial dispensation from the laws in one of his bills. See Ascon. *In Cornel.* p. 58 C. I was mistaken in my interpretation of the evidence, *CPh* 36 (1941) 129, n. 69.

[60] That is, *inter trinum nundinum.* On the period indicated by this phrase see Mommsen, *op. cit.* 3.375 f.; Kroll s.v. "Nundinae," *RE.*

[61] The *lex Caecilia Didia* of 98 (see Lange, *op. cit.*, 3d ed., 2.471) required an announcement *ante trinum nundinum* for proposals of laws as well as for elections. The general view is that this law was of advantage to the nobles since tribunes would have had to give warning before bringing in popular bills. But it may have worked also against the nobles, who could not, without due notice, take advantage of the presence of Italians immediately after the elections to propose laws.

[62] Appian, *B.C.* 1.10–14 and 29–32. These incidents occurred before the passage of the *lex Didia Caecilia*.

[63] Cic. *Sest.* 109. Omitto eas <leges> quae ferunter ita vix ut quini et ii ex aliena tribu qui suffragium ferant reperiantur. See Mommsen, *op. cit.* 3.408.

[64] See n. 59.

[65] For full citation of the evidence see Gelzer s.v. "Tullius" (29) *RE* 913 ff.

[66] *Leg.* 3.45; *Sest.* 53: Lex erat lata vastato ac relicto foro et sicariis servisque tradito. See the orations of 57–56, *passim*.

[67] *Sest.* 77.

[68] *Leg.* 3.44–45, Keyes' translation, Loeb text. Cicero continues: Sed visum est et vobis et clarissimis viris melius de quo servi et latrones scivisse *se* aliquid dicerent de hoc eodem cunctam Italiam quid sentiret ostendere. L. Aurelius Cotta, the *consularis* who had expressed himself on Clodius' law, held that law invalid because it was passed by armed slaves and because the centuriate assembly alone could vote on a *privilegium*. The latter argument may have provided the pretext for calling the centuries to pass on Cicero's restoration. Cf. also *Sest.* 65 and 73.

[69] See Cic. *Post red. ad sen.* 24–25, 29, 31 and many other passages of the orations of the next two years.

[70] *Dom.* 90: cum denique homines in campum non tabernis sed municipiis clausis venerant. The great crowd at Rome was, according to Clodius, responsible for the shortage of grain which ensued.

[71] *Pis.* 3 (see n. 47 above); *post red. ad sen.* 27: eaedem centuriae quae me consulem fecerant. See the letters of commendation for business interests of Volaterrae and Atella, two municipalities which had aided Cicero in his *honores* and his *labores*, *Fam.* 13.4.1; 13.7.4. For the repeated references to the support that *Italia cuncta, Italia tota,* gave to Cicero see Merguet's *Lexikon* to the orations s.v. *cunctus* and *totus*. Before the attack on him began, Cicero was confident that all Italy would rally to his aid. See *ad Q. Fr.* 1.2.16 (end of 59): Si diem nobis dixerit tota Italia concurret. According to *Sest.* 26 a throng from all Italy did come, but according to Cicero's accounts of the voting, his supporters seem not to have been in the assembly. Clodius' gangs presumably kept them out.

[72] There has geen general recognition of the influence of the tribal assembly in the late republic, but, as far as I know, there has been no attempt to analyze the difference of the role of urban plebs and Italians in the centuries and the

tribes. Yet my results are implicit in Last's brief discussion, *CAH* 9.8–9, 91, where he points out that the rural tribesmen resident in Rome had special influence on legislation rather than on elections.

[73] There is no information about the sites of tribal headquarters in Rome, but expressions like *prandia tributim data* and *libellos circum tribum missos* (Suet. *Iul.* 41) indicate their existence. From *Murena* 72, *spectacula sunt tributim data et ad prandium vulgo vocati,* one would conclude that tribal headquarters had enough space for shows and banquets. One of the rural tribes, the Pollia, possessed a tribal burial site outside the Porta Salaria. Cf. *CIL* 6.33992–6 (*ILS* 6054–5). The regular officers of the tribes were *curatores,* possibly chosen from the *tribuni aerarii,* who in the late republic seem to have been tribesmen of high census rating.

[74] See Mommsen, *op. cit.* 3.196–197.

[75] Cic. *Mur.* 73: Quid statuent in viros primarios qui in circo totas tabernas tribulium causa compararunt? On one occasion, when Cicero was in Arpinum during the Ludi Romani, he assured his brother that Philotimus (freedman of Cicero's wife, Terentia) was looking out for their *tribules.* See *ad Q. Fr.* 3.1.1.

[76] Domitius, who, as his offers of gifts to his soldiers at Corfinium show, was one of the richest men of Rome, supported Cicero for the consulship (*Att.* 1.1.3–4) while Caesar canvassed for Catiline. Another prominent man in the Fabia was P. Scipio Nasica (after his adoption, Q. Metellus Scipio). For the tribes of Domitius and Scipio see Cael. apud Cic. *Fam.* 8.8.5–6.

[77] See Q. Cicero, *Comm. Pet.* 17; Cic. *Mur.* 69; *Vatin.* 39; *Planc.* 43; *Har. resp.* 56.

[78] *Op. cit.* 370 ff. and *passim.* As Last points out, *AJPh* 58.471 f., some of Marsh's comments on the various types of "machines" imply party caucuses such as certainly did not exist at Rome.

[79] Thus M. Aemilius Scaurus, son of the *princeps senatus* of the Marian period, is described as having a good chance for the consulship because *est pondus apud rusticos in patris memoria* (Cic. *Att.* 4.16.6).

[80] Cicero asserts that not Murena but his friends gave shows and meals to the tribes (*Mur.* 72). See also Q. Cicero, *Comm. Pet.* 44.

[81] *Planc.* 48. On Curio's assistance in obtaining the augurate for Mark Antony see *Phil.* 2.4: Poteras autem eo tempore auguratum petere, cum in Italia Curio non esset, aut tum, cum es factus, unam tribum sine Curione ferre potuisses?

[82] *Planc.* 45. Cf. Q. Cicero, *Comm. Pet.* 18: Nam per hos annos homines ambitiosi vehementer omni studio atque opera elaborant ut possint a tribulibus suis ea quae petierint impetrare. See also the phrase *ad conficiendas centurias* in 18. The reference there seems to be to the centuries of *equites equo publico.* When the consular elections are spoken of, *tribus* and *centuria* are used almost indiscriminately. The *centuria* is *unius tribus pars.* Cf. Cic. *Planc.* 49.

[83] *Comm. Pet.* 53: Nec tamen in petendo res publica capessenda est neque in senatu neque in contione. Occasionally a program was announced. Thus Pompey before his election to the consulship of 70 promised to restore the full powers of the tribunate. See Appian, *B.C.* 1.121; cf. Pseudo-Ascon. on *Verr.* I.45, p. 220 Stangl.

[84] See Mommsen, *op. cit.*, 3d ed., 1.197; 3.392. In 67, tribunes forced the consul Piso to state in a public meeting whether he would announce the candidacy of M. Lollius Palicanus, an adherent of Pompey, and Piso declared that he would not do so. Cf. Val. Max. 3.8.3. The presiding magistrate had the privilege of holding a *contio* before the election, but he does not seem usually to have done so. See, however, Livy 10.21.11–15 and the accounts of speeches (n. 40) after the *praerogativa* had voted. These instances all come from times of peril. It is not unlikely that in 52, a period of revolution, the *interrex* who held the *comitia* communicated to the people the recommendation of the senate that Pompey be made sole consul.

[85] *Mur.* 43–46; cf. Q. Cicero, *Comm. Pet.* 56.

[86] The magistrates, especially the consuls and the tribunes, are described as men *excellenti gratia ad conficiendas centurias*. See n. 82 above. Cf. *Fam.* 11.16.3 (a request to Decimus Brutus for support of a candidate for the praetorship in 43): Quoniam equitum centurias tenes in quis regnas, mitte ad Lupam nostrum ut is nobis eas centurias conficiat.

[87] *Comm. Pet.* 5.

[88] *Comm. Pet.* 51.

[89] Suet. *Iul.* 23.2: In magno negotio habuit obligare semper annuos magistratus et e petitoribus non alios adiuvare aut ad honorem pati pervenire quam qui sibi recepissent propugnaturos absentiam suam.

[90] *Ad Q. Fr.* 3.1.10; 3.8.3; cf. 3.2.3 on Caesar's influence.

[91] Suet. *Iul.* 41.

[92] *ILS* 8205–8207.

[93] *ILS* 6398–6438. See Frank Frost Abbott's delightful essay, "Municipal Politics in Pompeii," *Society and Politics in Ancient Rome* (New York, 1909) 3–21.

[94] *Att.* 1.1.1. Cicero had not held a province after his praetorship and therefore was on hand to start the campaign long in advance. Sometimes expraetors returned from their provinces just in time to present themselves *ante trinum nundinum* before the election. Caesar did so in 60, and M. Aemilius Scaurus in 54 (Ascon., p. 19 C).

[95] Cic. *Planc.* 9–16; *Mur. passim.* Compare Cicero's frequent use of the phrase *supplicare populo*. He chides Antony for asking (*rogare*) rather than begging (*petere*) votes for the consulship (*Phil.* 2.76). On Cicero's activity for Plancius see *Planc.* 24: Appellavi populum tributim, summisi me et supplicavi. Cato is said to have been defeated for the consulship because he had the senate pass a decree forbidding friends to canvass for a candidate and then

himself lived up to the decree, refusing to have his friends canvass for him. Cf. Plut. *Cato min.* 49.

⁹⁶ Often, in campaigns for the consulship, only three candidates seem to have been in the running at the end. That was true of the contests for 94 (*Comm. Pet.* 11), 63 (Cicero, C. Antonius, and Catiline), 59 (Caesar, Lucceius, and Bibulus), and 51 (Cato, M. Marcellus, and Servius Sulpicius Rufus).

⁹⁷ Cic. *Verr.* I.22. On laws concerning *ambitus,* a term which covered all manner of malpractices, see Mommsen, *Strafrecht* 865 ff.

⁹⁸ Ascon. pp. 75–76 C; on the *divisores* see Mommsen, *Staatsrecht* 3.196; Liebenam s.v. "Divisor," *RE.*

⁹⁹ Cic. *Att.* 1.16.12; 1.18.3; cf. Plut. *Pomp.* 44.

¹⁰⁰ Suet. *Iul.* 19.

¹⁰¹ The crime of *sodalicium,* attacked by the *lex Licinia de sodaliciis,* concerned clubs that were said to have been formed within the tribes and organized into *decuriae,* a characteristic feature of Roman associations (Cic. *Planc.* 45, 47). By means of these clubs, bribes were distributed on a large scale throughout the tribes. Cf. Cic. *Cael.* 16, *infinito ambitu; Planc., passim; Schol. Bob.* p. 152 Stangl. See Mommsen, *De Collegiis et Sodaliciis Romanorum* 32 ff.; *Strafrecht* 873. De Robertis, *op. cit.* (n. 37 to chap. ii, above) 110 ff., has made what seems to me a valid distinction between the decree of the senate of February 56 and Crassus' law. My explanation is based in part on his discussion. The senatorial decree (*ad Q. Fr.* 2.3.5) provided *ut sodalitates decuriatique discederent lexque de iis ferretur, ut qui non discessissent ea poena quae est de vi tenerentur.* The decree, to be followed by a law, apparently attempted to dissolve the guilds in the urban tribes which Clodius used for his terrorizing bands. The law of Crassus was designed to curb the formation of clubs mainly within the rural tribes, where the voters were organized for elections and kept in line by tribes for the elections. How ineffective the law was in accomplishing the desired purpose is shown by the fact that Plancius, who as the son of a prominent publican had ties with Crassus, was prosecuted under it by Iuventius, a strong optimate. Cicero's defense was that there was no organization within the tribes. On Crassus' law as an attempt to check the power of the *optimates* in the elections see Mommsen, *History of Rome* 5.136–138. Cf. chap. vii, esp. n. 52.

¹⁰² On the *coitio* see Gelzer, *Nobilität* 102 f. The *lex de sodaliciis* seems also to have been concerned with *coitiones.*

¹⁰³ Cic. *Planc.* 53.

¹⁰⁴ See Cic. *Mur.* 70–73, with the reference there to a *lex Fabia* (probably of 64 B.C.) which limited the number of *sectatores.* Quintus divides Cicero's own *sectatores* into *voluntarii* and *qui tibi debent* (*Comm. Pet.* 37).

¹⁰⁵ Ascon. p. 20 C.

¹⁰⁶ Plut. *Crass.* 14; *Pomp.* 51; on a later election see *Att.* 4.16.6.

[107] Plut. *Luc.* 5–6; Sall. *Hist.* 1.77 M (line 20); Cic. *Parad.* 40, with Plasberg's emendation, *Rh. Mus.* 53 (1898) 81. The static condition of the voting body under the Sullan constitution, when the suspension of the censorship prevented extensive registration of new voters, may have contributed to Cethegus' power.

[108] On the *custodes* see Cic. *Pis.* 36; *Post red. ad sen.* 28; *Lex Malac. (ILS* 6089) 55. Cf. Mommsen, *Staatsrecht* 3.403, 406; Botsford, *op. cit.* 389 and 466 f.

[109] Pliny, *N.H.* 33.31.

[110] To restrict the power of the *custodes* who electioneered on the *pontes* over which citizens passed from each tribal division to deposit their ballots, Marius as tribune in 119 made the *pontes* narrower. Cf. Plut. *Mar.* 4; Cic. *Leg.* 3.38–39. In the *De Legibus* Cicero disagrees with his brother's objections to the written ballot but maintains that the ballots should be seen by the *optimates:* Habeat sane populus tabellam quasi vindicem libertatis dummodo haec optimo cuique et gravissimo civi ostendatur ultroque offeratur ut in eo sit ipso libertas, in quo populo potestas honeste bonis gratificandi datur. Montesquieu praises this idea of Cicero, *De l'esprit des lois* 2.2.

[111] On the presiding magistrate in the republic see Münzer, *RA* 14 ff. and *passim.* Münzer is inclined to exaggerate his influence. But for our period see Ascon. p. 89 C; Cic. *Leg.* 3.40.

[112] See n. 84 above.

[113] See Tacitus' account of Roman legislation, *Ann.* 3.27.

[114] On the *contio* see Botsford, *op. cit.* 139 ff.

[115] Cic. *Att.* 1.16.11: Illa contionalis hirudo aerari, misera ac ieiuna plebecula.

[116] Val. Max. 6.2.3.

[117] Cic. *Flacc.* 17.

[118] *De Lege Agraria* 2, delivered in January, 63. Another important oration of Cicero delivered from the Rostra was the *De Lege Manilia,* in support of Pompey's command against Mithridates. Pompey was at the time such a popular figure that support of his command was in itself popular.

[119] *Leg. Agr.* 2.15.

[120] *Leg. Agr.* 2.71. In a private letter to Atticus (1.19.4), written a little later, Cicero recognizes the need of cleaning out the urban populace.

[121] Cf. Cic. *Leg.* 3.24: Quod enim est tam desperatum collegium in quo nemo e decem sana mente sit?

[122] Dio 36.30.

[123] Plut. *Pomp.* 47.3, τρόπον τινὰ δημαρχίαν τὴν ὑπατείαν καθιστάς.

[124] See n. 59 above.

[125] Ascon. *In Cornel.* pp. 57–59 C. For the bill finally passed see p. 59: ne quis in senatu legibus solveretur nisi CC adfuissent neve quis, cum solutus esset, intercederet cum de ea re ad populum ferretur.

NOTES TO CHAPTER IV

[1] Polyb. 6.56 (Shuckburgh's translation). There is no other evidence to show that Polybius is right in thinking that belief in punishment in Hades played a role in the Roman state religion. The Roman concern was for the present and future in this world. This is not the view of Professor Benjamin Farrington, *Science and Politics in the Ancient World* (London, 1939); see especially p. 225: "The essential was to foster the belief that the oligarchical nobility were where they were by the will of heaven, and that any effort to dislodge them would be rewarded by condign punishment in this world and the next." Farrington's discussion of Polybius, Scaevola, and Varro is interesting, but he pushes his conclusions too far. See n. 56 below.

[2] Augustin. *C.D.* 4.27. Of Scaevola, Augustine says *expedire igitur existimat falli in religione civitates.* It is possible that this statement is to be attributed not to Quintus Scaevola, consul of 95, but to his father Publius, consul of 133 and also *pontifex maximus.*

[3] Augustin. *C.D.* 4.31 (cf. 27); also Bks. 6 and 7 *passim.* Cf. Dionys. 2.18, from the passage on Romulus' organization of the state, now considered to be based on a monograph of the time of Caesar. See n. 55 to chap. ii, above.

[4] The entire second book of Cicero's *De Divinatione* deals with the subject. See also the discussion of religious laws in *De Legibus* 2.

[5] See G. Wissowa, *Religion and Kultus der Römer* (2d ed., Munich, 1912) 435; for the calendars see 568 ff.

[6] See Kroll s.v. "Nundinae," *RE.* In connection with the effort to keep the voters outside Rome from attending certain assemblies (see chap. iii) it may be noted that the elimination of the *nundinae* from comitial days had a similar effect in an earlier period of the republic. The country people regularly came in on the *nundinae* for the market. Cf. Pliny, *N.H.* 18.13: Nundinis urbem revisitabant et ideo comitia nundinis haberi non licebat ne plebes rustica avocaretur. See Lange, *Röm. Altertümer,* 3d ed., 2.518 ff.

[7] For legislative assemblies the prohibition against submitting laws during the period before and, in effect, immediately after the election (see n. 59 to chap. iii, above) made a further reduction of the number of comitial days.

[8] Censorin. 20.7: Sed horum <pontificum> plerique ob odium vel gratiam quo quis magistratu citius abiret diutius*ve* fungeretur aut publici redemptor ex anni magnitudine in lucro damnove esset, plus minusve ex libidine intercalando rem sibi ad corrigendum mandatum ultro ... depravarunt. Cf. Macrob. 1.14.1; Solin. 1.43; Ammian. 26.1.12. See J. Marquardt, *Römische Staatsverwaltung* 3 (2d ed., Berlin, 1885) 286 f. Cf. also Cic. *Leg.* 2.29.

[9] Dio 40.62.1; cf. Cael. apud Cic. *Fam.* 8.6.5.

[10] *Ad Q. Fr.* 2.4.4–5. See 2.4.6 for opposition to Lentulus from the tribune C. Cato at a public meeting: C. Cato contioniatus est comitia haberi non siturum si sibi cum populo dies agendi essent exempti.

[11] On reasons for repeating ceremonies see Cic. *Har. resp.* 23. On repetitions in the time of Plautus see my discussion, *TAPhA* 68 (1937) 291–296.

[12] *B.G.* 2.35.

[13] Cael. apud Cic. *Fam.* 8.11.1–2; cf. also *Fam.* 2.15.1; 15.11.1.

[14] Plut. *Sulla* 8; App. *B.C.* 1.55 and 59. Cf. Mommsen, *Staatsrecht,* 3d ed., 1.263 n. 6.

[15] The best discussion of the auspices is still that of Mommsen, *op. cit.,* 3d ed., 1.76–116. Botsford's excellent treatment, *The Roman Assemblies* 100–118, is based on Mommsen. S. Weinstock, s.v. "Obnuntiatio," *RE,* has presented some new interpretations, but they are not convincing.

[16] The evidence is fully stated by Mommsen, *op. cit.,* 3d ed., 1.101–106.

[17] Plut. *Cato Min.* 42; *Pomp.* 52; cf. Dio 39.32.1.

[18] Cic. *Phil.* 2.82–84.

[19] For these laws (*leges Aelia et Fufia*) see n. 22 below.

[20] On the requirement that plebeian officers should always be elected see Cic. *Leg.* 3.9, *neve plebem orbam tribunis relinquunto;* Livy 3.55. Cf. Mommsen, *op. cit.,* 3d ed., 2.279 ff.

[21] *Leg.* 3.27, Keyes' translation, Loeb text.

[22] Clodius' law, according to Cicero's doubtless exaggerated statements, invalidated the *leges Aelia et Fufia.* These were apparently two separate laws passed about the middle of the second century (Cic. *Pis.* 10; *Vatin.* 23). They gave both the regular magistrates and the tribunes the right of *obnuntiatio* in the centuriate and the tribal assemblies. (One or both laws contained a section forbidding the presentation of laws in the *trinum nundinum* before the election. See n. 59 to chap. iii, above.) Cicero regards these laws as a protection against demagogic tribunes. Cf. *Pis.* 9: Propugnacula murique tranquilitatis ac otii; *Post red. ad sen.* 11: Legem tribunus plebis tulit ne auspiciis obtemparetur, ne obnuntiare concilio aut comitiis, ne legi intercedere liceret, ut lex Aelia et Fufia ne valeret, quae nostri maiores certissima subsidia rei publicae contra tribunicios furores esse voluerunt. In actual practice the laws seem to have provided advantages for the tribunes as well as for the consuls. Just how Clodius' law affected the provisions of the *lex Aelia et Fufia* we do not know. A. H. Greenidge, *CR* 7 (1893) 158–161, and W. McDonald, *JRS* 19 (1929) 164–179, have attempted to answer the question, and to show that Clodius' law remained in effect, but the results, as Weinstock has pointed out (*JRS* 27 [1937] 215–222), are not conclusive. Weinstock's solution is that Clodius' law was invalidated by the college of augurs, but the two passages he cites in favor of that view (*Dom.* 40; *Har. resp.* 48) seem to me to show that the augurs as a college took no such action. Cicero is referring to a question directed by Clodius in a *contio* to a group of augurs. But to in-

validate a law the senate had to act on the recommendation of the board of augurs to whom the question had been referred by senate or magistrate. If the senate or the augurs had taken any such action Cicero would certainly have told us about it, for it would have supported his argument that Clodius' laws were invalid. On the inconclusiveness of the evidence on the *leges Aelia et Fufia* and on Clodius' law see Mommsen, *op. cit.*, 3d ed., 1.111 ff.

[23] Cic. *Sest.* 129.

[24] Cic. *Att.* 4.3.4.

[25] The examples are collected by McDonald, *op. cit.*

[26] Perhaps on that account Q. Metellus Scipio (formerly known as P. Scipio Nasica) served as *interrex* in that year. He was a patrician by birth but had been adopted into a plebeian family and had held the tribunate of the plebs in 59. For the *tessera* that records him as *interrex* see Münzer, *Hermes* 71 (1936) 222 ff.

[27] *Leg.* 2.31, Keyes' translation, Loeb text.

[28] For the evidence see Münzer, s.v. "Sempronius" (53) *RE* 1408–1409, and Pease's notes (*op. cit.* in n. 39 to chap. iii, above) on Cic. *Div.* 1.33 and 2.74–75. Cf. Degrassi, *Inscriptiones Italiae* 13 (Rome, 1947) p. 462, under 162 B.C.

[29] Cic. *Div.* 1.29, with Pease's note. See A. D. Simpson, *TAPhA* 69 (1938) 532–541.

[30] Dio 39.15.2; see Meyer, *Caesars Monarchie*, 2d ed., 126 ff.; Tyrrell and Purser, *The Correspondence of Cicero*, 2, 2d ed., xxix–l.

[31] *Fam.* 1.4.2: *nomen inductum fictae religionis;* cf. 1.7.4: *quemadmodum homines religiosi Sibyllae placere dixerunt.*

[32] *Fam.* 1.7.4–5.

[33] Dio 39.57–63. The abundant evidence in Cicero's letters of 54 for the suits brought against Gabinius is cited by Tyrrell and Purser, *op. cit.*, 2, 2d ed., xliv ff.

[34] Cic. *in Catil.* 3.19 ff.

[35] See n. 22.

[36] See Walter Allen, *TAPhA* 75 (1944) 1–9.

[37] *Har. resp.* 8–9, N. H. Watts' translation, Loeb text. This speech to the senate has been convincingly dated in September, 56, by P. Stein, *Die Senatsitzungen der ciceronischen Zeit* (Dissertation, Münster, 1930) 97–100 and by Gelzer, *Klio* 30 (1937) 1 ff. With the *de domo sua ad pontifices* this oration presents the fullest evidence for the religious strife between Cicero and Clodius. See also the two orations in which Cicero thanked senate and people for his restoration, and the *Pro Sestio,* the *In Vatinium,* and the *In Pisonem.* Other details of the struggle could have been added to my discussion, for instance Clodius' attack on Cicero as *hostis Capitolinus* (*Dom.* 7) and Cicero's attack on Clodius for defiling the temple of Castor by storing arms there. See *Pis.* 11: Arma in templum Castoris, o proditor templorum omnium, vidente te constituebantur ab eo latrone cui templum illud fuit te consule arx civium perditorum ... bustum legum omnium ac religionum.

[38] Until shortly before the Gracchi it was customary for the *pontifex maximus* to remain in Italy because of his sacred duties. Cf. Mommsen, *op. cit.,* 3d ed., 1.491 n. 2; on the career of P. Crassus Mucianus, who broke the tradition, see Münzer, *RA* 261 ff. Caesar's immediate predecessor, Q. Metellus Pius, was absent for years in Spain while he was *pontifex maximus.*

[39] The pontifices by this time had lost much of the power they had once possessed in civil law. See Marquardt, *op. cit.,* 2d ed., 3.317 ff.

[40] See Mommsen, *op. cit.,* 3d ed., 2.18 ff.

[41] Cf. Münzer, *RA* 414, and *passim.*

[42] Cic. *Fam.* 3.10.9.

[43] Documentation for this discussion will be found in my paper, "Caesar's Colleagues in the Pontifical College," *AJPh* 63 (1942) 385–412. See also "The Election of the Pontifex Maximus in the Late Republic," *CPh* 37 (1942) 421–424, and, for Caesar's priesthoods, *CPh* 36 (1941) 113 ff.

[44] Dio 39.17. Since two members of the same *gens* could not hold membership in the augurate, Lentulus, to obtain the priesthood for his son, had him adopted by the Manlii Torquati.

[45] Cic. *Att.* 2.5.2.

[46] Cic. *Ad Brut.* 1.5.3.

[47] See n. 60 to chap. i.

[48] The name, given simply as M. Crassus (*Har. resp.* 12), might of course be that of the elder Crassus, but the man in question had acquired the office shortly before 57 B.C., a year or two before Crassus' younger son, Publius, was elected to the augurate. See *AJPh* 63.393 f. The elder Crassus, a man of sufficient prestige to win the censorship, would almost certainly have been elected to a priesthood before that time. I suggest that he may have been a member of the *quindecimviri sacris faciundis.* That might account for his activity, through his tribune C. Cato, in making known the Sibylline oracle that concerned the Egyptian king in 56. If Crassus belonged to that priesthood, the "triumvirate" was made up of members of the three chief colleges.

[49] See *AJPh* 63.409 n. 83. Cf. C. Bardt, *Die Priester der vier grossen Collegien aus römisch-republikanischer Zeit* (Berlin, 1871). Other members of the augurate at this period were L. Julius Caesar, consul of 64, M. Valerius Messalla, a *praetorius,* and probably Q. Mucius Scaevola, tribune of the plebs in 54, member of a house famous for its priesthoods. The son of P. Lentulus Spinther was elected in this year (see n. 44 above), and Crassus' younger son Publius was probably chosen in 56 to succeed L. Lucullus. Cicero succeeded Publius Crassus in 53.

[50] Cato was chosen a member before he had held any public office. See Plut. *Cato Min.* 4. Other members were L. Aurelius Cotta, consul of 65, and L. Manlius Torquatus, son of the consul of 65.

[51] Altheim, *A History of Roman Religion,* translated by Harold Mattingly (New York, 1937) 331.

[52] P. Vatinius, tribune of 59, had ambitions for the place in the augurate left vacant by the death of Q. Metellus Celer in that year, though he seems not actually to have presented himself. Cf. Cic. *ad Att.* 2.9.2 and the frequent references in the letters of the period to the contest for the augurate. The "triumvirs" apparently did not support Vatinius. See *Vatin.* 19–21. Later, perhaps about the time he became consul (47), Vatinius was elected to this priesthood. C. Lucilius Hirrus, a cousin of Pompey, was an unsuccessful competitor of Cicero for the augurate in 53. Neither of these men belonged to a consular family.

[53] Among men known to have obtained a priesthood after the *lex Labiena* the only staunch optimate was L. Domitius Ahenobarbus, elected to the pontificate in the period 56–51 (see *AJPh* 63.405) and defeated for the augurate in 50. Elections of priests usually took place between the consular and the pratetorian *comitia,* at a time when Italians were in Rome. They were thus not decided by the urban plebs alone, but, as was pointed out in chapter iii, the nobles were less powerful with the tribes than with the centuries.

[54] Cic. *Vatin.* 14.

[55] Cic. *Dom.* 39–40; *Har. resp.* 48. See n. 22 above.

[56] *Op. cit.* 172 ff. Farrington's Marxist interpretation is that the Epicureans championed the common man against the state religion both of the Greek cities and of Rome. Of the passages he cites from Lucretius, only one seems to me to have specific bearing on the Roman state religion. After giving a rational interpretation of lightning, Lucretius says (6.379–382):

> Hoc est igniferi naturam fulminis ipsam
> perspicere et qua vi faciat rem quamque videre,
> non Tyrrhena retro volventem carmina frustra
> indicia occultae divum perquirere mentis.

Lucretius may have had in mind the decrees of the *haruspices* who were consulted on lightning in 65 and 56.

[57] See Momigliano's review of Farrington (*JRS* 31 [1941] 151 ff.) for some interesting comments on the Epicureans in politics.

NOTES TO CHAPTER V

THE CRIMINAL COURTS AND THE RISE OF A NEW MAN

(Pages 98–118)

[1] Only two cases are known to have been brought to the people in the years 70–50. M. Lucullus was tried and acquitted by the tribal assembly in 66 on a charge of illegal acts committed under Sulla. C. Rabirius, condemned by special judges for *perduellio* in 63 (see chap. vi), appealed to the *comitia centuriata,* but the assembly was dissolved before the voting took place. Tribunes and aediles still threatened to bring men to trial before the people, but the

threats were not carried out. For the evidence see Botsford, *The Roman Assemblies* 322 ff.

[2] See Harriet Dale Johnson, *The Roman Tribunal* (Baltimore, 1927); A. H. Greenidge, *The Legal Procedure of Cicero's Time* (Oxford, 1901) 456 ff.

[3] Cic. *Brut.* 192: Ego vero . . . in eis etiam causis in quibus omnis res nobis cum iudicibus est, non cum populo, tamen si a corona relictus sim, non queam dicere. Cf. also 289–290; *N.D.* 2.1; *Tusc.* 1.10; Catullus 53.

[4] Cic. *Dom.* 41. See Meyer, *Caesars Monarchie,* 2d ed., 73 n. 3.

[5] *Verr.* II.2.181.

[6] *Off.* 2.50: Non est saepe faciendum nec umquam nisi rei publicae causa . . . aut ulciscendi . . . aut patrocinii ut nos pro Siculis . . . Semel igitur aut non saepe certe. In the discussion of Cicero's prosecution of Verres, I am constantly under obligation to Gelzer's biography of Cicero, s.v. "Tullius" (29) *RE* 839 ff., and to Richard Heinze's "Ciceros politische Anfänge," *Sitzber. säch. Akad.,* phil.-hist. Kl. 27 (1909) 947–1010 (reprinted in Heinze, *Vom Geist des Römertums* [Leipzig and Berlin, 1938] 59 ff. My references are to the original publication). See also T. Petersson, *Cicero: A Biography* (Berkeley, 1920) 123–170, and F. H. Cowles, *Gaius Verres* (Ithaca, 1917).

[7] *Div. in Caec.* 18; cf. *Verr.* II.5.126–127. Except where otherwise noted, the translations are from the excellent Loeb version of L. H. G. Greenwood. I take the liberty of altering "judges" to "jurors" as a translation of *iudices.*

[8] *Verr.* II.2.2–5.

[9] *Verr.* II.4.81–82.

[10] Cicero was not, as is generally believed, curule aedile; he held the plebeian aedileship. See my discussion, *AJPh* 60 (1939) 194–202.

[11] *Div. in Caec.* 44.

[12] *Verr.* I.44–45.

[13] *Verr.* I.16 ff.

[14] *Verr.* I.44–45; II.2.102 and 113; II.3.45; II.5.5 and 153.

[15] 36.43.5: τοὺς γοῦν βελτίους πρότερον προαιρεῖσθαι λέγων, καὶ διὰ τοῦτο καὶ ἀγορανομῆσαι μᾶλλον ἢ δημαρχῆσαι ἐθελήσας, τότε πρὸς τοὺς συρφετώδεις μετέστη.

[16] *Verr.* I.2. Compare the appeal to Glabrio, the praetor in charge, I.51.

[17] *Verr.* I.46–49.

[18] *Verr.* I.44.

[19] *Verr.* I.49.

[20] *Verr.* II.1.23.

[21] *Verr.* I.47.

[22] *Verr.* II.1.13–14; II.5.173.

[23] See *Verr.* II.1.135 and the frequent references, especially in II.4, to the ancestor of the Marcelli, the conqueror of Syracuse. On Cotta see note 44 below. For other moderates see the list of upright jurors who would be disqualified if the case were postponed to the next year (*Verr.* I.29–30).

[24] As supporters of the knights and the *publicani* Cicero and Crassus had much in common. In the letter of reconciliation which Cicero wrote to Crassus in 54 he spoke of *vetus nostra necessitudo* (*Fam.* 5.8.1). The two men had been enemies for at least a decade before late 55, but nevertheless, because of interest in the knights, they coöperated in 61–60 in seeking to have the senate revise the publicans' contracts in Asia (*Att.* 1.17.9). Cicero had apparently broken with Crassus when in 66, at the insistence of the knights of Asia (*Manil.* 4), he decided to support Pompey's command against Mithridates. He is probably referring to Crassus when he speaks of the enmity his support of Pompey has aroused (*Manil.* 71: *simultates partim obscuras, partim apertas*). On Crassus as a middle-of-the-road man see nn. 10 and 11 to chap. vi, below. The only reference to Crassus in the *Verrines* is in II.5.5: *fortissimi viri virtute consilioque.* In this passage Crassus and Pompey are given joint credit for settling the gladiatorial war.

[25] Heinze, *op. cit., passim,* protested against the usual view that Cicero was a member of the "popular party" until his candidacy for the consulship. Gelzer, *op. cit.* 843 ff., accepts Heinze's view on Cicero's associations at the time, though he objects to Heinze's conception of parties. Gelzer is in general less favorable than Heinze in judging Cicero. Neither scholar suggests a connection between Cicero and Crassus.

[26] *Verr.* II.5.180 (my translation); cf. *Leg. Agr.* 2.100; *Att.* 4.8A.2.

[27] *Verr.* II.5.182. Cf. Heinze, *op. cit.* 978.

[28] *Verr.* II.2.64.

[29] See Gelzer, *op. cit.* 844 ff.

[30] *Verr.* I.19. The friend was C. Scribonius Curio the elder, consul of 76. Like his son, he was an uncertain quantity in politics. He was allied with Hortensius and the Metelli in 70 and with Pompey in 66; later he was an ally of Clodius, but he broke with Clodius and worked with the *optimates* against Caesar in 60 and succeeding years.

[31] *Verr.* I.27.

[32] *Verr.* I.24–25.

[33] *Verr.* I.8.

[34] *Verr.* I.53–54.

[35] *Verr.* I.55.

[36] Cf. *Verr.* II.3.10–11. It is noteworthy that in the rather technical discussion of this subject there are far fewer appeals to public opinion than there are in other portions of the *Actio Secunda*. I am not convinced by the arguments of Carsten Hoeg that the *Actio Secunda* was actually delivered. See *Dragma Martino P. Nilsson dedicatum* (Lund, 1939) 264 ff. Cf. Gelzer, *Abh. preuss. Ak. Wiss.,* phil.-hist. Kl. 1943, 1.24 n. 3.

[37] *Verr.* II.1.151–153. For Cicero's attitude toward popular demagogues see Gelzer, s.v. "Tullius" (29) *RE* 849.

[38] Quintil. 6.3.98; cf. Plut. *Cic.* 7.

[39] Cic. *Orat.* 129; Pseudo-Ascon. p. 205 Stangl.

[40] *Verr.* II.5.163.

[41] *Cic.* 8.

[42] On Catulus see particularly *Verr.* I.44 and the passages in which Cicero tries to rouse Catulus by describing Verres' theft of a candelabrum intended for the Capitolium which Catulus was restoring (II.4.69–71, cf. 82).

[43] *Op. cit.* 847.

[44] There were various factors which led to the compromise. Some senators had felt the onus of jury service and were apparently glad to be relieved of it. See *Verr.* II.1.22. At the same time the number of knights with residence in Rome had been diminished by Sulla's proscriptions and by the election of many of the remaining knights to the senate. There may not have been a sufficiently large body of knights residing in Rome to provide the number of jurors needed for the lists. That may explain the inclusion of the *tribuni aerarii,* tribal representatives who were apparently just below the knights in census rating (see n. 13 to chap. iii, above). The *tribuni aerarii* were regarded practically as members of the equestrian order. T. Rice Holmes' suggestion, *The Roman Republic* 1.165, that Crassus was the moving spirit in the compromise, seems to me likely. Pompey is usually credited with sponsorship of this law, but there is no ancient evidence to support this view. Pompey would probably have used a tribune to propose the law if he had been responsible for it. A Ciceronian scholiast (*Schol. Bob.* p. 328 Stangl) says that Cotta coöperated with the tribune Quinctius or with Palicanus, the latter of whom was an adherent of Pompey. But the report is obviously unreliable, for neither man was tribune in 70. It is clear from Cicero's comments on this law (*Verr.* II.2.174; II.3.223–224; II.5.177–178) that he had no part in sponsoring it, but he may nevertheless have welcomed it as a compromise. See Heinze, *op. cit.* 979.

[45] See Hitzig s.v. "Calumnia," *RE;* E. Levy, *Zeitschr. d. Sav. Stift.,* Roman. Abt. 53 (1933) 151 ff. I have had the advantage of a discussion of this subject with Professor Max Radin.

[46] Aristotle, *Pol.* 1268a.

[47] *Ibid.* 1268b (see Newman's note *ad loc.*): περὶ δὲ τοῦ τοῖς εὑρίσκουσί τι τῇ πόλει συμφέρον ὡς δεῖ γίνεσθαί τινα τιμήν, οὐκ ἔστιν ἀσφαλὲς τὸ νομοθετεῖν, ἀλλ' εὐόφθαλμον ἀκοῦσαι μόνον· ἔχει γὰρ συκοφαντίας καὶ κινήσεις, ἂν τύχῃ, πολιτείας.

[48] *Strafrecht* 504–511; cf. 253; 820 n. 2.; *Staatsrecht* 3.642, 971. In the first passage there are full citations from the jurists, most of which concern financial rewards. See also Ruggiero s.v. "Delator," *Diz. Epig.*

[49] *Lex Repetundarum, CIL* 1.2, 2d ed., 583, 76–77 and 83 ff. For mention of men who received such rewards (perhaps most common in extortion cases, in which noncitizens were apt to have an important role) see Cic. *Balb.* 53.

[50] *Lex Ursonensis, ILS* 6087.124. Modestinus, *Digesta* 48.14, says that rewards of this type still apply to the municipalities but not to the city where

the *princeps* has the choice of magistrates. Qua lege damnatus si alium convicerit in integrum restituitur, non tamen pecuniam recipit.

[51] *Balb.* 57: Obiectum est etiam quod in tribum Clustuminam pervenerit; quod hic adsecutus est legis de ambitu praemio minus invidioso quam qui legum praemiis praetoriam sententiam et praetextam togam consequuntur. Pompey's law on *ambitus* in 52 provided for *praemia*. See Appian *B.C.* 2.24: Μέμμιος δὲ ἁλοὺς ἐπὶ δεκασμῷ, τοῦ νόμου τοῦ Πομπηίου διδόντος αὐτῷ φήναντι ἕτερον ἀφεῖσθαι τῆς καταδίκης, τὸν πενθερὸν τοῦ Πομπηίου Λεύκιον Σκιπίωνα προεκαλέσατο ἐς ὁμοίαν δεκασμοῦ δίκην. Cf. Ascon. *In Milon.* p. 54 C (of the condemnation of Milo *in absentia* for *ambitus*). Illa quoque lege accusator fuit eius Appius Claudius et cum ei praemium lege daretur, negavit se eo uti. (Appius was a nephew of the consul of 54; as a representative of an old patrician house, he evidently scorned the reward.) Next, as Asconius goes on to say, Milo was found guilty of *sodalicium:* accusante P. Fulvio Nerato cui e lege praemium datum est. There were also provisions for rewards in the *lex Pedia* which provided for the prosecution of Caesar's murderers. Cf. Dio 46.49: συχνοὶ δὲ καὶ ὑπὸ τῶν ἄθλων προσαναπειθόμενοι κατηγόρουν· χρήματά τε γὰρ ἐκ τῆς τοῦ ἁλόντος οὐσίας καὶ τὴν τιμὴν τήν τε ἀρχὴν τὴν ἐκείνου, εἴ τινα ἄρα ἔχων ἦν, τό τε μηκέτι μήτ' αὐτὸν μήτε τοὺς υἱεῖς τούς τε ἐγγόνους αὐτοῦ στρατεύεσθαι ἐλάμβανον.

[52] Dio 36.40.3–4.

[53] Cic. *Sulla* 50: Honos ad patrem, insignia honoris ad te delata sunt. Tu ornatus exuviis huius venis ad eum lacerandum quem interemisti, ego iacentem et spoliatum defendo et protego. Münzer, s.v. "Manlius" (80) *RE* 1203, misunderstands the passage. The young Manlius Torquatus was apparently not yet in the senate, for he did not hold the praetorship until 49. The passage may therefore indicate that even a man not yet in the senate could secure senatorial *ornamenta* from such an accusation.

[54] He planned to accuse Aulus Gabinius in 54. See Cic. *Att.* 4.18.3; *ad Q. Fr.* 3.2.2.

[55] See Cic. *Cluent.* 98 and Quintil. 11.1.79. Et ambitus quidam damnati reciperandae dignitatis gratia reos eiusdem criminis detulerunt. See n. 50 above.

[56] Acquisition under this method of the *insignia* of a man of higher rank provides republican precedent for the frequent bestowal under the empire of the *ornamenta* of public office. Such *ornamenta,* as well as financial rewards, were sometimes given to the *delatores* of the empire. Thus under Tiberius the senators who accused Libo Drusus, a *praetorius,* received *praeturae extra ordinem* (Tac. *Ann.* 2.32).

[57] *Verr.* II.1.21 (my translation).

[58] *Verr.* II.5.173.

[59] *Rosc. Am.* 8: ut spoliis ex hoc iudicio ornati auctique discedant. The *spolia* in this case consisted of Roscius' property.

[60] *Rosc. Am.* 83.

[61] Cf. Cic. *Brut.* 317–324. See the lively account of Cicero's rise in H. J. Haskell, *This Was Cicero* (New York, 1942) 139 ff.

[62] Cicero accused T. Munatius Plancus Bursa in late 52 or early 51. See chap. vii above.

[63] *Comm. Pet.* 2; cf. 38 and *passim*.

[64] Cic. *Cluent.* 144, 157 ff.

[65] See n. 47 to chap. vi, below.

[66] On this question see Gelzer, *op. cit.* 858.

[67] Ascon. *in Cornel.* p. 60 f. C. See n. 3 to chap. vi, below. Asconius expresses admiration for the skill with which Cicero avoided doing violence to the *dignitas* of his eminent opponents. Note also the praise of Lucullus in the *De Lege Manilia*.

[68] *Att.* 1.2.1.

[69] In later years Cicero shamelessly charged that Catiline was acquitted because Clodius was bribed. See *Har. resp.* 42; *Pis.* 23.

NOTES TO CHAPTER VI

CATO AND THE "POPULARES"

(Pages 119–139)

[1] In chapters vi, vii, and viii no attempt is made to give full citation of sources. The material is available in the documented histories of E. Meyer, T. Rice Holmes, and Carcopino, and in the biographical article in the *Real-Encyclopädie*. For Pompey and Cato see Drumann-Groebe, *Geschichte Roms* 4.332 ff.; 5.164 ff. Syme's *Roman Revolution* has much valuable prosopographical material.

[2] Cicero never refers to the group as a *factio* or a club. Usually he refers to the men in the coalition as *homines nobiles* or as *boni* or *optimates*. Sallust calls them *factio* or *factio nobilitatis* or simply *pauci*. See nn. 22 and 30 to chap. i, above. Suetonius speaks of them as *optimatium factio* or *conspiratio* (*Iul.* 11 and 15) or simply as *optimates*. Dio usually describes them as οἱ δυνατοί.

[3] On the identity of the leading optimates see the list of men who bore witness against C. Cornelius in 65 (Ascon. p. 60 C; cf. n. 67 to chap. v, above). They were Catulus, Metellus Pius, M. Lucullus, Hortensius, and M'. Aemilius Lepidus, consul of 66. All these men except Lepidus, who was a neutral in the civil war, remained unswerving *optimates* as long as they lived. To this group we can add Lucius Lucullus and the three Metelli in the clique supported by Verres in 70. The most important of the three was Q. Metellus Creticus, consul in 69, who clashed with Pompey in the pirate war. (Two other Metelli, Q. Metellus Celer and Q. Metellus Nepos, related to Pompey's wife Mucia, were

for a time in Pompey's orbit, but after Pompey's divorce of Mucia in late 62 Metellus Celer became a strong optimate.) C. Calpurnius Piso, consul in 67, was one of the most vigorous opponents of Pompey and of Caesar. For further details see *TAPhA* 73 (1942) 1–24.

⁴ Occasionally the senate voted decrees favorable to the chief enemy of the *optimates,* Pompey, but usually for special reasons. See the excellent dissertation (prepared under Münzer's direction) of Paul Stein, *Die Senatsitzungen der ciceronischen Zeit* (Münster, 1930) 1–25. The following decrees are known to have been passed in favor of Pompey in the years 67–60: certain arrangements to carry out the Gabinian law, already passed by the tribes in 67; at least two thanksgivings, one in 63 and one in 62, which undoubtedly served to cut down comitial days in years when Pompey's tribunes were very active (see chap. iv above); presumably a decree in favor of Pompey's triumph, a distinction that could hardly have been refused. Finally, Stein has shown (19 n. 99) that the senate actually did postpone the consular *comitia* in 62 until the arrival of Pompey's candidate, M. Pupius Piso. This man, commended by Pompey to his friends and enemies alike (Dio 37.44.3), had close relations with his kinsman, Pompey's bitter foe, C. Calpurnius Piso, and Piso may have helped secure the postponement. See Cic. *Att.* 1.13.2.

⁵ On Pompey's methods see Vell. 2.29: potentiae quae honoris causa ad eum deferretur, non vi ab eo occuparetur, cupidissimus.

⁶ *Manil.* 62–63.

⁷ See T. R. S. Broughton, *TAPhA* 77 (1946) 40 ff.

⁸ Cic. *Fam.* 5.7.1; see *TAPhA* 73.19.

⁹ See the terrific indictment of Crassus in Cic. *Parad.* 6.46.

¹⁰ On Crassus as a man who wished to be considered a *popularis* see Cic. *in Catil.* 4.10; cf. Ascon. p. 76 C. Crassus may have been responsible for the tribunitial action of 69–68 which removed Asia and Cilicia from Lucullus' command.

¹¹ For Crassus as a middle-of-the-road man who cultivated all groups see Dio 37.56.5, 39.30.2; Plut. *Crass.* 7.

¹² Crassus' elder son Marcus married a daughter of Metellus Creticus, probably about the time (shortly after 67) that Creticus was quarreling with Pompey over the Cretan pirates. Groag, s.v. "Licinius" (58) *RE,* suggests that the son of this marriage, consul in 30, may have been born about 67, but there is no reason why his birth cannot be placed a year or two later. Crassus' younger son Publius married Cornelia, daughter of P. Scipio Nasica, probably a few years later. Crassus and Scipio may have been associated as early as the time of the Catilinarian conspiracy. See Plut. *Cic.* 15.1–2. On Crassus' alliances with the *optimates* see Syme, *JRS* 34 (1944) 96 f.

¹³ Cn. Piso, reportedly an agent of Crassus in the conspiracy planned for early 65, was sent by senatorial decree on a special mission to Spain and was murdered there, allegedly by Pompey's agents. See Sall. *Catil.* 19.1; Ascon. p. 92 C; Dio 36.44.5; *ILS* 875.

[14] In the years immediately after Sulla pardoned him Caesar seems to have coöperated with the Sullan senate; otherwise, members of the high nobility in the college of the pontifices would hardly have chosen him as a member of their priesthood. Cf. *CPh* 36.117 ff. Caesar began after that, probably in 72 or 71, to support the restoration of the tribunate. In speaking from the Rostra for the *lex Plautia,* which restored to the state the exiled adherents of Lepidus, he may have sponsored the first bill presented to the people under the revived power of the tribunes (*ibid.* 121 n. 32). After that he seems to have been consistently *popularis.* Cicero (*Catil.* 4.9 and *Att.* 2.1.6) provides strong evidence for the view of Plutarch and Dio that Caesar persistently cultivated the masses. Against that view see H. Strasburger, *Caesars Eintritt in die Geschichte* (Munich, 1938) *passim.* On Caesar's relations with Pompey in the seventies and sixties see *TAPhA* 73.9 ff. One point not stressed there is Pompey's interest in winning over the old Marians whom Caesar championed. Pompey was generous in his treatment of the adherents of Sertorius who surrendered in Spain and he burned unread correspondence from prominent Romans discovered there. Cf. Plut. *Pomp.* 20.4; *Sert.* 27.1–3; App. *B.C.* 1.115.

[15] See Strasburger, *op. cit.* 107 f.; cf. *TAPhA* 73.16 ff. See also nn. 24 and 30 to chap. vii, below.

[16] See n. 43 to chap. iv, above.

[17] T. Rice Holmes, *The Roman Republic* 1.252, suggests that Metellus was in collusion either with Cicero or with Caesar; since he was still at this time an adherent of Pompey, it is probable that he was acting in the interests of Caesar and Labienus. The problems created by this trial (cf. Meyer, *Caesars Monarchie,* 2d ed., 549 ff.) need not concern us here.

[18] The only tribunitial action with which Catiline is known to have been associated was the veto of a senatorial decree in 64 which recommended a more stringent bribery law. See Ascon. pp. 83 and 86 C.

[19] See Artur Rosenberg, *Geschichte der römischen Republik* (Leipzig, 1921) 91 f. (cf. 64 f. for an indictment of C. Gracchus for advancing the capitalists, and 77 ff. for praise of Sulla, who is said to have saved the state from the capitalists). For praise of Catiline see also E. S. Beesly, *Catiline, Clodius and Tiberius* (London, 1878). For a graphic description of the social conditions that led to Catiline's revolution see R. von Pöhlmann, *Geschichte der sozialen Frage und des Sozialismus in der antiken Welt* (3d ed., Munich, 1925) 2.352 ff., 375 ff., 429 ff., and *passim.*

[20] In the very probable view of E. T. Salmon, *AJPh* 56 (1935) 309 ff., the news of the death of Mithridates led Crassus to abandon support of Catiline for the consulship of 62. The author has some interesting suggestions on the schemes of Crassus at the time.

[21] For Pompey's legates see Drumann-Groebe, *op. cit.* 4.420 ff.

[22] On Catiline and the nobility see Gelzer, s.v. "Sergius" (23) *RE* 1695 and *passim.* One of Catiline's old friends was Catulus, whose father's death

Catiline had avenged by the murder of Marius Gratidianus. See the letter of Catiline to Catulus, Sall. *Catil.* 35.

[23] On Cicero see n. 24 to chap v, above. The careers of the two Curios, father and son, and of C. Memmius, patron of Catullus and Lucretius (see Münzer, s.v. "Scribonius" [10 and 11] and "Memmius" [7] *RE*), are even more extraordinary. P. Servilius Vatia, consul in 78 and *triumphator,* and his son P. Servilius Isauricus, also seem to have shifted in their alignments. Apparently because of enmity with his cousins, the Luculli, the father supported Pompey's command against Mithridates. He was Caesar's competitor for the office of *pontifex maximus* in 63 and doubtless split the opposition in the final vote. After 59 he made up his quarrel with the Luculli and seems to have been counted among the good men. But he got the censorship in 55 when elections were controlled by the triumvirs. He was a neutral in the civil war. His son had once been a close associate of Cato, but joined Caesar in the Civil War and held the consulship in 48. See Münzer, s.v. "Servilius" (67) and (93) *RE*. Even though the *optimates* by their prestige controlled senatorial decisions, the majority of the senators seem to have shifted or compromised. Of the twenty consuls of 69–60 only four, Metellus Creticus (69), his brother Lucius (68) who died in office, his colleague Hortensius, and C. Calpurnius Piso (67), can be put down as consistent *optimates*. Some of the less-known men may have had as "good" a record, but their influence was not great. The strength of Pompey, particularly after the revision of registration carried through by the censors of 70–69 (see nn. 8–10 to chap. iii, above), is indicated by the men he brought to the consulship. They certainly included M. Pupius Piso (61) and L. Afranius (60) and probably also L. Volcatius Tullus (66) and L. Manlius Torquatus (65). Perhaps Q. Marcius Rex (68) was a supporter of Crassus, for he had difficulties both with Lucullus and with Pompey. Certainly P. Autronius and P. Sulla, elected for 65 but removed because of conviction for *ambitus,* were Crassus' men, as was C. Antonius (63) until Cicero won him over. L. Aurelius Cotta (65) and L. Julius Caesar (64) were relatives and in later times associates of Caesar.

[24] From Plutarch, *Cic.* 21, one might conclude that Cicero was not so firm in his actual speech, which he doubtless rewrote before he published it in 60 (*Att.* 2.1.3). See Gelzer, s.v. "Tullius" (29) *RE* 888.

[25] Vell. 2.35.3–4; App. *B.C.* 2.6.

[26] Cic. *Mur.* 62.

[27] Cic. *Fin.* 3.7; Val. Max. 8.7.2; Plut. *Cato Min.* 19.

[28] Dio, 47.6.4, provides some substantiation for Plutarch's doubtless exaggerated account of Cato's quaestorship (*Cato Min.* 16–18). On Cato as the guardian of the treasury see Cic. *Off.* 3.88.

[29] Plut. *Cato Min.* 17.4; Dio 47.6.4. Cato's attack on Sullan profiteers may have brought him into actual coöperation with Caesar, who as *iudex quaestionis* in 64 was passing judgment on the men who profited from the Sullan murders.

[30] Cic. *Mur.* 31: bellum illud omne Mithridaticum cum mulierculis esse gestum.

[31] Plut. *Cato Min.* 28.2.

[32] Plutarch's account, *Cato Min.* 20–21, is probably influenced, as much of the biography is, by the Cato legend. On the support that all the *boni* gave to Cato's candidacy see Cic. *Mur.* 81.

[33] *Att.* 2.1.8.

[34] Plut. *Cato Min.* 26.1; *Caes.* 8.4.

[35] Val. Max. 2.8.1; cf. Cic. *ad Q. Fr.* 3.2.2. The law placed a penalty on false reports of losses both of the enemy and of the Romans, and required commanders to take oath on the numbers reported. Cato may have had Caesar's prospective governorship in mind when he proposed the law. Another law, passed between January of 63 and about July of 62, may have been either proposed by Cato or inspired by him. It required *professio* in person for candidates for office. It affected Pompey's candidate for the consulship of 61, M. Pupius Piso (see n. 4 above), and it would have affected Pompey himself if, as was feared, he had sought a second consulship on his return. It was from this law that Caesar sought exemption in 60 so that he might triumph and also seek the consulship for 59. Cato prevented the exemption from being granted. On the law see Mommsen, *Staatsrecht,* 3d ed., 1.503 n. 3.

[36] Plut. *Cato Min.* 26–28; *Cic.* 23; Dio 37.43; Suet. *Iul.* 16; Cic. *Sest.* 62; *Schol. Bob.* p. 134 Stangl. In his life of Cato, Plutarch says that Cato first faced the armed mob, unarmed himself, and was rescued by Murena; then Metellus, who had withdrawn, saw the space about the tribunal empty and returned without armed followers to pass the law; then his opponents advanced with such confidence that Metellus' men, thinking they were armed, turned and fled. Sallust, *R.P.* 2.2.4, evidently gives the Caesarian version of this story, though the fact has not been recognized: Sin in te ille animus est qui iam a principio nobilitatis factionem disturbavit, plebem Romanam ex gravi servitute in libertatem restituit, in praetura inimicorum arma inermis disiecit etc.

[37] Suet. *Iul.* 16. Plutarch, *Cato Min.* 29.2, says that Cato prevented the senate from suspending Metellus Nepos from office.

[38] Plutarch (*Cato Min.* 30, *Pomp.* 44) is the only source for this story, but we know from Cicero (*Att.* 1.12.3) that Pompey had divorced Mucia shortly before his return. On the credibility of the story see Meyer, *op. cit.* 45 f.

[39] Cic. *Att.* 1.14.2.

[40] One might be tempted to suppose that Cato had secured a more favorable position in the order through a successful prosecution, but Velleius (2.35.3) is against such a view. He says that at the session on the Catilinarians Cato was *paene inter ultimos interrogatus.*

[41] Cic. *Att.* 1.17.9: Atque erat dicturus, ad quem propter diei brevitatem perventum non est, heros ille noster Cato.

[42] On the use of the filibuster see Groebe, *Klio* 5 (1905) 229–235.

[43] *Att.* 1.16.12. Cato made the proposal in association with his brother-in-law L. Domitius Ahenobarbus.

[44] *Op. cit.* (in n. 7 above).

[45] Pompey was not a member of the senate until he became consul in 70. After his consulship, as Meyer notes (*op. cit.* 44, see Plut. *Pomp.* 23), Pompey withdrew from active participation in affairs, making only rare appearances before he went off to his eastern commands.

[46] App. *B.C.* 2.9; Plut. *Luc.* 42.

[47] Cic. *Att.* 1.17.8; 2.1.8.

[48] *Att.* 1.17.9; cf. 1.18.7. See Strasburger, *Concordia Ordinum* (Dissertation, Frankfurt am Main, 1931) 43 ff.

[49] Cic. *Att.* 2.1.6: *cuius nunc venti valde sunt secundi.* I have given the phrase in Strachan-Davidson's rendering. See *Cicero and the Fall of the Roman Republic* (New York, 1894) 188.

[50] This detail is reported only by Suetonius, *Iul.* 19.2.

[51] Suet. *Iul.* 19.2: ne quid ageretur in re publica quod displicuisset ulli e tribus.

[52] *Att.* 2.19.2; 2.20.4.

[53] *Att.* 2.3.3–4; *Prov. cons.* 41. See H. A. Sanders, *Memoirs of the American Academy in Rome* 10 (1932) 55 ff., for the suggestion that the deal was not a matter of general knowledge until after the Council of Luca.

[54] M. Valerius Messalla, consul in 61, described in that year as a "good" man (Cic. *Att.* 1.13.2–3; 1.14.6). He became one of Caesar's land commissioners in 59 (*ILS* 46) and was censor in 55 when the triumvirs controlled the elections. His daughter seems to have married Caesar's nephew Q. Pedius (Pliny, *N.H.* 35.21).

[55] Dio 38.3.1. On the sources for this period see Meyer, *op. cit.* 68 ff.

[56] Dio 38.4.1–3.

[57] Dio 38.7.1–2; Plut. *Cato Min.* 32; Appian, *B.C.* 2.12; Cic. *Sest.* 61.

[58] It is often stated by modern historians that Bibulus began his watch of the heavens during the passage of the first agrarian law. But the claim that the legislation of Caesar's consulship was invalid was based on disregard not only of auspices but also of laws and of vetoes. (On this point see Suet. *Iul.* 30.3: adversus auspicia legesque et intercessiones.) Cicero indicates that the first agrarian bill disregarded the veto, while Vatinius' law restoring Ptolemy Auletes to his throne violated the auspices. See his report of a conversation with Pompey in May 59, *Att.* 2.16.2: se leges Caesaris probare, actiones ipsum praestare debere; agrariam legem sibi placuisse, potuerit intercedi necne nihil ad se pertinere; de rege Alexandrino placuisse sibi aliquando confici; Bibulus de caelo tum servasset necne sibi quaerendum non fuisse. My view is that immediately after the passage of the first agrarian law Bibulus withdrew to "watch," and that when he was doing so he would not have appeared in the Forum, as he did when the first bill was proposed, to protest the legislation.

[59] Plut. *Caes.* 14.1; *Pomp.* 47.3.

[60] Cic. *Sest.* 135; *Vatin.* 29; *Pis.* 37, 50, 90; Dio 38.7.6. Many more references could be added.

[61] See Camille Jullian, *Histoire de la Gaule romaine* (Paris, 1909) 3.196 f.

[62] Cic. *Sest.* 63; Plut. *Caes.* 14.8. Cf. Cic. *Brut.* 219.

[63] Suet. *Iul.* 22: Quo gaudio elatus non temperavit quin paucos post dies frequenti curia iactaret invitis et gementibus adversariis adeptum se quae concupisset, proinde ex eo insultaturum omnium capitibus. See the passage that follows for replies made to Caesar.

[64] Caes. *B.G.* 1.35.

[65] Suet. *Iul.* 54. Cf. n. 58 above. See Meyer, *op. cit.* 76, for further evidence.

[66] Cic. *Att.* 2.20.4: Populare nunc nihil tam est quam odium popularium. For Bibulus' edicts see the rest of that letter and 2.21; cf. also Plut. *Pomp.* 48.4 and, for quotations from the edicts, Suet. *Iul.* 9, 10, and 49.

[67] Cic. *Att.* 2.19.3–4. The incident took place at the *Ludi Apollinares,* when many Italians had probably arrived, expecting the elections to be held on time.

[68] The elimination of candidates seems to have been the chief object of the famous Vettius affair. The major source for it is Cic. *Att.* 2.24. See Meyer, *op. cit.* 84 ff.

[69] *Att.* 2.20.6; 2.21.5.

[70] Suet. *Iul.* 23; Cic. *Sest.* 40; *Vatin.* 15; *Schol. Bob.* pp. 130 and 146 Stangl.

[71] Suet. *Iul.* 23.

[72] Cic. *Sest.* 59–60; Dio 38.30; App. *B.C.* 2.23.

[73] Cicero (*Sest.* 60–63; cf. *Dom.* 65) discusses Cato's reasons for accepting. See the significant suggestion in *Sest.* 61 that Cato was already committed by his oath to observe Caesar's land law.

[74] Cic. *Dom.* 22.

[75] Plut. *Cic.* 34; *Cato Min.* 40. See Meyer, *op. cit.* 138 ff.; Gelzer, s.v. "Tullius" (29) *RE* 948.

[76] *Att.* 2.9.1; 2.21.1; *Off.* 3.88. Cicero blamed Cato particularly for his attack on the knights (see nn. 47 and 48 above), for it destroyed the *concordia ordinum* which Cicero believed he had created in his consulship. That attack had certainly united Crassus with Pompey, and ended the possibility of a compromise between the *optimates* and Crassus. The attack on the knights was morally justified, but the stubborn resistance to the land law, which provided a well-deserved bonus for Pompey's troops and relief for the city plebs, is less defensible.

NOTES TO CHAPTER VII
"OPTIMATES" AND DYNASTS
(Pages 140–161)

[1] *Pro Sestio* 96 ff. See n. 46 to chap. i, above. The case, which was tried in March, 56, demonstrates, as does the trial of M. Aemilius Scaurus (see chap. ii),

the confusion in the political relationships of the time. The accusation was inspired by Clodius and Vatinius, and the counsel for the defense included Clodius' ally Crassus, along with Hortensius, Calvus, and Cicero. Pompey, who at this time was opposing Crassus, and Clodius' enemy Milo appeared as witnesses for Sestius. Cicero evidently reworked his speech for publication (see Meyer, *op. cit.* 135 n. 1), attempting in answer to a question of the accuser (cf. 96, *quae esset nostra natio optimatium*) to explain to the youth of the land who the *optimates* were. On the speech see Gelzer, s.v. "Tullius" (29) *RE* 935 ff., and P. Boyancé, "Cum Dignitate Otium," *Rev. Ét. Anc.* 43 (1941) 172–191.

[2] *Prov. cons.* 38. See n. 57 to chap. i, above. The speech is perhaps Cicero's παλινῳδία (*Att.* 4.5.1), composed to guarantee his subservience after the Council of Luca.

[3] *Har. resp.* 40, with Gelzer's comments, *op. cit.* 946.

[4] See n. 12 below.

[5] Favonius may actually have been a new man; at any rate, he is the only member of his house known to have held office in the republic. He may have come from Tarracina. In adhering to principle he was at times even firmer than Cato. Thus he was the last of the senators to take oath to observe Caesar's agrarian law in 59 (Dio 38.7; Plut. *Cato Min.* 32.6), and he was the only one in January, 49, to object to any dealing with Caesar (*Att.* 7.15.2). For a jest he made at Pompey's expense compare Val. Max. 6.2.7. See Münzer, s.v. "Favonius" (1) *RE*.

[6] Of the older leaders of the senate only Hortensius, often an unreliable figure in politics, was still active. The Luculli had retired to their luxurious villas, and most of the other prominent men were dead.

[7] *B.G.* 4.4–13. See also Suet. *Iul.* 24.3; App. *Celt.* 18; Plut. *Caes.* 22.3; *Cato Min.* 51.

[8] Val. Max. 6.2.8.

[9] From the speech of Cn. Lentulus Marcellinus, quoted by Val. Max. 6.2.6. Marcellinus had been Pompey's legate, but had turned against him. See Münzer, s.v. "Cornelius" (228) *RE*.

[10] Demonstrations in the theater, such as had taken place in Caesar's consulship, doubtless continued. Cicero (*Sest.* 115 ff.) describes the favor that actors, and particularly the famous tragic actor Aesopus, showed him during his exile. The audience seems to have responded enthusiastically. For Cato's activity in the games celebrated by Favonius as aedile in 53 see Plut. *Cato Min.* 46.

[11] See Mommsen, *History of Rome* 5.136. Cf. n. 52 below.

[12] L. Marcius Philippus married Caesar's niece Atia, mother of Augustus, whose first husband C. Octavius died shortly after 59. It is assumed by Münzer, s.v. "Marcius" (76) *RE,* that the marriage took place about 57, but there is no sure indication of the date. The unwillingness of Pompey and Crassus to have the consular *comitia* for 55 held by either of the consuls of

56 suggests that Marcius was not then on friendly terms with the "triumvirs." Plutarch (*Cato Min.* 39) says that both consuls were favorable to Cato, and the records of senatorial action, including the special honors voted to Cato, indicate that such was the case after Cato's return. See Stein, *op. cit.* (in n. 4 to chap. vi, above) 42–44. I believe that it was after 56 that Caesar won Marcius by the marriage with Atia. Marcius was neutral in the Civil War.

[13] One of them was Cn. Domitius Calvinus, who as tribune had vetoed Caesar's first agrarian law. He was later won over by Caesar, but at this time he was still among the good men. Another praetor of 56 was a second "good" tribune of 59, Q. Ancharius. See Cic. *Sest.* 113; *Vatin.* 16; *Schol. Bob.* p. 135 and 146 Stangl.

[14] Dio 39.31.1; Plut. *Cato Min.* 41–42. This flight of Domitius, rather than, as has often been held, his attempted flight from Corfinium, is in Sallust's mind when he speaks of Domitius' *pedes fugaces* (*R.P.* 2.9.2). Cf. Carlsson, *op. cit.* (in n. 2 to chap. i, above) 9 note 2. See n. 50 below.

[15] See n. 41 to chap. iii, above.

[16] Curio's attack on Pompey's second consulship (see n. 72 below) shows that his enemies made capital of Pompey's employment of force at this time.

[17] See n. 101 to chap. iii, above.

[18] A result of this cultivation of the Italians was that when Pompey was ill in 50 the Italian cities passed public vows for his recovery. See Cic. *Att.* 8.16.1; 9.5.3. Pompey was in these years, as always, concerned with the increase of his *clientela*. His curatorship of the grain supply, conferred for five years in the autumn of 57, made him Caesar's rival for the favor of the urban plebs.

[19] Cicero, in defending Caesar's agent Balbus in the autumn of 56, protests against attacks on the friends of one's enemies. Cf. *Balb.* 60: Et erit aequa lex et nobis, iudices, atque omnibus qui nostris familiaritatibus implicantur vehementer utilis, ut nostras inimicitias ipsi inter nos geramus, amicis nostrorum inimicorum temperemus. For the prosecution of Crassus' associate Plancius see n. 101 to chap iii, above.

[20] Cic. *Pis.* 94; Ascon. p. 17 C. See Greenidge, *op. cit.* (in n. 2 to chap. v, above) 448. Pompey perhaps counted on influencing the lists through the censors then in office, but they were unable to complete the *lustrum*.

[21] Among adherents of the dynasts accused in this year were Messius, Vatinius, Gabinius (several accusations), Cn. Domitius Calvinus, C. Memmius, and C. Cato.

[22] Dio 38.7.6. During the hot summer of 54 Cato appeared in court clad only in toga and loin cloth without tunic. It was, he pointed out, the costume of statues of Romulus, Titus Tatius, and Camillus. For the evidence and the interpretation of Cato as a true Stoic in this incident see Meyer, *op. cit.* 219.

[23] See Münzer, s.v. "Licinius" (113) *RE.* Cf. n. 25 below.

[24] Suetonius' life of Caesar is the chief source for these attacks. See 9–10,

49–50, and *passim*. Cf. n. 30 below and n. 15 to chap. vi, above. The historian was Tanusius Geminus, who, like a writer of the next decade, M. Actorius Naso (Suet. *Iul.* 9.3 and 52.1), was hostile to Caesar. For a suggestive but not always convincing analysis of the sources for Caesar's life see H. Strasburger, *op. cit.* (in n. 14 to chap. vi, above). Among attacks on Pompey may be mentioned Marcus Brutus' pamphlet, *De dictatura Pompeii*. Cf. Meyer, *op. cit.* 210 n. 5. There was of course a great deal of counterpropaganda from adherents of the dynasts, not only in the speeches of their tribunes and their representatives in the courts but also in pamphlets. One example of the latter type was Metellus Scipio's brochure attacking Cato's administration of Cyprus. It was later used by Caesar in his *Anticato*. See Meyer, *op. cit.* 436 n. 2.

[25] See Morel, *Frag. Poet. Lat.* (Leipzig, 1927), Calvus, frg. 17 (against Caesar) and 18 (against Pompey). Cf. Suet. *Iul.* 49.1 and 73. Calvus was the son of the tribune C. Licinius Macer, active as a *popularis* in 73 and author of a history which glorified the struggle of the plebeians against the patricians. The son might have been expected to be favorable to Caesar's popular activity. For suggestions on the reasons for his opposition see Frank, *AJPh* 40 (1919) 396 ff.

[26] *Catullus: The Complete Poems* (Broadway Translations, London, n.d.). I have quoted from Catullus 29, 54, and 93.

[27] For the suggestion that Titus Labienus is lampooned in a group of Catullus' poems see Frank, *op. cit.* 407 f. For other political allusions see Frank, *Catullus and Horace* (New York, 1928) chap. iv and *passim*.

[28] Suet. *Iul.* 49. Catullus 11 was written before the reconciliation. See Mommsen, *History of Rome* 5.142 n. 1.

[29] This pact (Cic. *ad Q. Fr.* 2.14.4) had been a matter of general rumor for some time when it was revealed by Memmius in the senate in early September (*Att.* 4.17.2); that may have been why Cato was too ill that month to preside over the extortion court (*ad Q. Fr.* 3.1.15; *Att.* 4.17.4). Cato had been very active that year in trying to curb bribery, and the candidates for the tribunate had deposited with him a sum of money to be forfeited to their competitors if any of them should be caught bribing. See Cic. *ad Q. Fr.* 2.14.4.

[30] See *op. cit.* 107 ff. for an analysis of the reports in Suet. *Iul.* 9 and 11.1; cf. *TAPhA* 73, 16 f.

[31] The only source for the passage of an "extreme decree" at the time is Dio 40.45.2; cf. Meyer, *op. cit.* 210 and n. 3. Dio, who treats the Parthian disaster separately, accounts for the end of anarchy by Pompey's own decision not to seek the dictatorship that the tribunes were trying to give him. Pompey seems to have made such a decision, but not until he had been commissioned to defend the state under the "extreme decree." The reason for the decree was, I think, the news of the battle of Carrhae, which occurred on June 9 (Ovid, *Fasti* 6.465). According to Dio (40.45.1), the elections took place in July; according to Appian (*B.C.* 2.19, a vivid account of the disorders), they were

held either in August or in early September. That the news of Carrhae had reached Rome by election time is indicated by the fact that Cicero in this year was elected to the augurate to succeed P. Crassus, who met his death in the disaster. Elections of priests, usually followed immediately the consular *comitia*.

³² On Pompey's commission to set the state in order see Tac. *Ann.* 3.28: *Cn. Pompeius tertium consul corrigendis moribus delectus;* cf. App. *B.C.* 2.28 (from a letter of Pompey): ἐς θεραπείαν τῆς πόλεως ἐπικληθείς. See Syme, *RR* 316.

³³ Tac. *Dial.* 38: tertio consulatu Cn. Pompeius ... imposuit ... veluti frenos eloquentiae.

³⁴ Cato, who was a juror in the trial of Milo, was said to have voted against the condemnation of Milo, but Asconius (p. 53 f. C) is doubtful about the report. Cato had previously defended Milo in the senate. Cf. Cic. *Fam.* 15.4.12. In subsequent trials there were more condemnations of Clodians than of Milonians. Pompey did not interfere, although he did intervene to prevent the trial of his new father-in-law Metellus Scipio and at the end of the year sought in vain to prevent the conviction of his adherent Plancus Bursa. See n. 40. On the trials of this year see Meyer, *op. cit.* 234 ff.; Holmes, *op. cit.* 2.169 ff.

³⁵ Caes. *B.C.* 1.32; Cic. *Att.* 8.3.3. For the date of the law see Meyer, *op. cit.* 233 n. 1.

³⁶ For recent bibliography on the *Rechtsfrage* see G. R. Elton, *JRS* 36 (1946) 18–42. The author accepts Mommsen's date 49 for the termination of the Gallic command. In the vast bibliography I have found the analysis of C. E. Stevens particularly illuminating, although I do not accept all his interpretations. See *AJPh* 59 (1938) 169–208.

³⁷ Tac. *Ann.* 3.28. According to Dio 40.56, Pompey's command was lengthened after his law on the provinces had been passed.

³⁸ Unlike Gaius Gracchus' law on provinces, which it superseded, Pompey's law did not ban the use of the veto, and Caesar was able to offer resistance to the new regulation through the vetoes of his tribunes. Another law of Pompey, *de iure magistratuum,* restated the requirement of candidacy in person, and thereby affected the *privilegium* accorded to Caesar by the law of the ten tribunes earlier in the year. When the matter was called to his attention, Pompey had an exception in Caesar's favor written into the law which had already been deposited in the treasury. Cf. Dio 40.56; Suet. *Iul.* 28. Meyer, *op. cit.* 243 f., interprets Pompey's insertion recording Caesar's exemption from the law as a sign of unwillingness for a complete break with Caesar.

³⁹ Caesar, *B.C.* 1.4, seems to take the credit for Cato's defeat.

⁴⁰ This was the trial of T. Munatius Plancus Bursa, adherent of Pompey. See Cic. *Fam.* 7.2.2: In primisque me delectavit tantum studium bonorum in me extitisse contra incredibilem contentionem clarissimi et potentissimi viri.

[41] Evidently Caesar did not like Cicero's course at the time, for he began to press through his agents for the return of the money he had lent Cicero. See Cic. *Att.* 5.1.2; 5.4.3 (both written in May, 51). The subject is mentioned from time to time in Cicero's correspondence from Cilicia.

[42] Only the *prooemia* of the six books, preserved for Book 1 and in part for Book 5, are directly related to Cicero's own times. The *prooemium* of Book 1 admonishes the citizen on the duty of taking an active part in politics. One may doubt whether Cicero wrote that passage in the period before 52 when he was in despair over his own position in politics.

[43] *Rep.* 1.34 (Laelius is speaking): Memineram persaepe te cum Panaetio disserere solitum coram Polybio ... multaque colligere ac docere optimum longe statum civitatis esse eum quem maiores nostri nobis reliquissent.

[44] This discussion is from the incomplete *prooemium* of Book 5.

[45] According to Meyer (*op. cit.* 174 ff.) and Reitzenstein (*Nachr. Gött. Ges. d. Wiss.* 1917, 399 ff. and 436 ff.), Cicero in these books was advocating a monarchical republican constitution in which Pompey was to be the first citizen, the *princeps*. Cicero's *Republic* would thus forecast the principate of Augustus. Heinze has convinced me that Cicero is speaking not of a single *princeps* but of the ideal statesman, not necessarily unique in his age. See "Ciceros Staat als politischer Tendenzschrift," *Hermes* 59 (1924) 73 ff. (reprinted in Heinze, *Vom Geist des Römertums* 142 ff.).

[46] See Gelzer, *op. cit.* 975; Radin, *Marcus Brutus* 92 f., who suggests that Cicero also has Cato in mind; Carlsson, *op. cit.* 103 ff., who has a special interpretation of Cicero's "leading statesman," a role which Cicero himself was to fill.

[47] On the date of the *De Legibus* see E. A. Robinson, *PAPhA* 77 (1946) 321 f.

[48] *Rep.* 1.68: Quos <tyrannos> si boni oppresserunt, ut saepe fit, recreatur civitas; sin audaces, fit illa factio, genus aliud tyrannorum, eademque oritur etiam ex illo saepe optimatium praeclaro statu, cum ipsos principes aliqua pravitas de via deflexit.

[49] See nn. 23–25 to chap i, above. Boas, *Rh. Mus.* 83 (1934) 181 ff., provides evidence to show that the word *potentatus* (*Rep.* 2.14, with Boas' comments on the manuscript reading) came into use in the party strife of this period.

[50] *Op. cit.* See n. 2 to chap. i, above. The date 51 was proposed by L. Hellwig, *De genuina Sallustii ad Caesarem epistula cum incerti alicuius suasoria iuncta* (Dissertation, Leipzig, 1873). Since then, scholars who have accepted the letter as the work of Sallust have dated it either in 50 or in 49 (on that date see n. 14 above). Before I had had an opportunity to read the work of Carlsson, I had independently reached the conclusion that the letter should be dated in 51. The bases of the dating are as follows: the letter was written after Pompey set the state in order in 52 and after the law of the ten tribunes had given Caesar the privilege of being a candidate for the consulship *in absentia*

(cf. *beneficia populi*, 2.3); one consul was opposed to Caesar (*adversum consulem*, 2.3). These conditions would fit either 51 or 50. But the former year is indicated by the fact that Caesar was still fighting at the time (2.2 *inter labores militiae interque proelia victorias imperium*), for 51 was the last year of resistance in Gaul. I agree with Carlsson that the *terminus ante quem* for the letter is September 29, when Marcus Marcellus' efforts to have the senate consider the Gallic succession failed. I do not feel sure that he is right (*op. cit.* 60 f.) in holding that a *terminus post quem* is provided by the publication of Cicero's *Republic* about May, 51, for I am not convinced that Sallust in chapter 9 is echoing Cicero, *Rep.* 6.1. Carlsson has shown that much in the letter fits the conditions of 51. Particularly important is the discussion of the activity of Marcus Marcellus against the Transpadanes. There are, I believe, other reflections of the times that Carlsson does not mention. In 11.6 Sallust refers to absences from the senate because of *iudicia publica*. One of the decrees of September 29, 51 (Cael. apud Cic. *Fam.* 8.8.5), attempted to curb such absences. For other connections with the times see discussion in the text and notes 57–59.

[51] See *R.P.* 2.7–8. The *tribuni aerarii* seem to have had a census between 300,000 and 400,000 sesterces, while the first class was composed of men possessing a minimum census probably of 50,000 sesterces or more (according to Mattingly, of 100,000 sesterces or more). See n. 36 to chap. iii, above.

[52] See nn. 17 and 20 above. It is interesting that Mommsen, who considered the letter of Sallust a *suasoria* written under the empire, regarded the juries and the electoral assemblies as the strongholds of optimate power. See *History of Rome* 5.136 (where he is speaking of the efforts of the "triumvirs" to control the state): "But if the guidance of the state was at the absolute disposal of the regents, there remained still a political domain . . . which it was more easy to defend and more difficult to conquer; the field of the ordinary elections of magistrates, and that of the jury courts."

[53] *R.P.* 2.10.5. Nam ceteris salva urbe tantum modo libertas tuta est: qui per virtutem sibi divitias decus honorem pepererunt, ubi paulum inclinata res publica agitari coepit, multipliciter animus curis atque laboribus fatigatur.

[54] *R.P.* 2.3.1–2. Specific details follow on the power put into the hands of the *factio*.

[55] Cf. Caes. *B.C.* 1.4.4: Ipse Pompeius . . . cum communibus inimicis in gratiam redierat. See Carlsson's illuminating interpretation, *op. cit.* 19 ff. Particularly significant is Sallust's designation of the *factio* as *hostes,* not *inimici.* A *factio,* in his view, is composed of *hostes* of the *res publica.* See *R.P.* 2.10.8.

[56] *R.P.* 2.4.2. See Carlsson's defense of the reading *at hercule M. Catoni L. Domitio* (ms. *atherculem catonem*), *op. cit.* 41 ff. To his parallels for this exaggerated language add Cic. *Sulla* 50 (cf. n. 53 to chap. v, above). Cicero's letters from exile show that, when deprived of rank and citizenship, he considered himself practically dead. Sallust may have exaggerated the number of

men condemned, but there were certainly many trials in 52 (*iudicialis annus,* Cic. *Brut.* 243) and they continued into the next year (Cic. *Fam.* 7.2.4) and perhaps longer. See n. 58.

[57] *R.P.* 2.4.2: Quein acerbius in dies male faciundo ac dicundo dignitate alios alios civitate eversum irent. Carlsson, *op. cit.* 50 ff., associates the passage with the trials under Pompey's laws of 52, but does not relate the penalties directly to the laws.

[58] *R.P.* 2.4.3–4 (following immediately on the discussion of trials which seem to be under the *leges Pompeiae* of 52): Cuius contumeliam homines ignavissimi vita sua commutare volunt, si liceat—quein optatius habent ex tua calamitate periculum libertatis facere, quam per te populi Romani imperium maximum ex magno fieri. Compare the warning in 2.8.7 against the *dolus* of the *factio:* quoius si dolum caveris, alia omnia in proclivi erunt. I think Sallust has in mind a possible trial of Caesar for *ambitus* under Pompey's law and with the jurors selected by Pompey. (Cf. *R.P.* 2.3.3; in 2.7.11 he seems to be thinking of the jurors of Pompey's law of 55.) Trials under the *leges Pompeiae* were still going on in 51 (see n. 56 above). See Caesar's comments on Pompey's jurors, *B.C.* 3.1.4. Caesar was of course liable to prosecution under other laws, and a tribune had tried to bring him to trial in 58 (see n. 71 to chap vi, above). Cato may have made his first threats as early as that time, and may have repeated them when he spoke in the senate in 56 against Caesar's attack on the German tribes (see n. 7 above). The charge in that case would probably have been *maiestas.* Suetonius, in reporting Cato's threat of a trial, seems not to have had Pompey's law of 52 in mind. Cf. *Iul.* 30.3.

[59] Caelius may be reflecting such charges of *inertia* against the *optimates* when he tells Cicero (*Fam.* 8.2.2) that Marcus Marcellus' attacks have calmed down *non inertia sed, ut mihi videbantur, consilio.* Cf. also 8.10.2.

[60] *R.P.* 2.9. For Postumius see Cic. *Att.* 7.15.2 (January, 49). In that passage Cicero mentions Postumius' unwillingness to go to Sicily without Cato. The reference to the little-known Postumius is one of the strongest proofs that the letter was not composed under the empire.

[61] See Carlsson, *op. cit.* 58 ff., 86. The characterization of Cato does not take account of Cato's energy in political life, but the emphasis seems to be on lack of achievement in war. Sallust in his glorification of Cato in the *Catiline* (see chap. viii above) presents him again as a man of thought rather than of action.

[62] For this type of document, the συμβουλευτικόν (Cic. *Att.* 12.40.2), see Carlsson, *op. cit.* 118 ff.

[63] Barwick, "Zum Bellum Gallicum," *Philol.* Suppl. 31 (1938) 100 ff., has presented strong arguments for the view that Caesar wrote the successive books of the commentaries in successive winters and published them immediately. Barwick (124 ff.) associates the publication with Caesar's provision

in his consulship for making the *acta senatus* public (Suet. *Iul.* 20.1; see chap.
vi).The yearly commentary, Barwick holds, would have provided a welcome
means of presenting to the people in the most favorable light the greatness of
Caesar's achievements. Caesar would thus not have to depend on an unfavorable report from his enemies in the senate. Against the interpretation of
Caesar's commentaries as propaganda see Norman J. Dewitt, *TAPhA* 73
(1942) 341 ff.

[64] *B.G.* 6.1; 7.6.

[65] *B.G.* 1.44.12.

[66] Through the letters of Caelius to Cicero we are well informed on senatorial meetings from May, 51, to September, 50. Except in the discussion of
Cicero's triumph, Cato does not figure in the accounts. It is noteworthy that
even the *optimates,* according to Caelius, did not vote for Favonius in his contest for the praetorship for 50. Cf. *Fam.* 8.9.5. There were evidently divisions
among the *optimates* such as persisted in the Civil War. Some of them may
have been won over by Metellus Scipio to support Pompey. Appius Claudius,
related to Pompey through the marriage of their children, was back in Rome
upholding Pompey's position.

[67] Cael. apud Cic. *Fam.* 8.4.2; 8.8.10; 8.10.3–4.

[68] Cael. apud Cic. *Fam.* 8.6.5 (February, 50): Quod tibi supra scripsi Curi-
onem valde frigere, iam calet; nam ferventissime concerpitur. levissime enim,
quia de intercalando non optinuerat, transfugit ad populum et pro Caesare
loqui coepit legemque viariam, non dissimilem agrariae Rulli, et alumenta-
riam quae iubet aediles metiri, iactavit.

[69] See Caesar's sympathetic account of Curio's African disaster and of his
courageous death, *B.C.* 2.23–42. On Curio's career see Münzer, s.v. "Scribonius" (11) *RE.*

[70] Cf. Lucan, *Phars.* 4.819–820.

> Momentumque fuit mutatus Curio rerum
> Gallorum captus spoliis et Caesaris auro.

[71] On Curio as an orator see Cic. *Brut.* 280–283.

[72] Cael, apud Cic. *Fam.* 8.11.3: *totus eius secundus consulatus exagitatur.* It
is not clear whether the speech was made in the senate or in a *contio.* At the
end of the year Mark Antony, who had replaced Curio as Caesar's tribune,
continued the attack. Cf. Cic. *Att.* 7.8.5: *accusatio Pompei usque a toga pura.*

[73] Caelius is an example. In the process of going over to Caesar he wrote
Cicero in September, 50 (*Fam.* 8.14.3), that one should follow the better side
in politics until it came to civil war, and that then one should choose the
stronger side. Later, when he was sorry he had joined Caesar (*Fam.* 8.17.1),
he said that he had been persuaded by Curio. Curio, who before this time had
had great influence in elections (Cic. *Fam.* 2.6), is given the credit by Cicero
for bringing about Antony's election to the augurate in 50 (*Phil.* 2.4; cf. n. 81
to chap. iii, above). In spite of Curio's aid, Caesar's candidate for the consul-

ship failed to win in that year. Caesar and Pompey each obtained the election of a supporter in the censorship. They were Caesar's father-in-law, Piso, and the father-in-law of Pompey's son, Appius Claudius. Appius tried without success to expel Curio from the senate and actually succeeded in expelling Sallust.

[74] *Att.* 7.5.4; 7.6.2.

[75] *B.C.* 1.2.6: minis amicorum Pompei plerique compulsi inviti et coacti.

[76] On the course of events see Holmes, *The Roman Republic* 2.247–255; 323–327.

[77] Asinius Pollio apud Suet. *Iul.* 30.4. See n. 58 above for the passage which precedes.

[78] *Ep. Mor.* 104.30–31; 95.69–70; cf. 14.13.

NOTES TO CHAPTER VIII

CATONISM AND CAESARISM

(Pages 162–182)

[1] Premerstein, *op. cit.* (in n. 41 to chap. ii, above); Syme, *The Roman Revolution.*

[2] Compare Sallust's reference to the *clientelae* of the *factio, R.P.* 2.11.3; see the end of chap. ii. For Pompey's cultivation of the Italian cities see n. 18 to chap. vii, above.

[3] *Op. cit.* 13 and index s.v. "Dignitas." See H. Wegehaupt, *Die Bedeutung und Anwendung von Dignitas* (Dissertation, Breslau, 1932). The word is constantly used in the early chapters of Caesar's *Civil War.* See Bk. 1, chaps. 4, 7, 8, 9, 32. Cicero, *Att.* 7.11.1 (written in January, 49), shows that Caesar emphasized *dignitas* in his dispatches: Atque haec ait omnia facere se dignitatis causa. Ubi est autem dignitas nisi ubi honestas? On *dignitas* as a leading motive for the formation of the "triumvirate" a decade earlier see Florus 4.2.11: Caesare dignitatem comparare, Crasso augere, Pompeio retinere cupientibus.

[4] Caes. *B.C.* 1.9.2; 1.32.3; Sall. *R.P.* 2.2.3; cf. Cic. *Att.* 9.11A.2 (written to Caesar): iudicavique eo bello te violari contra cuius honorem populi Romani beneficio concessum inimici atque invidi niterentur.

[5] *B.C.* 1.22.5; see nn. 31 and 32 to chap. i, above.

[6] Cic. *Att.* 10.15.2 (May, 49): Unum C. Marcellum cognovi timidiorem; quem consulem fuisse paenitet.

[7] See Syme, *JRS* 28 (1938) 113 ff.

[8] See n. 36 to chap. ii, above.

[9] *Att.* 8.11.2: Dominatio quaesita ab utroque est, non id actum beata et honesta civitas ut esset.

[10] *Att.* 8.16.2.

[11] Caes. apud Cic. *Att.* 9.7 C.1.

[12] *Att.* 9.16.2.

[13] Cf. Lucan, *Phars.* 2.519–521 (of the pardon of leaders who surrendered at Corfinium):

> Poenarum extremum civi, quod castra secutus
> Sit patriae Magnumque ducem totumque senatum
> Ignosci.

[14] *Ibid.* 5.14. For an interesting interpretation of Pompey's relations with the *optimates* at the beginning of the war see Kurt von Fritz, *TAPhA* 73 (1942) 145 ff. Professor von Fritz believes that Pompey deliberately concealed from the senate his plan for evacuating Italy, and that Domitius, who was ignorant of Pompey's plan, has been too harshly judged for his stand at Corfinium.

[15] Plut. *Cato Min.* 52.2; *Pomp.* 57.1. On the award of the supreme command to Pompey see Holmes, *op. cit.* 3.432 f.

[16] Even in February of 49 Cicero thought Caesar might succeed in winning Pompey. Cf. *Att.* 8.11.2.

[17] *Att.* 7.15.2 (of Cato, January, 49): Ita quod maxime opus est, in Siciliam ire non curat; quod metuo ne obsit, in senatu esse vult.

[18] Plut. *Cato Min.* 53.4.

[19] *Ibid.* 54.3–5.

[20] *Cato Min.* 55; *Cic.* 39; cf. Cic. *Div.* 1.68–69. See Gelzer, s.v. "Tullius" (29) *RE* 1003.

[21] *Bell Afr.* 87. See the following chapter on the death of Cato.

[22] *Cato Min.* 66–72.

[23] Cic. *Rep.* 1.39.

[24] Cic. *Leg.* 3.40. See nn. 40–42 to chap. vi, above. On Cato's eloquence see Cic. *Brut.* 118; Plut. *Cato Min.* 5.

[25] Plut. *Cato Min.* 23; Sall. *Catil.* 52. See n. 25 to chap. vi, above.

[26] See, for instance, Cic. *Parad.* 1: Animadverti, Brute, saepe Catonem, avunculum tuum, cum in senatu sententiam diceret, locos graves ex philosophia tractare abhorrentes ab hoc usu forensi et publico, sed dicendo consequi tamen, ut illa etiam populo probabilia viderentur.

[27] *Parad.* 2; compare Plutarch's story (*Cato Min.* 54.5–6) of the speech filled with abstractions by which Cato incited the troops to battle at Dyrrachium.

[28] Cic. *Fam.* 15.3–6. On Cato's attitude toward the problems of empire see Gelzer, "Cato Uticensis," *Die Antike* 10 (1934) 59–91. See also Gelzer, s.v. "Tullius" (29) *RE* 982, for the suggestion that Cato had, perhaps in connection with Pompey's law on the provinces, made a particular appeal to all governors for just and upright rule.

[29] *Fam.* 15.5. Cato had as tribune introduced a law regulating triumphs. See n. 35 to chap. vi, above.

[30] *Fam.* 15.6.1.

[31] *Att.* 7.2.7.

[32] *Ep. Mor.* 104.32.

[33] Plut. *Cato Min.* 53.1.

[34] *Att.* 12.4.2.

[35] Cic. *Brut.* 4–6, 330; cf. 53, 157, 250, 266, 273. See O. E. Schmidt, *Der Briefwechsel des M. Tullius Cicero* (Leipzig, 1893) 38 ff., and Gelzer, "Ciceros 'Brutus' als politische Kundgebung," *Philol.* 93 (1938) 128–131. In Gelzer's view, Cicero in the *Brutus,* as in the *Pro Marco Marcello,* was trying to influence Caesar.

[36] *B.C.* 1.4: Catonem veteres inimicitiae Caesaris incitant et dolor repulsae.

[37] For the fragments see Klotz, *C. Iuli Caesaris Commentarii* (Leipzig, 1927) 3.185–190. Cf. Meyer, *op. cit.* 435 ff.; H. Drexler, *Hermes* 70 (1935) 203–205.

[38] See, however, Meyer, *op. cit.* 437 n. 1.

[39] Cic. *Top.* 94.

[40] See Gelzer, *Caesar,* 3d ed., 318 ff., 349.

[41] On Sallust, *R.P.* 1, see Meyer, *op. cit.* 388 ff., 582 ff. Of particular interest is Sallust's frank criticism of Caesar's party.

[42] Cic. *Att.* 13.40, written about August 17, 45. For the date see *CPh* 32 (1937) 228–240

[43] See the frequent references in Cicero's letters of the spring of 49 to the disaffection of the urban plebs from Caesar. There were even demonstrations in the theater. Caesar's representatives in Rome continued to have constant trouble. The *senatus consultum ultimum,* which had been passed only ten times between 121 and 49, was passed by Caesar's senate three times in the years 48–47. For the evidence see Plaumann, *op. cit.* 371 f. (in n. 62 to chap. i, above).

[44] Suet. *Iul.* 77: nihil esse rem publicam, appellationem modo sine corpore ac specie. Sullam nescisse litteras, qui dictaturam deposuerit. The remark is quoted from T. Ampius Balbus, an adherent of Pompey who dabbled in historical writing. Cf. Cic. *Fam.* 6.12.5. See Klebs, s.v. "Ampius" (1) *RE.*

[45] When, in his Gallic proconsulship, Caesar made plans for a great marble structure to house the tribal assembly (Cic. *Att.* 4.16.14), he could hardly have expected to humiliate the assembly as he did in his dictatorship.

[46] *Fam.* 7.30.

[47] *Fam.* 9.15.4 (written in the autumn of 46 before Caesar went to Spain).

[48] On the importance of the new men from Italy who became members of the senate and reached high office under Caesar see Syme, *BSR Papers* 14 (1938) 1 ff., and *RR,* chap. vi.

[49] See Premerstein, *op. cit.* 32 ff. Cf. Suet. *Iul.* 84.2, 85; App. *B.C.* 2.106, 124, 137, 139, 144 ff.

[50] See App. *B.C.* 2.137–146 for the speeches of Brutus and Antony. On Antony's speech see M. E. Deutsch, *Univ. Calif. Publ. Class. Philol.* 9 (1928) 127 ff.

[51] See Meyer, *op. cit.* 508 ff.; L. R. Taylor, *Divinity of the Roman Emperor* (Middletown, Conn., 1931), chap. iii; J. Carcopino, *Points de vue sur l'impérialisme romain* (Paris, 1934) 89 ff. For a different view see Adcock, *CAH* 9.718 ff.; cf. Last, *JRS* 34 (1944) 119. Cicero, *Phil.* 2.110, seems to me conclusive evidence against the view of Adcock. Syme, who accepts his interpretation, admits that it is "a difficult passage" (*RR* 54, n. 4).

[52] See Radin, *Marcus Brutus,* chaps. x–xii.

[53] Aug. *R.G.* 25.

[54] *Op. cit.* 53.

[55] *C.* 4.14.6.

[56] See L. R. Taylor, *op. cit.*, chap. vii.

[57] Premerstein, *op. cit.* 53.

[58] See Syme, *RR* 276 ff., 288 ff.

[59] Tac. *Ann.* 1.9, a chapter purporting to give favorable comment on Augustus.

[60] *R.G.* 34.

[61] Syme, *RR* 313–524, *passim.* On the memory of Cato and Julius Caesar see 317 ff., 506 f.

[62] W. H. Alexander, "Julius Caesar in the Pages of Seneca the Philosopher," *Trans. Royal Soc. of Canada* 35 (1941) Sec. II, 15–28; "Cato of Utica in the Works of Seneca Philosophus," *ibid.* 40 (1946) Sec. II, 59–74 (referred to hereafter as Alexander, "Caesar" and "Cato"). I have had the advantage of discussing the material in these papers with Professor Alexander.

[63] "Cato" 59.

[64] Sall. *Catil.* 51–52, for speeches of Caesar and Cato; 53, for comparison of the two men. For recent bibliography see Lämmle, *op. cit.* (in n. 1 to chap. i, above). H. Drexler (*Neue. Jahrb.* N.S. 4 [1928] 393 ff.) has pointed out the criticism implied in the characterization both of Caesar and of Cato. The picture of Cato as a man of thought rather than of action disregards the facts of Cato's energetic and courageous political career. On the influence of the Cato legend on Sallust's Catiline see T. R. S. Broughton, *TAPhA* 67 (1936) 34–46.

[65] Verg. *Aen.* 8.670; Hor. *C.* 1.12.35–36, *Catonis nobile letum.*

[66] *C.* 2.1.24.

[67] *C.* 3.3.1–8. See Bernhard Busch, *De M. Porcio Catone Uticensi quid antiqui scriptores aequales et posteriores censuerint* (Dissertation, Münster, 1911) 43 f. Busch compares Cic. *Tusc.* 5.4 and *Off.* 1.112. Catoni cum ... semper ... in proposito susceptoque consilio permansisset, moriendum potius quam tyranni voltus aspiciendus fuit.

[68] Hieronymus, *in Hoseam* 2, prol. (frg. 45, Weissenborn).

[69] *Aen.* 6.835: Proice tela manu, sanguis meus. See Syme, *RR* 317; Alexander, "Caesar" 18 n. 1. Caesar is included with the Julii in *Aen.* 6.789 f. Servius says that Vergil has Caesar in mind in *Aen.* 1.286 ff. Frank, *Vergil:*

A Biography (New York, 1922) 71 f., accepts Servius' statement and sees in the passage the reflection of an epic that Vergil had started some years earlier.

[70] Seneca, *N.Q.* 5.18.4 (frg. 48 Weissenborn).

[71] *Georg.* 1.468.

[72] *C.* 1.12.46–48; 1.2.44. Propertius' only allusions to Caesar also concern the Julian star. See 3.18.34; 4.6.59.

[73] *Met.* 15.745–870. In the *Fasti* all references to Caesar except the account of his reform of the calendar (3.155–166) and an allusion to his victory in Africa (4.379 ff.) are immediately related to Augustus. See 1.533; 1.600 ff.; 2.144; 3.699 ff.; 5.569 ff.

[74] Macrob. *Sat.* 2.4.18 (from a collection of sayings of Augustus): Non est intermittendus sermo eius, quem Catonis honori dedit. venit forte in domum in qua Cato habitaverat. dein Strabone in adulationem Caesaris male existimante de pervicacia Catonis ait 'quisquis praesentem statum civitatis commutari non volet et civis et vir bonus est.' satis serio et Catonem laudavit et sibi, nequis adfectaret res novare, consuluit. See also Suet. *Aug.* 87.1 with Shuckburgh's note.

[75] Suet. *Aug.* 85.1: Multa varii generis prosa oratione composuit, ex quibus nonnulla in coetu familiarium velut in auditorio recitavit, sicut rescripta Bruto de Catone, quae volumina cum iam senior ex magna parte legisset, fatigatus Tiberio tradidit perlegenda. Gelzer, "Cato Uticensis" (see n. 28 above) 64, assumes that Augustus had written his work on Cato early in life, but in that case one might expect *recitabat* instead of *recitavit* in the second line of the passage. It would have been natural for Augustus to deal with the subject late in his life, for by that time, as we know from Seneca Rhetor (see Busch, *op. cit.* 49 f.), Cato's life and death were frequent themes of rhetorical exercises.

[76] See Syme, *RR* 426 ff., 511 ff.

[77] Seneca, *Dial.* 2.7.1. See Alexander, "Cato" 63 ff. The praise of Cato is not confined to Stoic writers. See the indexes of Velleius Paterculus and Valerius Maximus. Cf. Busch, *op. cit.* 46 ff.

[78] *Ann.* 16.21.

[79] B. M. Marti, "The Meaning of the Pharsalia," *AJPh* 66 (1945) 352–376.

[80] "Cato" 68 ff.

[81] *Phars.* 9.601–604.

[82] See Seneca, *Dial.* 9.7.5; cf. 2.1.3.

INDEX

The notes are in general indexed separately only when they introduce new material. Under biographical articles the dates given for consulships (*cos.*), praetorships (*pr.*), and tribunates of the plebs (*tr. pl.*), are in every case B.C.

"Triumvirate," first, 21, 48, 71, 132 ff.; called a *factio* by Cicero, 10, 21, 23; dissensions in, 141 f.; and Council of Luca, 144 f.; and election of priests, 93
Tullia, 196
Tullius, see Cicero
Tyranny, 23, 72, 143; Caesar charged with, 155, 163 f. See also *Regnum*

Varro, M. Terentius, 77, 96
Vatinius, P. (*cos.* 47): tribunate, 135; prosecution, 145; and trial of Sestius, 208, 228; and augurate, 216
Velina, tribe, 200
Vergil, 25, 27, 179
Verres, C. (*pr.* 74), 100 ff.; and bribery in elections, 59, 67, 104, 108
Veterans, colonies of, 47. See also Soldiers
Vicinitas, 63
Violence, 2, 6; in elections, 68 f.; in legislative assemblies, 60 f., 74 f.; Pompey's law on, 148 f., 156